Strictly Speaking
Cynthia B. Johnson

Table of Contents

Chapter 1
The Foundation of Public Speaking

Strictly speaking, there are rules to almost everything we can think of. You stay within the speed limit, wear your seat belt, don't cut in front of others in line, and use your manners with a 'please' or a 'thank you'. For the most part, when we stay within the known guidelines, the outcomes are positive. However, we've all heard the old saying, "Rules were meant to be broken". There is no doubt that in some circumstances, it is downright fun to break the rules. Yet, we also know that sometimes when we do, the outcome doesn't bend to our favor.

It is with this intent that **Strictly Speaking** begins its education of public speaking with you; for the understanding that even 'speaking' has rules. We've learned from a great deal of research and in learning from history that some things work better than others, and when used correctly, create success. With this in mind, hopefully you can recognize that effective public speaking also succumbs to rules. Our goal is for you to educate yourself and implement the strategies that have become effective and created success in the art of public speaking. As is true in many cases, we can learn from the opposite of right, or in other words, the way in which it didn't work, in order to recognize how it could have been done correctly. Let's begin here.

Baseball is an American pastime; loved by man and disliked by few. As a Chevrolet commercial echoes, "Chevrolet. It's as American as baseball and apple pie." With this, we get a mental visual of red, white and blue, pride and hard work. So, consider back in February of 2009 when then baseball star, Alex Rodriguez, held a press conference to address an interview that he had conducted with an ESPN reporter just a few weeks earlier. It was expected that A-Rod (as he is known by baseball fans) would not only own, but also explain why he had used banned sports-enhancing substances and failed a drug test while playing with the Texas Rangers.

Baseball fans wanted to see him apologize. Their trust in his hard work and dedication to an American pastime was broken and until the latest surfacing of a failed drug test, Rodriguez was considered to be a lock for the Baseball Hall of Fame. Near the end of his formal statement he said, "To all of my teammates…," then paused, appearing to tear up, before adding, "…thank you."

The before and after pictures of A-Rod at his press conference were like night and day. Few questions were addressed or answered, and he went from being a baseball superhero to just another fallen sports hero. What went wrong? Let's consider another example.

It's almost common, current day trivia to know the assault on Rihanna by Chris Brown in 2009. With the force of social media in the 21st century, we were privy to details given by the famous female pop star and of photographs on the internet of the horrific assault. The cultural breaking of a very static norm of men not abusing women had rocked those that follow pop culture, and at the very least, followers expected a committed apology by Chris Brown.

> "When I look at it now, it's just like, wow, like, I can't believe that actually happened.
> I've told Rihanna countless times and I'm telling you today, I'm truly, truly sorry that I wasn't able to handle the situation both differently and better" (2009).

According to some sources, there may be at least two concerns in terms of his apology to his ex-girlfriend. In fact, one concern came directly from Rihanna, stating that the apology denied immediate responsibility, rather scapegoating with a perceived sense of insincerity. It seems that of greater concern was protecting his fan base. But the second concern was that Brown came up short in terms of making good on his apology in the sense that even two years later, he failed to meet the terms of 'making good' on his intentions to right the wrongs.

What do an athlete and a pop star seem to have in common? To begin, because of their chosen profession, they are in the public eye. This means the public scrutiny of their behavior and actions. Fans expected an explanation for both individual's behaviors. Such explanation came to fruition via a public presentation where the words and intent behind the words were judged.

In his famous book on rhetoric, Aristotle, the famous Greek teacher of public speaking, spoke of the important relationship between words and self-defense. Aristotelian scholar George Kennedy commented on Aristotle's public speaking philosophy, stating:

> Both animals and human beings have a natural instinct to preserve and defend themselves, their territory, and their group and families. They do this by physical acts and by the use of signs, including utterances such as howls, cries, and human speech. *Rhetoric*, in the most general sense, is the energy inherent in emotion and thought, transmitted through a system of signs, including language, to others to influence their decisions or actions. In developed human societies, such as ancient Greece, social and political contexts emerge that mold speech into certain conventional forms shaped by the

psychology and expectation of audiences. Both literature and public address develop in this way (1991, p.7).

Just as a person has the capacity to defend themselves with their fists, so too does a person have the capacity to defend themselves with words. While most of us no longer need to defend ourselves with fists, Aristotle's admonition still rings true two thousand years later: all of us should be able to fine tune our symbolic capacity to defend ourselves effectively and explain our actions with words. In truth, those words are scrutinized and perceptions are formed of the individual and perhaps too, their character.

Being a college student, there is an inherent understanding that when you take particular courses, the nature of the subject is obvious. When studying geology, you study earth science, rocks and formations. Mathematics delves into quantities, space, changes, and more. However, few have a grasp of the importance of studying communication. What do you study in a communication class, let alone, in a public speaking course? In this chapter, we will discuss what communication is, investigate the ingredients that compose the communication process, and finally, address how public speaking is a special kind of communication endeavor that yields specific rewards but also requires particular aptitudes different from other forms of communication.

The Essential Elements of Communication

Ingredient #1: Separation

Have you ever considered the purpose or 'why' there is a need to study the field of communication? It's not a question we often ask because communication is something we engage in all the time, consciously or unconsciously. Communication can be compared to breathing: we don't' think about it unless it becomes difficult for us.

Simply put, we desire to communicate because we are separated, or distanced from one another. We each have unique physiological structures, separate nervous systems and are biologically distinct from one another. This is a biological fact of the human condition we cannot deny. If we completely understood one another, like the mystical powers of the mind reading character Mel Gibson demonstrated in the movie, "*What Women Want*" (2000), there would be no need to open our mouths to speak or gesture with our body. But, we are not mind readers. In fact, most of us have had the thought that relationships would indeed be a great deal easier if we could read one another's mind. However, it is one of the great ironies of life that we communicate as a consequence of our inability to completely understand one another and because of our natural instinct to be understood.

It is no surprise then that one of the basic motives of human beings is to be understood. We all have a desire for those important individuals in our lives to 'get us' like those more superficial others in our lives do not. Consider the move, *"The Break Up"* (2006) where Jennifer Aniston's character, Brooke, stages a break up with Gary, her boyfriend, in hopes to make him better understand her needs. However, she never becomes clear on her intentions. That, coupled with listening to bad advice, creates a comical view of breaking up and the societal perceived war of the sexes. However, in reality, the perception of needs and the desire to be understood is very real.

While we are physiologically separated from one another, we spend our lives trying to overcome the distance (both physiological and metaphorical) between ourselves and others through communication. We want others to understand us. We want others to feel our pain. We want others to appreciate our life story, to pay attention to our goals for the future, to respect our beliefs, to listen to our fears, and so on. Each of us has a motive to communicate, a reason to open our mouths, a reason to listen and be listened to as each is a symptom of our desire to help others 'get' us and for us to 'get' others. As a tragic example, think back or consider the 1999 Columbine high school shooting where two young men, both students at the high school, killed 13 fellow students and wounded more than 20 (2007). While there is little doubt and compiled evidence that these boys were influenced by particular video games and the Gothic lifestyle, the identified reason they asserted for the slaughtering of their fellow classmates was the absence of connection with their peers. Instead, they asserted that they were often bullied and left to 'feel' disconnected and not understood by others at the school. One can only speculate on the layered forces that lead to such a tragedy, but what we can decipher from their statements is that the lack of being 'gotten' by others was a large psychological component to this devastation.

Ingredient #2: Symbols

Moving forward, a rational question that would follow our understanding of separation as an essential element of communication is, "How do we overcome the physical reality of being separated from others"? What appears to be a simple answer is more complex than most give credit for: the use of symbols. We are symbol-users and our tools are verbal and nonverbal signs that allow us to communicate. Through agreement, culture and convention, for example, the letters c-e-l-l stand for what we put up to ear and carry around with us to contact people near or far. 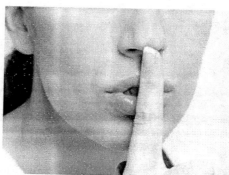 Yet it has layered meaning as well, doesn't it? When we say that we are texting someone, we automatically understand that to mean the communication comes from the cell phone. The latter term, phone, is often dropped now when we reference our cell, as it has now become a negotiated and accepted term. An exaggerated yawn in the midst of a class lecture, by agreement or convention, means that you may be tired but it also means that you may be bored. In each instance, specific letters in the alphabet and commonly understood nonverbal gestures help us understand or communicate about our feelings, thoughts, ideas, and experiences (Brummett, 2006).

For the sake of clarity, let's consider what our lives would look like without a symbolic tool we almost always depend on to communicate with one another: words. The importance of words to both speakers and audiences can only fully be appreciated when we consider a world without words:

- Without words, how else could you explain to your chiropractor where specifically in your back the pain is emanating from and what the pain feels like – is it a throbbing pain, is it a sharp pain, and how long have you experienced the pain?

- Without words, how could you express your likes and dislikes? Imagine sitting inside of a restaurant with your friends and not being able to explain what type of food you enjoy or what you'd like to order and drink. You could point and have them play guessing games, but imagine the time, energy and the vast amount of ambiguity in this method. The ease of explanation through symbols allows for communication to be expedited and less ambiguous.

- Without words, we wouldn't be able to share. Laughter, for example, is a byproduct of a shared meaning. Think of the last time you recalled a fun memory that evoked positive feelings that resulted in laughter. When you share that memory, the laughter is a consequence of understanding this shared meaning – common friends in the scenario, possible embarrassments or comedy within the circumstance, a commonly shared experience – that resulted in a laugh-out-loud funny because the situation was put into verbal words and then shared among the group. Wouldn't life be a very unfunny and lonely place without words?

- Without words, how would we unite to achieve collective action? Try inspiring hundreds and perhaps thousands of individuals, organize them, and direct them toward a common cause without the use of words. All public figures, religious and political alike, share something in common: words were necessary to their ministry as it was through words that they communicated, inspired, and led their followers.

- Without words, how would protest be possible? As symbol users, we have a remarkable capacity to say "no" to the status quo – a relationship we're unhappy in, a local curfew that you believe is unfair, a proposed tax increase on your college education, or even a war you believe is unjust or unworthy of human suffering.

To reiterate, without symbols or words, there would an endless variety of individuals but no possibility for achieving "We" or "Us." "We" and "Us" are the unique byproducts of communication (Burke, 1966).

Ingredient #3: Mystery

Unfortunately, complete understanding is impossible. There is always 'noise', ambiguity or misperceptions when individuals communicate. The good news is that this doesn't stop us from trying to be understood or to understand others. Inherent in every conversation you have with a friend or a stranger and in every email you send to a boss or a significant other, there will always be the mystery of how they will respond, how they will interpret the symbols in your email or the messages you impart on the phone. Mystery is the feeling in the pit of your stomach that emerges every time you ask someone for a job, ask a stranger for a favor, or the first time you call someone on the phone to set up a date, because you are unsure of how they will respond or what they might say in response. This mystery – that feeling in the pit of your stomach – is the universal communication situation all of us share together.

Even though you can attempt to describe accurately your headache to your doctor, the doctor may still not understand your pain or frustration. Your doctor may approximate what your headache feels like, but because she is physiologically distinct from you, understanding is always proximate as it is an ongoing process that is never complete. Granted, while some people seem to understand us more than others (family, spouse, partner, friends), communication is never finished because we are always changing, situations are always evolving, and so too are our feelings, ideas, and beliefs. There are two specific factors in particular that exacerbate the mystery between people that can partly explain why your life-long friend may understand you more than a stranger you pass on a busy street might: *noisem*.

External noise includes conditions of the physical environment where communication occurs that affects or prevents communication with another person. An example of such conditions is talking to a friend while a loud car drives by in the background or talking to a friend on your cell phone as your phone loses reception. External noises are those elements that impede or change what can be heard, said, or understood *between* you and someone else.

Internal noises, on the other hand, are physiological or psychological factors within us that inhibit or prevent us from fully understanding or communicating with others. Trying to listen to someone who is giving you directions to a job interview is difficult when you are already fifteen minutes late to an important interview. You may hear the words come out of the mouth of the person giving you directions, but you are likely to forget what they are saying because you are still angry that you left your home fifteen minutes later than you had scheduled and now may not get the job as a result of your tardiness. Likewise, concentrating on taking an exam when you have a migraine headache might inhibit your ability to recall important information and thus, diminishes your ability to communicate accurately your knowledge. *Psychological noise*, such as worry, fear, memories, anticipations, and expectations, always influences or affects how we interpret (what we attune to and what we ignore) and communicate.

External and internal psychological noise, therefore, draws attention to the reality that there are always variables at play in the physical surroundings or on our minds and in our hearts when we communicate with other people. While we may give the person we are talking to eye contact, nod our heads in approval, and remain silent while they talk, our mind is never completely focused because other factors are always competing and/or interrupting our complete and undivided attention. After all, when reflecting upon the above information, we can assess that communication does not take place in a vacuum. In other words, there are a myriad of factors that affect our processes within communication.

"Speech Class Noise Types Video"

Ingredient #4: Channel(s) of Communication

A communication channel is the manner in which communication is expressed. It can also be viewed as a means to an end – a tool that assists in the effectiveness of communication. Typically, the channels of communication are either visual or auditory. For example, the tenor and projection of your voice are auditory channels of communication and baggy jeans, jewelry and tattoos are visual channels of communication. The particular type of channel of communication can affect the communication encounter. For example, texting a professor to inform her that you are sick and will not be able to attend class is a different channel of communication than emailing, which is a different communication channel from writing a letter, which is a different communication channel from explaining the reason for your absence in person. In each communication situation, the channel of communication affects the message and the interpretation of the content.

Ingredient #5: The Invisible Past

Perhaps an example will help highlight the invisible factors at play in every communication encounter. No one carries an empty iPod. Our iPods are always full of play lists that we have created, songs our friends have sent us, songs that remind us of our past, songs that help motivate us to work out, and songs we play when we are depressed. We aren't objective, fully impartial judges of what we hear. In other words, we aren't blank slates. We have likes and dislikes reflected in the type of music on our iPod. We already have developed tastes. When we listen to a new song or new CD, we can't help but interpret that piece of music in light of what music is already on our iPod; evaluating the new music in terms of what genre it will fit into, determining whether we like that kind of music, assessing whether we have ever heard something similar before, and of course, determining whether we are in the right mood to appreciate the song itself.

In one important manner, we are like our iPods because we are never empty. In every communication encounter, we bring to the interaction an invisible past that affects how and in what we way we communicate. We can't help but bring our beliefs, previous experiences, attitudes, traditions, biases, prejudices and expectations to each speaking situation. Most of the time we're unaware of how our invisible past affects how we communicate but we cannot deny that the sum of our experiences affects how we communicate.

Ingredient #6: Source and Receiver(s)

When we communicate, we simultaneously play the role of source and receiver. When you create a verbal or nonverbal message (encoding) – from a simple "hello" to holding someone's hand – you are the communication source. The recipient of your messages, or receiver, tries to makes sense of your message by decoding each of your messages – "You're my friend, I haven't seen you in a week – Hello!" or "Why are you extending your hand to hold my hand – this makes me uncomfortable!" As both sources and receivers of messages, we exchange so much information through encoding and decoding that it is sometimes difficult to discern who originates a message.

To complicate matters just a bit, there are different types of receivers or audiences as well. The *self as audience* is the audience who never leaves us. We spend much of our time arguing with ourselves. For example, when your alarm goes off early in the morning and it's still dark and cold outside, you initiate a debate with yourself as to whether you should get out of bed and start your day or stay nestled warmly in your covers.

The other type of audience that we typically think of in everyday communication encounters is the *other as audience*. This includes everyone but you. This audience can be present physically when you speak – you can see the color of your audience's eyes while you talk – or they can be an audience that watches your latest rant on YouTube on their own cell phone, hundreds of miles away. Regardless of where this audience is located, one common feature of the *other as audience* is that recognizing the other changes how we think and communicate.

Here's a good test to help you remember how present the *other as audience* is in your own mind, even when an audience may not be physically present when you communicate. When you use the eraser on your pen or pencil, or when you push the delete key on your keyboard, you are acknowledging the presence of the *other as audience* because you are trying to translate what you believe or think in your own mind and make it understandable to someone else. You would never have to use your eraser if you were writing/speaking to yourself because your own ideas, thoughts, and beliefs always make complete sense to you. However, the moment you begin to think about how others might understand or interpret your beliefs and ideas, you know you are in the realm of the universal communication situation.

Ingredient #7: Feedback

In every communication exchange between source and receiver, there is feedback. Feedback is another way of acknowledging (verbally or nonverbally) that others influence how and what we communicate. Namely, a nod or raised eyebrows or a "Really?" from the person we are talking with (receiver) affects whether we continue with our story as originally planned, end our story, provide more detail to our story, and/or move onto another topic. Feedback is always present in communication interactions so we oftentimes forget its presence. However, it is only when the feedback we expected from others (audiences) is broken do we realize its impact. Have you ever told a joke and heard nothing but silence when you were expecting laughter? Have you ever tried to explain something and instead of a nod of approval, the person you were talking to showed facial expressions of confusion and exasperation? In each situation, the feedback from receivers affects what the communication source says or does not say, thereby creating an ongoing loop of correction or modification to the messages being sent and received.

The Rhetorical Situation:
How Public Speaking is Different than Conversation

Thus far we've discussed some important ingredients of the universal communication situation where there is a source and receiver connected and constantly adjusting to the other via feedback. While these ingredients apply to communication situations in general, it's important to address the unique elements that compose the public speaking situation by comparing and contrasting four specific differences within everyday conversation and public speaking.

Difference #1: Fluid vs. Formal Roles

Interpersonal conversation depends on the principle of reciprocity. When you communicate in informal contexts, both parties are expected to participate, each playing the role of source and receiver, encoding and decoding simultaneously. This creates a domino effect or cycle among participants. While we've all been stuck in conversations where one person dominates the conversation and does all the talking, most of us expect to speak *and* listen when conversing. Moreover, when you converse with friends, each party is considered an equal. Each of you expects to add something to the conversation and also acknowledges that the other person will have a comment to say in response. Thus, informal conversation is defined by the fluid roles we play as both speakers and receivers, as creators, active participants and audience members.

In public speaking, this rule of reciprocity is broken because of a very clear power difference. In traditional public speaking situations, speakers are expected to speak uninterrupted on a topic behind a podium while audiences are expected to listen, in relative silence, until the speaker is finished. As an audience member, you may want to interrupt, to disagree, or you may even know that what the speaker is saying is untrue. As an audience member, however, you accept the power distinctions between you and the speaker and are expected to allow the speaker to complete his or her presentation uninterrupted. As a professor of communication, I have witnessed first-hand that 'one' student who makes a random comment during another student's presentation. There is little doubt that it is responded to with awkward glances and negative non-verbals from others. Even the classroom environment has accepted social norms that are negotiated by acceptable and unacceptable symbols of communication.

In interpersonal conversations, feedback is interactive because it changes what is said or not said between two people. For example, when friends are laughing at your jokes, you tell more jokes. When friends are showing nonverbal signs of disinterest in your story, you will shorten the story or change topics all together. However, in traditional speaking situations, ongoing feedback is constrained by the expectation that verbal feedback will occur only after applause. The important point of distinction between conversation and public speaking is that feedback in conversation is expected to change the content and quality of the interaction whereas the feedback provided in public speaking settings is designed as a response to the completed speech or presentation.

Difference #2: Informal vs. Formal Rules

In everyday communication, conversation is oftentimes predicated on shared meaning. Interpersonal conversation encourages the kind of insider knowledge that only two life-long friends can share or two employees who have worked at the same company for years can fully understand. Simply put, shared knowledge means the use of specialized language, inside jokes, abbreviations, slang, colloquialisms, common expressions, and free-flowing movement from one topic to another. These informal aspects of interpersonal conversation are allowable (and understandable) because of the familiarity that each participant shares (or can share) with the other in the form of a shared history.

In public speaking settings, audiences are composed of different individuals from a variety of backgrounds. As expected, the speaker doesn't or can't know the audience members intimately. Because of that fact, public speaking is defined not by the familiarity of audience to speaker as much as it is by a formalized and rigid set of rules. Generally, there are three genres of rhetoric, or types of speaking situations, each with its own set of rules, replete with what subjects are appropriate to speak about and expectations about how to speak. These genres of rhetoric include: (1) deliberative speaking situations, (2) judicial situations, and (3) ceremonial situations.

In deliberative speaking situations, politicians in the House of Representatives or Senate, for example, argue over what the best means are to achieve a desired future – i.e. should this person be nominated to the Supreme Court, what is the best health care system for the U.S., and how best might our military fight and win the war against terrorism? In judicial speaking situations, like the OJ Simpson Trial, the Scott Peterson Trial, or even the Michael Jackson trial, prosecutors and defense argue over guilt or innocence in the context of a courtroom. Here, both sides attempt to determine justice by arguing over what occurred in the past. Finally, in ceremonial or epideictic rhetorical situations, speakers celebrate virtue or condemn vice. In these recurring situations, like wedding ceremonies, eulogy orations, keynote presentations or even award celebrations, etc., speakers attempt to draw attention to values they find worthy of emulation or positive critique vices that they believe are worthy of condemnation.

In each specific speaking situation, there are specific rules for what can and cannot be said, what should or should not be said, and what counts as evidence and effective reasoning. Whereas in interpersonal conversation, trust is determined by the opportunity to know or get to know one another, in the context of public speeches, evidence and reasoning replaces trust as the measure by which audiences believe or don't believe what a speaker says.

Difference #3: Spontaneous vs. Strategic Intention

When you communicate with a friend, you don't always have a clear purpose or agenda. Let's be honest, in interpersonal situations, we rarely have an agenda or purpose. Most of the time, communicating with a friend can be justified simply because it is enjoyable. We doubt you ask yourself if you were "successful" or "effective" after having a conversation with a friend. Successful at what? Effective based on what

criteria? These questions sound silly when considered in light of interpersonal and informal contexts, but they are essential questions all speakers must address when speaking in public.

As a public speaker, you always have a purpose. Audiences, or receivers, expect you to say something about some topic, in a logical manner, for some purpose. Speakers speak to respond to an implicit "question" in the minds of audiences (Bitzer, 1968). Speakers speak to provide information as well as help audiences to make sense of what just happened, to calm audience fears, and to give meaning to seemingly senseless acts. For example, after the 1995 Oklahoma City Bombing at the Murrah Federal Building in Oklahoma City, OK, where 168 people, including 18 children died, words are what audiences expected to hear to help answer the inevitable questions that emerged from the carnage. Why? Who would do such a thing? How did this happen in the heartland of America? And what can we do to prevent such tragedies from happening again?

Audience questions, whether implicit or explicitly stated, are the collateral damage that always seems to follow events that defy expectations. On the evening of September 11, 2001, after the world witnessed live images of the collapse of the Twin Towers in New York City, the crash of an airliner into the Pentagon and a downed airplane in the fields of Pennsylvania, President George Bush spoke to Americans to help them make sense of what had happened, reassure Americans and the world that essential government operations were in place to handle the crisis, and to remind Americans that we would endure this tragedy just as we had others in the past. In times of confusion, destruction, deliberation, and celebration, audiences look to speakers to help them make sense of the world by addressing the why and what and how of experiences that suddenly seem less than clear.

"CNN – Ex-President George W. Bush's Post 9/11 Speech"

Speakers and speeches don't always follow events, however. Sometimes, speakers and speeches attempt to preempt issues, events, or impending threats that might be overlooked, forgotten or underappreciated without the speaker's use of words and attention to the topic (Vatz, 1973). For example, less than a year after the Allied Victory in World War II, Winston Churchill delivered a speech at Westminster College in Fulton, Missouri, introducing the term "iron curtain" into the vernacular to highlight the growing schism between the democracies of Europe and the growing threat of Soviet Communism. More recently, Senator Al Gore's 2006 film *An Inconvenient Truth* attempted to draw attention the harmful effects of global warming and warn audiences of the imminent dangers of viewing ecological calamity as a mere political issue rather than as the overriding moral issue of the twenty first century.

"Churchill Sinews of Peace (Iron Curtain)"

Speakers attempt to preempt or answer the questions audiences have in their minds. Speakers speak for a purpose, and oftentimes, the speaker who is deemed the most credible and the most persuasive is the speaker who most effectively addresses audience fears, doubts, worries, and questions.

Difference #4: One to Many

In everyday conversation, communication is not similar to a ping-pong game, where the participants take set turns. Rather, communication is more like a dance, where interaction is featured and the movement between people is more important than the individuals themselves. Interruptions, laughter, and feedback keep the dance of conversation moving as the "we" becomes more important than the "I". On the other hand, in public speaking, the spotlight rarely shines on the audience because the center of attention is the speaker. For many of us, standing alone behind a podium and staring out into a sea of faces is the  subject of many nightmares because when we speak in public, we can't hide behind the "We", as it is the "I" that is on stage, and it is the "I" to which all eyes are looking at. This reality is why public speaking is unlike any other class you will take or any other academic and performance based experience. Before we get into the details in the *how to* part of this book, it is important to explore why taking a public speaking class will be unlike any other class you've taken in college, as well as why taking a public speaking class will positively impact the rest of your life.

Reason #1: Public Speaking is a Full Body Experience

The thought of speaking to a friend probably doesn't make you very nervous or apprehensive, especially if you know the other person intimately. When you hear the words public speaking, however, what feelings come to mind? Fear? Trepidation? Nausea? Disgust? Revulsion?

 You're not alone. Consider a 2001 Gallup Poll survey asking what people most feared in life. What do you believe was one of the most-feared objects or experiences? Incredibly, more people fear public speaking than spiders, heights and even death (Brewer, 2001). In fact, only snakes beat out public speaking on the most-feared list. Now, we dare not consider what would happen if your public speaking teacher made you speak in front of the class while your audience held needles, mice and spiders (the other top contenders on the most-feared list)! But seriously, what is it specifically about public speaking that makes us all so nervous?

In other classes, you are expected to attend regularly, take diligent notes, write papers, and fulfill assignments. In public speaking classes, the same is true but for one significant difference. In public speaking classes, you're most important assignments – speeches – aren't between you and your professor alone. Rather, you are expected to write speeches for your peers, and deliver your speeches *in front of* your peers.

Usually, we have no problem speaking to people. It's when we have to speak *in front of* people, especially our peers, that we become so very nervous. This anxiety does all kinds of strange things to our bodies – our faces turn red, our hearts beat faster, our mouths becomes dry, hands begin to shake, and sometimes, when we're really nervous, some of us feel like we're going to pass out. That's what we mean when we say public speaking is a full body experience. For the most part, public speaking is one of the few, if only, classes that isn't about you alone – there has to be an audience involved for speaking to become public speaking. In public speaking classes, you will be on stage. Your ideas will be on a platform in front of others. People will judge you. People will judge what you say and how you say it. Private correspondence – writing a paper or fulfilling an assignment that *only* the professor reads – isn't a luxury in public speaking.

The good news is that you are not alone – everyone feels nervous. Yes, even people who are extroverted become nervous. And yes, even people who look like they're not nervous become nervous (they just hide it better than others). And more good news: everyone in your class will be going through the same experience together, so hopefully you can empathize with your classmates as each of you makes the long and lonely walk to the podium where the room becomes silent, and all eyes and ears fix upon you.

Reason #2: Public Speaking is a Building Block of Community

Second, public speaking is necessary for the creation of community. Simply put: without public speaking, how would we celebrate our commonalities, highlight our differences, inform and educate others, change others' minds, and even change our own minds?

Our democratic political system is designed around several important premises that we too often take for granted: (1) each of us, as individuals, has something important and valuable to say, (2) our individual voices matter because the more voices we hear, the better our collective decision making, and (3) one voice can change the minds of millions of people. Here, think of many, many impactful individuals that utilized a public speaking forum as a means for change. We think of Lincoln, Churchill, Martin Luther King, Jr., Gandhi, and the list goes on and on. For each of these leaders, the use of sharing their desires for change in a public setting initiated the gathering of many like-minded people that impacted historic change.

For example, during the presidential campaign of 2008, town halls across this country highlighted the connection between public speaking and community. In both the Democratic and Republican Primary Campaigns, traditional town hall meetings, oftentimes broadcast on major television networks, allowed individuals from all walks of

life, all economic backgrounds, races, religious preferences, and political persuasions, to share their opinions publicly on various political topics, debate important issues, and help set the agenda for political behavior and policy making.

On the eve before Election Day, did you feel like you "knew" John McCain? What about Barack Obama? Interestingly, there is a unique relationship between speaker and audience that is only made possible through public speaking where we learn about the various presidential contenders through their performances in debates, interviews, and speeches. For the most part, public speaking is the means by which we come to know, assess, critique, ridicule (watch any episode of *Saturday Night Live* for evidence that we love watching public speakers as much as we do making fun of them), or support the various political candidates. Just like we develop relationships with our political candidates without having to meet them personally, so too will you feel connected and/or repulsed, inspired and/or disgusted, and, perhaps most importantly, a part of and/or excluded from a purpose/goal/cause as a result of listening and participating in the most basic of community building blocks: public speaking.

Reason #3:
Public Speaking is An Unavoidable Reality of 21st Century Citizenship

Public speaking might be easy to dismiss if it were important but avoidable. However, in the 21st century, it is both an important and inescapable reality in all aspects of life. Translation: If you've been putting this class off for years or you had a lump in your throat on the way to class – public speaking will find you whether or not you are ready for it. It is an unavoidable necessity.

At our institution, we offer a nursing program that requires their students to present case studies, rotation results and reports to fellow classmates. Because all of the nursing students are additionally required to successfully complete a Public Speaking class, we have constant contact and communication with these students. As a result, it is probably no surprise to you that these students continually inform us that they underestimated the need, use and importance of public speaking in the health care field. Whether they are presenting to the hospital Board, a team of doctors, or a family unit, they are 'on stage' with their communication skills.

Consider the following:

- For seniors who want a job after graduation, public speaking often makes the difference in getting the job and not getting the job. In formal job interviews, employers want to know if you can orally organize your thoughts about your previous experiences, articulate why you want to work at this particular organization, and most importantly, they want to hear how effectively you can persuade them that you would be a valuable asset to their organization. In fact, research shows that the use of poise, interest (e.g. eye contact) and expressiveness are large factors of success in a job interview (Riggio, 2011).

- For public officials working within the Center for Disease Control, the expertise of recognizing life-threatening flu strains must be matched with an understanding of what information should be released to the public.

- For the shop floor manager trying to make sense of a constantly changing health code required by local governments, ongoing training is a must.

- For the executive attempting to instill hope and comfort within employees during times of economic hardship, speeches must be matched with numerous public press releases explaining new projects and their positive effects.

- For technology directors confronted with an ever-expanding online universe and an explosion in online crime, press conferences regarding cyber terrorism must be balanced with clear and accessible language for the general public.

- For criminal justice professionals assessing an archaic justice system without DNA testing, explaining justice in terms of scientific method and the technological advancement of DNA testing will require skilled professionals who can explain science in everyday language to jury members.

- For teachers who must effectively adjust their instruction to various learning styles, regular communication with students and parents is an ongoing work in progress.

- For attorneys who must write and deliver arguments to win their cases, public speaking can mean the difference between court findings of innocence and guilt.

- For artists who attempt to sell their work, creating an authentic online presence is an essential and ongoing communication challenge.

- For young people of all majors, communication is a common ingredient. For example, as part of Marine Week Chicago, Maj. Shawn D. Haney, a public affairs officer from Anderson, S.C., taught the kids in the program about the importance of communication in their future careers. As part of the meeting, Haney discussed the multiple ways people communicated. She talked about the importance of body language, written reports and public speaking. She told the students, "I really feel that communication is important to everyone no matter what you think you're going to do in life." (BYLINE: States News Service).

- For the powerless and marginalized, public speaking is also essential. According to Kathleen Torrens, an associate professor of communication studies at the University of Rhode Island, public speaking is a vital part of citizenry for all students – especially those for whom college is not an option because of financial or academic reasons. She said:

  Knowing how to make a cogent, persuasive argument is important because this population should be able to stand up for themselves - whether in the courts, the school systems, or in other public forums where public advocacy is necessary to protect themselves and their families." (*US Fed News,* May 4, 2009 Monday 11:10 AM EST).

- For the betterment of its citizens, the city of Fontana issued the following news release:

  The Mayor and City Council invite the public to register for the new public speaking class at the Heritage Neighborhood Center located at 7350 W. Liberty Parkway. The Friday classes begin Friday, June 26 from 7 to 8:30 pm for ages 18 and older. Fees are $28 for 4 weeks. Fear Free Public Speaking will enable the student to identify, overcome, and transform their fear of public speaking into an opportunity to deliver amazing presentations. Students will work to eliminate stage fright and enhance their networking skills. For more information or to register, please visit any neighborhood center or call (*US State News,* June 4, 2009 Thursday 12:02 PM EST).

Public speaking transcends occupational differences. Whatever your particular major and however different your goals are in life from the person sitting next to you in class, each of us are constantly confronted with issues of facts, forced to make sense of these facts, and asked to provide audiences with an understandable translation of these facts. This is our modern reality. The question isn't if you will have to speak in public, but *when* and *how well.*

Reason #4: Public Speaking As Self-Help

Pause for a moment and think of an important leader or mentor in your life. Wasn't that individual you conjured in your mind an excellent public speaker? Someone who grabbed your attention? Someone who made logical arguments? Someone who used persuasion, emotion and compelling evidence? Someone whose delivery matched the intensity and passion of their topic or subject matter?

Throughout Western history, leaders and leadership can't be separated from public speaking. A famous Greek professor named Isocrates believed that the skills involved in public speaking, argument making, reasoning, and eloquence, actually fostered morality as speakers would be more committed to adhering to the very principles and ideas they advocated as speakers speaking to a community. He even went as far as to teach students to memorize and practice well known speeches so they could meet the challenges of a new occasion and draw from the past – a kind of ancient "best of speeches" series – and craft new, aesthetically pleasing and politically appropriate oratory.

From Plato, the famous Greek philosopher, we learn the lessons of his master, Socrates, regarding the use what was called dialectics, a spoken form of reasoning employing questions and answers in the search for truth. Maybe some of your professors today still use the question and answer technique oftentimes referred to as the Socratic Method. In the Socratic Method, a professor asks you a question about a subject of importance of which he/she expects you to know the answer. Then the professor takes your answer and asks you another question. Again and again this process of questions and answers continues until a mutual understanding of the topic at hand is fully exhausted. While this may not  sound like the traditional public speech format you are accustomed to, the use of public reasoning and examples served as an early model in the development of public communication.

Later, Cicero, the famed Roman teacher of all things public and political, was quick to point out to students of politics and law that they needed speech training. He explained that Aristotle, the famed Greek philosopher and great teacher of public speaking, relied on speech "tools" to help his students prepare for public deliberation and oration (Crowlee and Hawhee, 1999). As it turns out, Greek teachers included the study of public speaking along with language and reasoning to help round out a complete education. The public communication tools included skills such as how to generate a thesis, or main idea, how to provide helpful examples to support your points, and how to persuade audiences using comparison and contrast.

While Roman teachers borrowed heavily from the Greeks' speech training manuals, they also condensed these writings into "how to" manuals for later students. In addition, the Romans studied the Greek teachers' use of arrangement (how to organize your thoughts), style (how your words should sound), reasoning (how logically you connect evidence to claims), delivery (how well you present your speech to an audience) and memory (we don't use this one much anymore but the Greeks and Romans developed techniques for memorizing long and complicated speeches – imagine trying to memorize an hour-long speech without the help of any notes!), and codified these principles into a kind of training manual for students and statesmen of their new empires (Bizzell and Herzberg, 2000).

These 'pragmatic' tools, meaning to deal with things in a rational and sensible manner, for the public speaker meant that students did not have to rely solely on being born with a gifted tongue, perfect memory, or strong voice to participate. Rather, the emphasis on the teaching of public speaking made it possible for students (granted, these were privileged children of wealthy families) to learn, practice, and attempt to advance their ideas, arguments, careers, wealth, and reputations in public settings. In other words, for you this means that one doesn't need to be naturally gifted in the art of the tongue. Rather, it can be and is a skill one can learn and improve when they assert their effort in public speaking.

Later during the Medieval Period (490s-1700), teachers would congregate in cities and spiritual centers often with other teachers. These earliest universities were little more than students coming together – referred to as stadiums – and they almost always revolved around collectives of well-acknowledged teachers (Bizzell and Herzberg). The arrival of these academic groups helped inspire the Renaissance where the teaching of speaking found its way into early university, covering topics of grammar, logic and public speaking for persuasive means.

The teaching of public speaking has a long history in the development of citizenry and the self-development of public leaders. In other words, while the techniques of public speaking may have evolved over the years, one thing remains certain: oral communication practice is necessary if we are to advance as public persons (Morgan, 2003). If public speaking was deemed necessary to the educational and moral development of both teachers and leaders of the western world for the previous two thousand years, we believe you can gain something from the art of public speaking as well.

Reason #5: Public Speaking Isn't Only About Speaking

Too often, public speaking is only seen as helping people become better speakers. While speaking is an essential aspect of public speaking (and it's usually the part we focus on because it's the speaking in public part that we spend so much time worrying about), it is not the only skill you will gain after reading this book.

Taking a class in public speaking will help you become a more discerning audience member because you will develop a new language to assess the content of a speaker's messages and appeals, as well as the quality of their presentation. Consider the learning tool that your fellow classmates become for you. Public speaking can teach us both how to make arguments and how better to judge other people's arguments. While we rarely get nervous when listening and critiquing other people's messages (like we do when speaking in public), learning how to be better judges of other people's arguments is an invaluable skill.

In his 2009 Notre Dame address President Obama asked graduates to be forward thinking, critical consumers, and users of facts. He stated:

Now, you, Class of 2009, are about to enter the next phase of your life at a time of great uncertainty. You'll be called to help restore a free market that's also fair to all who are willing to work. You'll be called to seek new sources of energy that can save our planet; to give future generations the same chance that you had to receive an extraordinary education. And whether as a person drawn to public service, or simply someone who insists on being an active citizen, you will be exposed to more opinions and ideas broadcast through more means of communication than ever existed before. You'll hear talking heads scream on cable, and you'll  read blogs that claim definitive knowledge, and you will watch politicians pretend they know what they're talking about. Occasionally, you may have the great fortune of actually seeing important issues debated by people who do know what they're talking about – by well-intentioned people with brilliant minds and mastery of the facts. In fact, I suspect that some of you will be among those brightest stars.

"President Obama: Notre Dame Commencement"

While the rest of President Obama's speech regarded both the need to maintain civility in the ongoing abortion debate and the need to find common ground, this moment in the speech is particularly enlightening because the President calls on graduates to recognize the appropriate usage of facts and encourages students to achieve such "mastery" in public discourse as well. Learning about public speaking will not only help you become a better speaker, it will also help improve your decision making abilities in discerning between truth and fiction, right and wrong, and good and bad.

Conclusion

Public speaking is an important, and some may contend essential, part of communication. It is an inescapable part of modern life, and an essential component of both leadership and good citizenship. The following chapters will provide the necessary details to help you better learn, understand, and practice the essential elements of effective public speaking. For additional information and visual example on the foundation of public speaking, visit: https://www.youtube.com/watch?v=RANhF66GEio.

References

Aristotle. (1991). *On rhetoric: A theory of civic discourse.* George Kennedy (trans.). New York: Oxford University Press.

Ballif, M. & Moran, M.G. (Eds.). (2005). *Classical rhetorics and rhetoricians: Critical studies and sources.* New York: Praeger Publishers.

Bizzell, P. & Herzberg, B. (2000). *The rhetorical tradition: Readings from classical times to the present* (2nd ed.). New York: Bedford/St. Martin's Press.

Bitzer, L. (1968). The Rhetorical Situation. *Philosophy & Rhetoric, 1,* 1-15.

Brewer, G. (2001). Snakes top list of Americans' fears. Retrieved June 22, 2009, from http://www.gallup.com/poll/1891/Snakes-Top-List-Americans-Fears.aspx

Brummett, B. (2006). *Rhetoric in popular culture 2nd ed.* Thousand Oaks, CA: Sage Publications, Inc.

Burke, K (1966). *Language as symbolic action: Essays on life, literature and method.* Berkeley, CA: University of California Press.

Gwynn, A. (1926). *Roman education from Cicero to Quintilian.* Oxford: Clarendon Press.

Hawhee, D. & Crowley, S. (2008). *Ancient rhetorics for contemporary students.* New York: Longman.

Lentz, T. M. (1989). *Orality and literacy in hellenic Greece.* Carbondale: Southern Illinois University Press.

May, J.M. (2002). *Brill's companion to Cicero: Oratory and rhetoric.* Boston: Brill Leiden.

Morgan, M. (2003). *Presentational speaking.* Boston: McGraw Hill.

Rebhorn, W. A. (Ed.). (2000). *Renaissance debates on rhetoric.* Ithaca, NY: Cornell University Press.

Vatz, R. E. (1973). The myth of the rhetorical situation. Philosophy & Rhetoric, 6, 154-157.

Suggested Websites

http://www.nydailynews.com/entertainment/gossip/rihanna-chris-brown-fight-started-text-message-woman-article-1.369542 (2009)

http://www.history.com/topics/columbine-high-school-shootings (2007)

https://www.psychologytoday.com/blog/cutting-edge-leadership/201101/using-effective-nonverbal-communication-in-job-interviews (Riggio, 2011).

Chapter 2
Understanding the Audience

Imagine that you're in your home or dorm room and you're jolted by an emergency broadcast announcement on your satellite radio feed. The latest weather forecast indicates that a tornado is fast approaching: sirens blaring, wind blowing, and rain pouring. Will giving a speech or holding a press conference prevent the tornado from heading your way? Not likely. While words can be used to help save lives by alerting citizens as to the exact location and expected path of the tornado, words alone won't change its course. The wrath of the tornado is an uncontrollable factor.

However, consider this: words matter when they can affect, modify, and change audiences (Bitzer, 1968). Much like the announcement above that would alert people to the impending direction of the tornado. This is why it is impossible to study and practice public speaking without acknowledging the importance of the audience. When audience impact is the goal, audiences become an essential factor in all aspects of the speech process, from the very reason for the speech itself, to audience expectations about what the speech should look and sound like, and finally, in determining the overall impact of the speech performance. To this end, it is important and essential to note that public speaking is intended 'for' inclusion of the other; in this case, the audience.

The Audience Calls for a Speech

Some situations call forth the need for speakers and speeches. For example, after the 1995 Oklahoma City Bombing at the Murrah Federal Building in Oklahoma City, Oklahoma, audiences naturally wanted answers to the inevitable questions that emerged from the carnage. Why did this happen? Who would do such a thing? How could such a horrific event happen in the heartland of America? What can we do to prevent such tragedies from happening again? Audiences felt the need to 'be in the know' of information, as this was a tragic event that affected not only those close to the crisis, but also to Americans in general.

On April 23, 1995, Bill Clinton attempted to address many of these audience-inspired questions in a speech at the Oklahoma Bombing Memorial Prayer Service. In an attempt to make sense of the tragedy, Clinton said:

> To all my fellow Americans beyond this hall, I say, one thing we owe those who have sacrificed is the duty to purge ourselves of the dark forces which gave rise to this evil. They are forces that threaten our

common peace, our freedom, our way of life. Let us teach our children that the God of comfort is also the God of righteousness: Those who trouble their own house will inherit the wind. Justice will prevail.

Let us let our own children know that we will stand against the forces of fear. When there is talk of hatred, let us stand up and talk against it. When there is talk of violence, let us stand up and talk against it. In the face of death, let us honor life. As St. Paul admonished us, let us "not be overcome by evil, but overcome evil with good."

"William J. Clinton: Oklahoma Bombing Memorial Speech"

In times of confusion, destruction, deliberation, and celebration, audiences look to and expect speakers to help them make sense of the social, cultural and political landscape by addressing the why, what, and how of events and experiences. Consider the following landmark event, that will forever have an impact upon all Americans.

On the evening of September 11, 2001, only hours after America and the world witnessed live images of the collapse of the Twin Towers in New York City, the crash of an airliner into the Pentagon and a downed airplane in the fields of Pennsylvania, President George Bush spoke to the American people in an attempt make sense of what had happened, reassure Americans and the world that essential government operations were in place to handle the crisis, and to remind Americans that we would endure this tragedy just as we had others in the past. In his final words to the nation on the evening of September 11, 2001, President Bush said:

This is a day when all Americans from every walk of life unite in our resolve for justice and peace. America has stood down enemies before, and we will do so this time. None of us will ever forget this day, yet we go forward to defend freedom and all that is good and just in our world. Thank you. Good night. And God bless America.

"CNN – Ex-President George W. Bush's Post 9/11 Speech"

Speakers and speeches do not always, however, simply respond to audience expectations. Sometimes, speakers and speeches attempt to preempt issues, events, or impending threats that might be overlooked, forgotten or underappreciated without the speaker's use of words and attention to the topic (Vatz, 1973). Less than a year after the Allied Victory in World War II, the Prime Minister of England, Winston Churchill, delivered a speech at Westminster College in Fulton, Missouri, and introduced audiences to the term "iron curtain" to highlight the growing threat of Soviet Communism. Of this impending menace, Churchill said:

> From Stettin in the Baltic to Trieste in the Adriatic an iron curtain has descended across the Continent. Behind that line lie all the capitals of the ancient states of Central and Eastern Europe. Warsaw, Berlin, Prague, Vienna, Budapest, Belgrade, Bucharest and Sofia, all these famous cities and the populations around them lie in what I must call the Soviet sphere, and all are subject in one form or another, not only to Soviet influence but to a very high and, in some cases, increasing measure of control from Moscow. Athens alone – Greece with its immortal glories – is free to decide its future at an election under British, American and French observation. The Russian-dominated Polish Government has been encouraged to make enormous and wrongful inroads upon Germany, and mass expulsions of millions of Germans on a scale grievous and undreamed-of are now taking place. The Communist parties, which were very small in all these Eastern States of Europe, have been raised to pre-eminence and power far beyond their numbers and are seeking everywhere to obtain totalitarian control. Police governments are prevailing in nearly every case, and so far, except in Czechoslovakia, there is no true democracy.

"Churchill Addresses People at the Westminster College in Fulton, Missouri"

Upon receiving the 1963 National Book Award for *Silent Spring*, environmentalist Rachel Carson indicted the modern mindset by highlighting what she referred to as a dangerous world threatening the health and security of human existence:

> Mankind has gone very far into an artificial world of his own creation. He has sought to insulate himself, in his cities of steel and concrete, from the realities of earth and water and the growing seed. Intoxicated with a sense of his own power, he seems to be going farther and farther into more experiments for the destruction of himself and his world. There is certainly no single remedy for this condition and I am offering no panacea. But it seems reasonable to believe – and I do believe – that the more clearly we can focus our attention on the wonders and

realities of the universe about us the less taste we shall have for the destruction of our race. Wonder and humility are wholesome emotions, and they do not exist side by side with a lust for destruction.

Similarly, over forty years later, Senator Al Gore and former presidential candidate, attempted to draw attention to what he argues is the ignored but deadly effects of global warming with his 2006 film, "An Inconvenient Truth". countless graphics in the form of PowerPoint presentations were also released to world-wide audiences with the intent to inform others of his perspective, as well as to provide emotional visuals of support.

Speakers speak to explain what has happened, warn audiences about what might happen, and argue for the right way to live. In each instance, the goal of the speaker is to interpret a situation while acknowledging, changing, correcting, and responding to audience expectations. Thus, for every speech, there is an audience that constrains or empowers the speaker to accomplish his/her goals. For this reason, speakers must not only understand who is in their audience, but also adjust their messages to account for audience beliefs and expectations. Without the ability to do this, speaker and the speech itself becomes self-serving.

From a Hearer to an Audience Member

Imagine you are on a crowded bus or subway and there's only one available seat. As you listen to your music on your iPhone or cellular device, the person next to you overhears the music you are listening to. In fact, you notice the person moving his feet to the rhythm and beat of the music that you thought only you could hear. Does this mean that the person sitting next to you on the bus is an audience member?

The simple, one-word answer to the question is No. The person next to you is capable of being influenced by your music because he can hear your music. But your music wasn't intended for him and you had no expectation that he would respond to your music or change his behavior as a result of overhearing your music. In addition, that person sitting next to you isn't an audience member because you didn't think about him in advance of your chance meeting on the bus. Simply put, your intent was not meant for the 'other'.

A person is transformed from a hearer to an audience member when you, the creator, begin to think about that person (or that type of person) and adjust your idea(s) to him/her in anticipation of how he/she might respond. If you've thought about the person or persons before they ever laid eyes on you as you stand behind your podium, then they're a part of your audience. You may not know the names of the people in your audience but you've hopefully thought long and hard about how an individual, or someone resembling that person's background, interests, desires, and expectations, might respond to your speech and have carefully considered strategies for overcoming possible audience objections and concerns to your ideas (Bryant & Wallace, 1947).

From Expression to Communication

Consider that if you've ever kept a diary, activity log, or a journal, your audience is you, and you alone. The intent is self-reflection. Therefore, spelling mistakes, transitions, and the logic and flow of your ideas are not overriding concerns because your goal is to express yourself to yourself. As long as you can read your own scribble and decipher spelling errors and grammar inconsistencies, then there's no reason to worry.

"Keeping a Journal"

With a diary, you don't have to use your eraser because our own ideas, thoughts, and beliefs always make sense to you. In fact, you may reflect back upon your journal years later and find some of those omissions or mistakes as funny, or perhaps emotionally purposeful. Yet, the moment you begin to think about how others might understand or interpret your beliefs and ideas, you know you are in the realm of a translation process that adapts your feelings and emotions and ideas (i.e. pure expression) into something comprehensible to audience members beyond yourself.  On the other hand, for a paper you write for your professor, you must ensure your paper has a clear point and thesis, each paragraph has a topic sentence with transitions linking one point to another, and spelling and grammar are correct and appropriate to maximize the professor's understanding of your ideas. The intent of clarity becomes of utmost importance.

When you know your work will be read or heard by others, the eraser and the delete key are important functions of acknowledging that you must translate for others because you want them to understand. Consider the author of the very book you are reading right now. These instruments are essential for my use as I review the contents, so you, the audience, understands the purpose and the content of the chapters within the book. Similarly, you must think about and anticipate how others might make sense or be confused by your thoughts, assertions, and/or evidence when you are presenting. Public speaking involves communicating your ideas and adapting them, or translating them, to that of audiences beyond yourself. When you contemplate these issues, you are now in the realm of communication. In fact, speakers who are most empathetic with what it is like to listen to and respond to other's ideas and words make the best speech writers and speakers. Think about this from your own perspective. When you are listening to others, you more than likely appreciate someone who is clear, connects to the audience members and uses 'your' time wisely to connect the logic and points of the presentations purpose. When you use this philosophy as a presenter yourself, you are implementing that sense of empathy that will connect your audience to you as the speaker. Consider speakers who neglect, underestimate, or ignore audiences, do so at their own peril because public speaking requires an intimate understanding of the translation process necessary to take what you believe and think and communicate it to others in a way that is understandable and compelling (Burke, 1931).

When you speak to an audience in a public speaking situation, what you say is always interpreted in light of audience members' previous experiences, expectations, needs, or interest level. Wouldn't it be too easy if audiences listened to our speeches and words in the very way we wanted them to, ignoring everything they knew, believed and held to be true? Clearly, this isn't the case, as people are not mind readers. If they were, there would be no need for a public speaking class because each time you opened your mouth, what you said would be understood, acted upon, and appreciated in the exact way you wanted it to be. But that ideal speaking situation rarely, if ever, happens. If you've ever said something that you thought was funny and the people you were speaking to didn't or if you believe you were remarkably clear about giving someone directions to your house but your friend got lost, you understand the endless challenges of translation (Burke, Counter-Statement, 1931).

Translation Process

Who's In My Audience?

The goal of any speech is to influence an audience. It is crucial to remember that the ultimate purpose of a public presentation is to offer an opportunity for the audience to learn. The speech needs to focus on the 'other', or in this case, the audience. Thus, in order to maximize the effectiveness of a speech, you should consider the following questions when constructing your speech:

(1) Who is in your audience?

Demographic analysis includes information about the characteristics of your audience that might help you better understand their particular background, interests, and perspectives so you can better anticipate audience objections, points of controversy, and possible confusion areas. Demographic factors include, but are not limited to the following variables:

a. **Age** – Will different age groups respond differently to my topic? How might someone's age predispose them to my topic?

   Example: On September 18, 2007, Randy Pausch, professor of computer science at Carnegie Mellon University, delivered his "Last Lecture." Though this was no ordinary lecture, it was both literally and figuratively his "last lecture." The "Last Lecture" series, originally conceived for top professors to think about what mattered most to them and then give a hypothetical "final talk," meant something more for Randy Pausch as only weeks prior to his "final talk", he had been diagnosed with terminal pancreatic cancer. The title of his lecture was, "Really Achieving Your Childhood Dreams."

"Randy Pausch Last Lecture: Achieving Your Childhood Dreams"

   Discussion Question: After watching the speech, who do you think Professor Pausch was directing his speech to? How do you know this? Use specific elements from his speech to prove your point. How might the speech have changed if he was directing the speech at a differently aged audience – much older than college-aged, for example?

b. **Gender** – Will my audience's conceptions of masculinity and femininity affect what I include/exclude from my speech? Should my language choices change given the gender composition of my audience? What assumptions am I making that may be incompatible with the gender composition of my audience?

   Then First Lady Hillary Rodham Clinton delivered a well-referenced speech concerning women's rights at the 1995 United Nations' 4th World Conference on Women. Aside from the obvious "we/our" language, Clinton voices assumptions about what is important to women's lives such as human rights, jobs, and healthcare. Here is an excerpt from her speech:

It is also a coming together, much the way women come together every day in every country. We come together in fields and factories, in village markets and supermarkets, in living rooms and board rooms. Whether it is while playing with our children in the park, or washing clothes in a river, or taking a break at the office water cooler, we come together and talk about our aspirations and concern. And time and again, our talk turns to our children and our families. However different we may appear, there is far more that unites us than divides us. We share a common future, and we are here to find common ground so that we may help bring new dignity and respect to women and girls all over the world, and in so doing bring new strength and stability to families as well.

By gathering in Beijing, we are focusing world attention on issues that matter most in our lives – the lives of women and their families: access to education, health care, jobs and credit, the chance to enjoy basic legal and human rights and to participate fully in the political life of our countries.

There are some who question the reason for this conference. Let them listen to the voices of women in their homes, neighborhoods, and workplaces. There are some who wonder whether the lives of women and girls matter to economic and political progress around the globe. Let them look at the women gathered here and at Huairou – the homemakers and nurses, the teachers and lawyers, the policymakers and women who run their own businesses. It is conferences like this that compel governments and peoples everywhere  to listen, look, and face the world's most pressing problems. Wasn't it after all – after the women's conference in Nairobi ten years ago that the world focused for the first time on the crisis of domestic violence?

"First Lady Hillary Rodham Clinton's Remarks to the Fourth Women's Conference in Beijing, China"

<u>**Discussion Questions**</u>: How would an audience comprised of more than homemakers respond to this speech? Do men feel connected to the speaker, to the topic? Why or why not? How are men included both in the demographic analysis and in the suggested call to action?

c. **Racial, Ethnic, and Cultural Background –** Will the racial and cultural background of my audience affect audience interest or relevancy of my topic? Does my audience have a different worldview based on their cultural or racial experiences? If so, how might this affect audience reception of my ideas?

Comedian Bill Cosby's 2004 controversial speech at the National Association for the Advancement of Colored People (NAACP), celebrating the 50th Anniversary of famous Supreme Court Decision, Brown v. Board of Education, illustrates the racial and cultural dynamics of audience analysis. Below is an excerpt from his controversial speech:

So, ladies and gentlemen, I want to thank you for the award – and giving me an opportunity to speak because, I mean, this is the future, and all of these people who lined up and done – they've got to be wondering what the hell happened. *Brown v. Board of Education* – these people who marched and were hit in the face with rocks and punched in the face to get an education and we got these knuckleheads walking around who don't want to learn English. I know that you all know it. I just want to get you as angry that you ought to be. When you walk around the neighborhood and you see this stuff, that stuff's not funny. These people are not funny anymore. And that's not my brother. And that's not my sister. They're faking and they're dragging me way down because the state, the city, and all these people have to pick up the tab on them because they don't want to accept that they have to study to get an education.

We have to begin to build in the neighborhood, have restaurants, have cleaners, have pharmacies, have real estate, have medical buildings instead of trying to rob them all. And so, ladies and gentlemen, please, Dorothy Height, where ever she's sitting, she didn't do all that stuff so that she could hear somebody say "I can't stand algebra, I can't stand..." and "what you is." It's horrible.

Basketball players – multimillionaires can't write a paragraph. Football players, multimillionaires, can't read. Yes. Multimillionaires. Well, *Brown v. Board of Education*, where are we today? It's there. They paved the way. What did we do with it? The White Man, he's laughing – got to be laughing. 50 percent drop out -- rest of them in prison.

You got to tell me that if there was parenting – help me – if there was parenting, he wouldn't have picked up the Coca Cola bottle and walked out with it to get shot in the back of the head. He wouldn't have. Not if he loved his parents. And not if they were parenting! Not if the father would come home. Not if the boy hadn't dropped the sperm cell inside of the girl and the girl had said, "No, you have to come back here and be the father of this child." Not "I don't have to."

Therefore, you have the pile up of these sweet beautiful things born by nature – raised by no one. Give them presents. You're raising pimps. That's what a pimp is. A pimp will act nasty to you so you have to go out and get them something. And then you bring it back and maybe he or she hugs you. And that's why pimp is so famous. They've got a drink called the "Pimp-something." You all wonder what that's about, don't you? Well, you're probably going to let Jesus figure it out for you. Well, I've got something to tell you about Jesus. When you go to the church, look at the stained glass things of Jesus. Look at them. Is Jesus smiling? Not in one picture. So, tell your friends. Let's try to do something. Let's try to make Jesus smile. Let's start parenting. Thank you, thank you

"Bill Cosby Famous Pound Cake Speech"

Discussion Questions: How might a person's race affect audience reception of Cosby's speech? How did Cosby's race and cultural standing in the African American community affect his message? How did Cosby's choice of language – "The White Man, he's laughing – got to be laughing. 50 percent drop out – rest of them in prison" – impact his message? Do you believe Cosby's indictment of his nearly all-black audience – "You're raising pimps" – was an effective strategy? If yes, why? If not, why not?

d. **Religious affiliation** – Religious values and traditions affect what we believe to be true/untrue, right/wrong, and good/bad. Understanding your audience's religious background will help you better understand their current attitudes and values as well as help you anticipate how they might interpret your message, word choice, and goals.

The Reverend Jeremiah Wright became a controversial figure in the 2008 Presidential campaign, partly because of controversial statements he made in several videotaped sermons to his church, Trinity United Church of Christ in Chicago. It was one of Reverend Wright's members, Presidential Candidate Barack Obama, who was asked to distance himself from many of Wright's controversial statements, including a quote from one of Wright's 2003 sermons, in which he said, "Not God bless America, God damn America. God damn America for treating its citizens as less than human." In another sermon, he called America, the "U.S. of KKA."

In 2008, at the National Press Club Breakfast, Reverend Wright defended himself and his sermons, and sought to articulate his religion's philosophy. What follows is an excerpt from his speech:

When using the paradigm of Dr. William Augustus Jones, Dr. Jones, in his book "God in the Ghetto," argues quite accurately that one's theology, how I see God, determines one's anthropology, how I see humans, and one's anthropology then determines one's sociology, how I order my society.

Now the implications from the outset are obvious.

If I see God as male; if I see God as white male; if I see God as superior, as God over us and not Immanuel, which means God with us; if I see God as mean, vengeful, authoritarian, sexist or misogynist, then I see humans through that lens.

My theological lens shapes my anthropological lens. And as a result, white males are superior; all others are inferior. And I order my society where I can worship God on Sunday morning, wearing a black clergy robe, and kill others on Sunday evening, wearing a white Klan robe (Cheers, applause).

I can have laws which favor whites over blacks, in America or South Africa. I can construct a theology of apartheid, in the Afrikaner church, and a theology of white supremacy in the North American or Germanic church.

The implications from the outset are obvious. But then the complicated work is left to be done, as you dig deeper into the constructs, which tradition, habits and hermeneutics put on your plate.

To say, I am a Christian, is not enough. Why? Because the Christianity of the slaveholder is not the Christianity of the slave. The God to whom the slaveholders pray, as they ride on the decks of the slave ship, is not the God to whom the enslaved are praying, as they ride beneath the decks on that same slave ship.

How we are seeing God, our theology, is not the same. And what we both mean when we say, I am a Christian, is not the same thing. The prophetic theology of the black church has always seen and still sees all of God's children as sisters and brothers, equals who need reconciliation, who need to be reconciled as equals, in order for us to walk together into the future which God has prepared for us.

Reconciliation does not mean that blacks become whites or whites become blacks or Hispanics become Asian or that Asians become Europeans. Reconciliation means we embrace our individual rich histories, all of them. We retain who we are, as persons of different cultures, while acknowledging that those of other cultures are not superior or inferior to us; they are just different from us.

We root out any teaching of superiority, inferiority, hatred or prejudice. And we recognize for the first time in modern history, in the West, that the other who stands before us with a different color of skin, a different texture of hair, different music, different preaching styles and different dance moves; that other is one of God's children just as we are, no better, no worse, prone to error and in need of forgiveness just as we are.

Only then will liberation, transformation and reconciliation become realities and cease being ever elusive ideals. Thank you for having me in your midst this morning (Applause.).
(http://www.chicagotribune.com/news/politics/chi-wrighttranscript-04282008,0,3113697.story)

"Jeremiah Wright Address to the National Press Club"

Discussion Questions: Given the noted applause, what demographic makeup would you say Reverend Wright's audience is? How does his message include or exclude audience members from different religious groups? Would Reverend Wright's message be recalibrated for a mostly white Methodist group in Connecticut? A mainly Hispanic Catholic group in El Paso? If so, how?

e. **Belonging/Group Membership** – Will my audience's membership in organizations and groups (i.e. company affiliation, volunteer organizations, social clubs, political party affiliation, hobbies) affect how they respond to my topic? Each of us belongs to organizations and each organization has a set of values of "instructions" that we typically adhere to. For example, if your audience is composed of registered Republicans, membership in that organization means they share particular values and attitudes. Likewise, if you were giving a speech to registered Democrats, you can assume certain beliefs and attitudes based on their party affiliation.

(2) What does my audience know about my subject?

The knowledge level (or lack thereof) is essential to know when constructing your speech. Accurately assessing the audience's knowledge level will help you know where to begin your speech and what you need to focus on in the speech to achieve your aim.

At a practical level, accurately assessing audience knowledge level of the topic will help you make better decisions about how much to assume about your audience:

a) If the audience is <u>familiar</u> with the topic and subject matter, audiences will expect:

- Your speech not to address information or material they are already familiar with.
- Your speech to tell them something new, go into more detail, provide more nuance to an already-familiar topic.
- Something to be added to their knowledge level.
- New angles or unique perspectives to be added to an already familiar topic.

b) If the audience is <u>unfamiliar</u> with the topic and subject matter, audiences will expect:

- Your speech to make the case that the topic is relevant.
- A proper and full contextualization of the topic.
- An introduction to the basic terminology of the subject.

Demographic analysis includes important knowledge about your audience. However, audience analysis *does not* provide all the necessary information a speaker needs to know about an audience's possible reactions and expectations about the topic and content of your speech. "Thoughtful audience analysis is one of the best habits you can develop as a speaker" author unknown. *Psychological* audience analysis helps a speaker anticipate how an audience feels about the topic of subject matter of your speech. In essence, the internal emotional and analytical state of an audience will help determine the positive and negative manner in which your message is received. Apathy and attention, support and rejection are all largely determined by the audience's mindset.

(3) Will my audience care what I am speaking about?

Anticipating audience interest in your topic is essential. Preparing a speech for an audience that might not initially find interesting doesn't mean you should give up on the topic. To the contrary, it simply means that that audience disinterest in your topic should guide your decisions throughout the speech making process. Expert speakers always consider the interest level of the audience because knowing (in advance) that an audience is relatively interested or disinterested in the topic matter doesn't mean you shouldn't construct the speech. Rather, it means you need to make strategic adjustments to create interest or increase interest.

a) If your audience is <u>interested</u> in the topic/subject matter:

- Less time needs to be devoted to establishing relevance
- Move quickly into the content of the speech
- Use already-established audience interest to delve deeper into detail about the subject matter.
- Rely on pre-approved evidence (already accepted by the audience) or sourcing that includes the legitimacy of the speaker.
- Emphasis may be placed on arguments in the body of the speech to build on existing audience support. If it is known than an audience already tends to agree with a point in your speech, it is ok to add evidentiary support.

If the audience is <u>uninterested</u> in the topic matter:

- The introduction (especially the attention getter) is very important.
- Relevance needs to be clearly articulated in the introduction and touched on throughout the speech in each main point.
- A diversity of outside evidence (i.e. expert testimony, quotations, examples, stories, and statistics) should be used throughout the speech to create and maintain interest.

Example and Discussion Question: Perhaps the biggest challenge for a novice speaker is helping the audience care about what you care about. In this excerpt from a student speech, pay particular attention to how the speaker attempts to: a) establish relevance and b) bring a topic that may be abstract and "bring it close" to the heart and minds of her audience.

…Unfortunately, for some Americans we may say tomato, but others say deporto. According to Contra Costa Times on July 29, 2005 there's an estimated 3 million to 6 million Muslims in the United States, and according to Talk of the Nation from August 9th, 2001, the number of mosques in the nation grew 25% since 1995 and now numbers more than 1,200….Not to mention, muslims work in all kinds of places. When I decided to go and get a new job I first went for "the look" (placed red dot on head) but all this did was make me think of a tampon commercial. Well, I got  fired (showed convenience store picture). I hate to drive (showed cabby picture), and I can't sew a pair of pants, much less the left and right ventricle (showed image of serious looking doctor). And I am not alone...or safe …at work or in my mosque. The Insight on the News of January 7th, 2003 released FBI hate-crime data show that crimes against Arabs and Muslims have increased more than 1,500 percent since last year. The Jerusalem Post of July 24th, 2005 states the best estimate of American Muslims is between 1.9 and 2.8 million, compared to the figure of six to seven million used by Muslim groups, the media, and many US officials.

Based on the student's speech thus far, answer the following questions: How specifically did this speaker attempt to make her topic relevant? How was this topic made interesting to an audience that may not have been familiar with crimes against Arab and Muslims? Please be specific.

(4) Does your audience agree or disagree with your topic (this pertains mostly to persuasive speeches)?

If the audience <u>strongly agrees</u> with the topic matter:

- Don't introduce points that they may not agree with
- Focus on reinforcing audience agreement
- Focus on intensifying audience agreement

If the audience <u>strongly disagrees</u> with the topic matter:

- Work to establish minimal points of agreement
- Focus the speech on commonalities rather than points of disagreement
- Remind the audience that you respect the points of difference

(5) What are common obstacles to audience understanding?

- The status quo, or what the audience currently believes to be true, is typically the greatest impediment to audience reception of new information. What audiences already hold to be true – whether right or wrong, good or bad, advantageous or not – must at least be addressed by a speaker.

Examples: If you are asking your audience to recycle paper and plastics, you must first overcome the fact that there is currently no recycling program on campus. Asking the audience to do something different, to change an attitude toward recycling – from "I don't care" to "I want a recycling program on campus" – means you must overcoming pure habits of thought. Habits of thought are powerful only because that's what's been done before. And, if that's what was done (or not done) before, then the first question an audience member will ask is: Why change now?

- For persuasive speeches in particular, when you are asking an audience to change a belief, attitude, value, behavior, there are recurring audience objections that you, as the speaker, must address and overcome, no matter what the topic. Common objections that you should address, either explicitly or implicitly in your speech often include: money (cost), time, effort, tradition.

(6) What kind of speech am I giving?

Is my general purpose to <u>inform</u>, <u>persuade</u>, or <u>entertain</u>? Knowing the type of speech genre required and expected, will help you answer the following questions:

- What type of evidence is expected?
- Is humor appropriate?
- How long is too long or how short is too short?
- Who came before me? What will follow me?
- Are questions and answers expected following the speech?

"Public Speaking: Types of Persuasive Speeches"

(7) Situational Analysis or Where am I speaking?

- Am I speaking to a small group of 5-7 people or a theater of hundreds?
- Will a microphone be available?
- Will there be a podium?
- Will I have access to audio and visual equipment for sound or power point?

Making the wrong decisions in assessing your audience will greatly limit your effectiveness both in terms of content and speaker credibility. Remember, your ethos, or credibility, is determined by what you do and don't do in your speech. This largely determines whether or not your audience will provide you the trust given to those that they perceived as ethical. This trust leads to a willingness to agree or follow a presenter. But, making wrong assumptions about your audience's knowledge level, interest, attitudes, or expectations is a sure sign to your audience that you don't care enough about your audience to have done the necessary homework in contemplating the audience's needs, desires, and expectations. Also, don't forget that the forms of audience analysis discussed thus far can be used to better understand your audience, the ultimate goal of any speaker is to create a "we" from the many "I's" in your audience.

Lastly, it is also imperative to take into account *Contextual* audience analysis. Here, the speaker takes into consideration how the context itself will affect the audience. From a sociological perspective, the social context theory investigates how social forces affect change in people (Briggs, 2015). Similarly, consider how changing a context for you would alter your ability to listen, understand and interpret communication. If you were invited by a friend to coffee so they could talk to you about a serious relationship issue they are having, the context helps or hinders the process of your ability to focus upon the dialogue. Consider a quiet, cozy shop versus a busy mall coffee shop. The context plays a large factor in changing attentiveness. So, as a speaker presenting to an audience, contextual audience analysis is very similar, but on a larger scale. It considers elements like: Are the audience members mandated to attend the presentation or is their attendance voluntary? What events have occurred for them in the past week that might influence their presence (e.g. company lay-offs or budget cuts)? What time of day is the presentation taking place, as it may affect the alertness of the audience members? What obstacles might the room have that prevent or assist in attentiveness? As well, contextual audience analysis also considers if the audience is expecting a formal or informal presentation (Dlugan, 2012). Thus, prior investigation of the context and application of this knowledge only provides for a greater opportunity of success with your presentation. As well, you increase your success of connecting with the audience due to your diligent attention of their needs and how the context will help or hinder the message they are receiving.

Targeting Your Audience

Given the differences and diversity of audiences, not everyone in the audience can be accounted for. Speakers must make strategic choices based on their target audience, or those toward which they are directing their speech to. If you attempt to adjust your speech to every single member of your audience, you may end up reaching no one. Targeting your audience helps speakers because it gives them direction by forcing them to remind themselves who they are speaking to and to whom their speech appeals, arguments, and evidence is directed toward.

<u>*Audience Analysis Exercise*</u>: Given what you know about the audience analysis questions every prospective speaker needs to ask, assess the choices the speaker made about his/her audience by examining the following speech. Based on the speech itself, answer the following relevant audience analysis questions:

(1) Based on the speech, can you tell what the possible demographics of the audience? How do you know?

(2) Based on the speech, what obstacles to audience comprehension did the speaker attempt to overcome?

(3) Based on the speech, did the speaker assume the audience was interested or uninterested in the subject matter? How do you know?

(4) Based on the speech, what was the knowledge level of the audience concerning the speech topic? How do you know? Be specific.

Sample Speech

On July 16, the Dyn-O-Mat company and a team of weather experts loaded 20,000 pounds of the storm-busting product into a C-130 jet at Palm Beach International Airport. During that day's test, team members removed a building thunderstorm completely from the atmosphere, a first-ever feat documented by Doppler radar. In the future, Dyn-O-Mat says its product will .... muzzle a hurricane.

Dyn-O-Mat, a Florida-based environmental products company, has successfully tested a formulated polymer substance capable of removing clouds from the sky. Dyn-O-Storm ... works by absorbing water from a brewing storm using a gel ... that drops harmlessly into the ocean. So it's no surprise that the St. Petersburg Times, August 24, 2003 believes that Dyn-O-Storm will take meteorology to a whole new level.

Because Dyn-O-Storm will most likely arm us to end threatening weather the likes of Hurricane Andrew and even tornadoes, we will first consider the history of cloud science that prompted Dyn-O-Storm, then we will "check our readings" on the current development and use of Dyn-O-Storm. And finally, we will make some predictions as to the future of this atmospheric wonder.

First, we have to go all the way back to a December evening in 1802. According to a Washington Post article of August 28, 2003, on that date, Luke Howard, a well-known London pharmacist, who practiced meteorology on the side, addressed the Askesian Society (weather hobbyists) and discussed his ideas for the classification and modification of cloud control. Since its inception, the classification of cloud study has aided the understanding of cloud formations and the conditions leading up to their dissolution ... or their violent eruptions. Over time, cloud study has been subverted to a

smaller sub discipline in weather science. Unlike Luke Howard's amateur morphology concerns, contemporary meteorology focuses more on the quantitative numerical weather prediction and weather manipulation. Detroit Meteorologist, Dr. Greg Mann explains in a Storm Warning interview October 2003, "Numerical weather prediction is a very different field: chaotic, dynamic, and the prediction of its trajectories is still limited by imperfect knowledge of the state of the atmosphere at some initial time." Consequently, we have seen a shift from the abstract prediction methods of weather forecasting, to a technical field, which allows a certain level of control. However, the control of our contemporary meteorological research is for predicting what our atmosphere is going to throw at us.

Enter... the concept of cloud seeding. Recent research has returned to yesteryear, to combine the quantitative study of contemporary prediction ... with the morphological study of clouds and their contents to reveal the details of how droplets and ice crystals interact to form precipitation. In a November 2003 email interview with Dr. William R. Cotton of the Colorado State University Department of Atmospheric Science, seeding of any clouds, requires that they contain super cooled water & the introduction of a substance, such as silver iodide, that has a crystalline structure similar to ice. When ice particles form in ...BIG...super cooled clouds, they grow at the expense of liquid droplets and become heavy enough to fall as rain from clouds that otherwise would produce none (big pause). Until recently, however, there has been no product that could seed clouds in an effective way...

Until now, with Dyn-O-Storm. See .. "weather modification" research has recently figured out a way to seed clouds theoretically .. using dust to encourage precipitation. But the August 2003 Case Study Weather Force, explains that climate modification and then severe storm control were "found ineffective" as just theory ... "until ... the creation of Dyn-O-Storm."

Peter Cordani, CEO of Dyn-O-Mat explains in New Scientist of November 20, 2003, that he hit on the idea in 1998 after using a gardening product that turns water into a gel so it will remain by a plant's roots for three of four days. Cordani said his cloud-busting, biodegradable granules don't contaminate the environment and dissolve when they come into contact with salt water."

A November 2003 filing of the United States Patent office reveals that Cordani's Dyn-o-Gel is "made of water absorbent polymer plastic called polyacrylamide, which the ...company uses in products like oil-absorbing mats ...[and] liquid absorbing disposable diapers." Dyn-O-Gel polyacrylamide as a – "super absorbent polymer resin capable of absorbing water up to several thousand times as its own weight. These super absorbent polymers are prepared from water-soluble polymers, but have cross-linking [molecular] structures that render the polymers water-insoluble." Dutch publication Polymer of June 2003 explains that ...by combining acrylamide – a vinyl substance – with water-soluble cross-linking molecular structures, a very strong, salt-soluble but water insoluble polymer can be produced with a uniform, small size, high gel capacity, and high water swell-ability. I.E.: Dyn-O-Storm hydrogel absorbs large amounts of moisture and then becomes a strong, gooey liquid...that falls safely out of clouds ... and dissolves cleanly in the ocean. And...because clouds are the engines for a storm, Dyn-O-Storm helps to weaken or destroy the storm itself.

In an earlier test, Dyn-O-Storm cut a cloud in half. The goal of more recent trials has been to knock down developing thunderstorms by using a bigger load of more absorbent powder. In the latest test, a large military aircraft scattered the powder through a storm cloud 1600 meters long and over 4000 meters deep. It took about 4000 kilograms of powder to soak up the moisture from the cloud. And what a soaking! The weather tower at Miami International Airport watched as "the cloud literally disappeared off the radar screen."

Well, with results like that, scientists predict that Dyn-O-Storm will be useful in the years to come ... for storm busting, fog diffusion, and general safety concerns. First, what about those pesky tropical storms? Dr. Jim Cornish of the Canada Environmental Organization explains in an October 2003 interview that hurricanes are severe tropical storms with torrential rain and winds above 74 miles per hour, and form under the 4 conditions of warm ocean water, quickly cooling atmosphere, vertical gale force winds, and at least 500 kilometers from the equator. The New Scientist October 2003 states that these conditions combined with the Coriolis Force – the spinning effect of big storms caused by the Earth's rotation – are needed to create the spin in a hurricane. Already ... Dyn-O-Storm has the ability to extract the moisture out of clouds being pushed up by a tropical depression's vertical winds ... or erase clouds already spinning in a hurricane! Hence, scientists are already measuring the amount of gel need for these huge weather disturbances.

Secondly, Dyn-O-Storm will be used for fog control! The New Scientist of August 2001, reported that early tests of Dyn O Gel in its infancy were deployed to test the efficacy of fog busting. And because Michael Allaby's 2003 book "Fog, Smog & Poisoned Rain" reports the continued, substantial health impacts of fog on our daily lives, Dyn-O-Mat predicts that fog busting will not doubtedly remain a primary use of Dyn-O-Storm.

Finally, Cordani explains that versions of the product are already under consideration by the federal Government in application to rainmaking and fire-fighting. Woman's World magazine of March 2003 points out that Dyn-O-Storm holds the potential to provide "perfect weather" rather than allow pesky "approaching storms" ... & it can "protect the lives of millions" who are in need of rain when dry conditions facilitate massive brush and timber fires.

Today, we've examined the study of ...and the erasure of clouds. Considering the study of clouds, the advent of Dyn-O-Storm for cloud-busting, and its future applications, it's obvious that this new-age hydrogel technology will soak up storms for years to come...giving meteorologists more than just numbers to think about!

Conclusion

Too often, novice speakers focus on the speaking aspect of public speaking without realizing that it is the public, or the audience, that distinguishes public speaking from other types of communication endeavors. Public speaking requires the art of translation so you can more fully account for the specific and particular demographic, psychological, and situational audience factors that distinguishes the particular needs and expectations of your audience from other audiences. For additional information and visual example of audience analysis, preview the videos on https://www.youtube.com/results?search_query=audience+analysis+in+public+speaking.

References

Bitzer, L. (1968). The Rhetorical Situation. *Philosophy & Rhetoric, 1*, 1-15.

Bryant, D. C. & Wallace, K. R. (1947). Fundamentals of public speaking. New York: D. Appleton-Century.

Burke, K. (1931). Counterstatement. Berkeley: Univ. of California Press.

Vatz, R. E. (1973). The myth of the rhetorical situation. Philosophy & Rhetoric, 6, 154-157.

Suggested Websites

http://sixminutes.dlugan.com/audience-analysis/
http://www.ehow.com/about_5414476_social-context-theory.html
https://www.youtube.com/results?search_query=audience+analysis+in+public+speaking

Chapter 3
Listening: More Than Meets the Ears

Recall being young. Certain lyrics or phrases seem to stick in your head. Ones that you repeated again and again.

Scott Westerfeld's "Ring around the rosie. A pocket full of posies. Ashes, ashes, we all fall down".

Neil Gaiman's "This little piggy went to the market. This little piggy stayed home. This little piggy ate roast beef. This little piggy ate none"

While we may not recall the authors of these rhymes when were young, note that as we mature, it became easier for most people to recite long stretches of dialogue from their favorite movie or lyrics from their favorite songs. Yet we often find it so difficult to remember what a speaker says on a topic that will have a direct and immediate impact on our life, like an upcoming test or an important job task?

Why is it that some statements survive in our collective memory? Most of us can't forget the following:

Franklin Roosevelt's, "You have nothing to fear but fear itself."

Patrick Henry's, "Give me liberty or give me death."

John F. Kennedy's, "And so, my fellow Americans: ask not what your country can do for you – ask what you can do for your country."

Martin Luther King's, **"I have a dream that my four little children will one day live in a nation where they will not be judged by the color of their skin but by the content of their character."**

"Nothing to Fear but Fear Itself"
"Ask Not What Your Country Can Do For You!"
"Martin Luther King 'I Have a Dream'"

Most of us don't remember what was said in each of these speeches other than these lone remaining phrases that, years after they were originally uttered, are still recited. Why do these phrases stay with us while so many other words, phrases and ideas fall into the delete file of "the forgotten"?

A professor recently delivered a speech to a local rotary club promoting a graduate-level academic program. He had been told that speaking to this group would be helpful in making contacts and providing a much-needed community endorsement. Half way through the 10-minute presentation, three of the older gentlemen in the attendance fell asleep. For most of the speech, the audience seemed more interested in eating their lunch than they did in listening to the speaker. Additionally, at the end of the presentation, the questions that were asked had nothing to do with the content of the presentation, but were about one single reference in the introduction to Hall of Fame pitcher Nolan Ryan.

Needless to say, the professor never heard from the group again regarding its desire to endorse the new academic program. He did, however, learn a valuable lesson regarding the process of listening – engaging in *effective* public speaking means understanding why audiences listen and why they don't!

According to the ever-present Webster's Dictionary, listening is a process whereby individuals both receive and comprehend sound. Additional definitions include, attending to the meaning of sounds, and a mental assessment of audible information. Hearing is different than listening. Hearing is the mere reception of sound waves while listening is the sense-making process that accompanies the sound reception. So, hearing can be understood as a physiological process, while listening can be understood as a psychological process. There's a big difference in hearing your professor's lecture

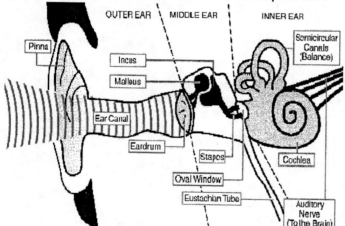

versus understanding what the professor is talking about.

As discussed in chapter one, communication as a behavior can be conceptualized in terms of senders and receivers deploying and making sense of information through symbolic means across a myriad of communication channels. Listening is that feature of the communication model whereby senders and receivers access and make initial sense of information as it is transmitted across channels.

Pearce, Johnson and Barker (1995) rely on a number of previous communication studies to point out two important issues concerning listening. First, consider this interesting fact: we rely on listening for more than a third of the time we are awake. Over thirty-five percent of our waking lives are spent listening! Second, as adults, we listen at approximately one-quarter efficiency. In other words, we do not attend to three quarters of the information we hear. Just as startling is the fact that information we hear is attended to less efficiently than when information is presented in written form. What this tells us is that we are more likely to remember what we read than what we hear. The stark reality is that we all are ineffective listeners, and unfortunately do not utilize the most of our skills or retain a great deal of the information we attend to. Therefore, the question still remains, why are we so ineffective at attending to information received through oral channels versus written channels of communication?

Perhaps, consider the following: first, reading is a solitary activity. Reading books, for instance, is a private engagement between you and the author (Postman, 1985). Have you ever noticed in a class when taking a test, some students seem to read more quickly, or more slowly than you. You look around to see if you are still the only person reading and/or taking the test, or how many students are still testing. This is a result due to the  fact that all readers proceed at their own pace. Some of us are slow readers and some of us are speed readers. Readers choose how fast their eyes dart from left to right, from paragraph to paragraph and from page to page. Second, readers can pick up a book anytime they want. Some of us, for example, are more alert and focused in the morning. Some of us are able to concentrate better at night. In each instance, the reader chooses when and how they read the text. Finally, when reading a book or even a magazine, a reader can actively remember content by underlining key phrases or words, writing notes on the side of the page, or even dog-earing the pages to remind themselves of a significant section.

 Contrast the above discussed facts of reading with the inefficiency of listening. Unlike reading the written word, speaking is not a private activity but, for the most part, a social engagement. And, because it is social and usually more spontaneous and feedback driven than the written word, listeners cannot proceed at their own pace. The speaker typically determines the pace. Sometimes a person speaks so slowly (i.e. 50-80 words a minute rather than the average of 130-150 words per minute) that their slow rate inspires inattention. Some speakers, on the other hand, speak too fast and we spend all of our time just trying to follow their rapid-fire speech pattern. Consider that Al Gore speaks at a rate of roughly 133 wpm, while Steve Jobs speaks at 158 wpm (Dlugan 2012). What accounts for such a variance? Dlugan concludes that genetic factors play a role, as well as the nervousness one experiences during the delivery, mental fatigue, the complexity of the words and content, as well as pauses that are self-induced or induced by the audience.

"How to Pace a Speech"

Second, when someone is speaking to us, it's hard to pay attention both to the person and to the content of their words. It's no surprise that we usually defer to people's nonverbal communication. According to research on nonverbal communication, 80% of communication is imparted through nonverbal means: eye contact, raised eyebrows, lack of eye contact, facial expressions, and much, much more. Sometimes, speakers are so persuasive in their delivery, so charismatic – the tenor of their voice, the movement of their body, the fluidity of movement from one idea to the next – that we become mesmerized into simply admiring. Admiration is great, but it is also an enemy of listening. It is no surprise then that listening is so challenging because it requires us to decode multiple levels of communication – voice, body, eyes, symbols, context, and relationship history – simultaneously.

"The Importance of Body Language in Presentations"

Third, unlike the act of reading, the speaker controls *when* listeners listen. Words remain on the page all day and all night, for you to read when and how you desire. Speakers, however, do not. Whether it be someone calling you on the phone right before you're going to sit down for lunch, or when you've have had a bad day, or when you feel sick, speakers chooses the time for your role as listener despite whether you are ready or whether you are in the right frame of mind to listen. Thus, attending to a speaker can either be a positive influence for the listener because variables such as timing, context and/or topic are all in line for the recipient. Or, perhaps the timing, context and topic is not something that aligns with their needs, thus the listener can be easily distracted or uninvolved.

Fourth, few of us carry around pen and paper every time someone speaks to us. Unlike reading a textbook where we know important information will be imparted to us as receivers of information, we have different expectations when we listen to someone orally speak to us. The relative fluidity of the encoder-decoder roles means that we don't expect to remember everything that is said in the course of a conversation because we

are both giving and receiving information. Moreover, when listening to someone, we can't press the rewind button. And, why take notes in your Blackberry or iPhone or jot down notes of what a speaker says unless you're required to do so, correct?

Janusik (2007) explains that traditionally we have had a very limited understanding of listening primarily because we have tested listening only as recall, perception and attention. In other words, we aren't 'trained' listeners. To this list, Janusik further adds working memory as a method of assessing the manner through which individuals both attend to and store information. Thus, listening can be assessed as sense-making and competent retention. For example, how well can you remember a conversation you had last week versus a conversation you engaged in 5 weeks ago? How much information from each conversation did you retain and how much of that information has eroded? According to the University of Missouri (2015), numerous studies show that after listening to a presentation, the average person only retains roughly 50% of the information. Within 48 hours, we lose still another 25%, therefore only retaining a mere 25% of the information. Have you ever had a communication experience that remained vivid even years later while more recent communication experiences disappeared very quickly? In addition to the variable of time, what qualities aided your recall of those experiences? What qualities aided in the erosion of your recall?

Beebe and Beebe (2005) provide a helpful template for understanding listening as a process. Building on Janusik's concerns with listening as a communication phenomenon greater than mere memory recall, they divide listening into the processes of selecting, attending, understanding, and remembering.

Selecting: Communicators must identify some sounds from others.

Attending: Communicators must spend mental time focusing on the sound phenomena. This is harder than it sounds (pun intended). There is so much competing for our attention, all the time, even when our bodies are physically present in one location. Although our bodies may be present, too often our minds are often wandering far away, worrying about the next day, the next test, the next weekend, the next meal, and so forth, making it difficult for any speaker to gain our psychological attention.

Understanding: Communicators must work to make sense of the phenomena. What does it mean? Why did this person say this and in this manner? What are the implications of what was just said? Did they contradict themselves?

Remembering: Communicators must recall the interpreted information. What was said? Who said it? When did they say it? Why did they say it?

To illustrate this effort-intensive process, let's consider an example of a fairly common example of inattentive listening. Often, my thirteen year old son wants to play his PS4 in the mornings before school. My husband and I are preparing for our day, attending to breakfast, etc. If my husband and I allow him this indulgence, his ability to listen to us is greatly compromised. For a while, it was not uncommon for us to ask our son three or four times to 'come to breakfast' or 'get his pack organized'. As a result, we instituted the no PS4 in the mornings and the 'one and done' request policy. Although he clearly isn't a fan of the changes we enforced, needless to say, the breakfast is eaten and his backpack is organized for the day, and he now listens to us because he isn't distracted by his game.

This example, unfortunately, is not much different than the challenges all public communicators must overcome when trying to reach. I often find the same challenges when I am lecturing to my college students. Too often, listening is discussed as an ideal when, in reality, listening never takes place in ideal circumstances. Therefore, it is important to acknowledge the types of listening habits that are less-than-effective, or otherwise stated, the type of listening that most of us engage in on a daily basis.

Harry Chambers (2001) states that there are four particularly problematic types of listeners public communicators should work to avoid.

(1) ***The "missing-in-action" listener:*** This type of listener is "detached" during communication exchanges. This is the person you meet at a dinner party who constantly looks over your shoulder at the front door, more concerned with observing who's walking through the front door, rather than focusing on your story.

(2) ***The "distracted" listener:*** This type of listeners is too mindful of distractions. This is the person at a political gathering more interested in getting a good picture of a speaker than listening to the speaker.

(3) ***The "selective" listener:*** This type of listener prejudges. This is the communicator who tells the school board that though they have asked for a smaller levy (due directly to public concern) they are really just more tax and spend nutjobs.

(4) ***The "contentious" listener:*** This is the listener who is so pre-prepared to reject others and their ideas before actually attending to the actual conversation, that they miss out on what the speaker actually says. This is the speaker who misses hearing a restaurant manager explain the meal is free because he is too busy yelling at the manager

If we know listening is so common and important, why is it that we are such ineffective listeners? According to Beebe and Beebe (1995), common listening barriers include, but are not limited to: internal, personal distractions, pre-judgement, external noise, parallel meaning between speaking and thinking, and too much information in the speech. For example, as a motivational speaker myself, I work on honing my craft by attending and listening to other coaches and speakers. I have personally witnessed speakers with wonderful work in terms of speaking craft, but somewhat deficient in their own listening skills. Although articulate, sharp and knowledgeable, the presenter was unable to answer questions form audience members, often times answering the wrong participant or confusing answers. Granted, some of this could be due to the nervousness of the presenter, but recall that this is a factor of ineffective listening. This example only serves to reinforce how difficult listening can be and 'is' affected by a variety of factors.

Hence Beebe and Beebe provide a checklist for becoming better listeners:

(1) Adapt to the speaker's delivery
(2) Listen with eyes and ears
(3) Avoid overacting
(4) Avoid jumping to conclusions
(5) Listen for major ideas
(6) Identify listening goals
(7) Practice listening
(8) Be a selfish listener
(9) Become active

Most of us worry about speaker apprehension. Fewer of us, however, think about listener apprehensions. Judi Brownell (2002) helps us recognize both the physical and mental signs that we may be suffering from listening apprehension – a condition of anxiety causing an inability to listen closely. Physically, an apprehensive listener may suffer from elevated blood pressure, increased heart rate, muscle tension, perspiration and back and neck pain in addition to difficulty breathing. Emotional signs of apprehensive listening may include stress and worrying, irritability, depression and fatigue, and tension and frustration. These factors aren't much different from those that suffer from speaker apprehension (which we will address later). Therefore, we can conclude that both speaker and listener apprehension impacts each and every person when in a presentational situation.

After a particularly complex, student-delivered informative speech a few years ago, one of our students in the audience had a very difficult time asking a question required of him. Here is the text of the speech followed by a transcript of the question. See if you can guess which of the physical or emotional symptoms of listening apprehension the student exhibited:

Student Speech Text:

> Take a look at your hands. No, seriously – take a look at your hands. See anything interesting or strange? Well, Canadian researcher Peter Hurd might just be able to, but it won't be through reading your palm or using tarot cards. Peter is a part of new research being done on what

are called digit ratios – or the difference in finger length - and he and colleagues have begun revealing startling information regarding how much our hands can tell about who we are – and who we are to become.

 To understand why **BBC News of March 4, 2005** believes that digit ratios could be nothing less than a biological window to the soul, we should first grab hold of the centuries of historical research behind these recent finds. Then, we'll point out the research that's currently underway, before discussing its future implications for our society and science as a whole. Take one last look at your hands – chances are, you'll never see them the same way again.

Trying to mine information from the hands is certainly nothing new. Since the beginning of recorded time, humankind has sought to discover more about itself using the most ubiquitous tools around – the hands. **According to the 1997 work entitled "Hand Book" by British researcher Tony Crisp**, hand analysis began several thousand years ago in ancient China as a simple science dedicated to observing traits like dirtiness and size of hands to determine characteristics about the people they were attached to. It didn't take long for this science to take on an air of mysticism, however, and soon hand analysis became little more than the reading of palms, used to predict the future.

The science of examining the hands with the purpose of research was all but forgotten until the turn of the 20th century. In 1901, New York physician Dr. William Benham's published *The Laws of Scientific Palmistry,* bringing hand analysis back under the study of science. **According to WebMD Medical News of March 3, 2005**, scientists soon began discovering strong correlations between certain characteristics and the relative lengths of the fingers – specifically, the ratio of length between the index and ring fingers. This field of research – known as "digit ratio" studies – have only recently begun making significant discoveries, but the ones that they have made will likely surprise, enlighten, and possibly even embarrass you.

Modern hand analysis has taken many forms and made several important findings – **the April 2004 issue of the Journal Early Human Development** reveals that autism, breast cancer risk, male and female fertility, and even penis size have all been linked to varying lengths between the index and ring fingers. Two of the most exciting discoveries have come in two areas – aggression and sexual orientation.

Now, contrary to popular belief, the middle finger is not the best indicator of aggressive tendencies. **According to BBC News of March 4, 2005**, researchers at the University of Alberta have recently discovered that the digit ratio between the index and ring fingers have a strong correlation to physically aggressive tendencies in men.

The research was conducted on over 300 undergraduates at the Alberta University, and was based on a series and surveys and subsequent hand measurements. The data provided some startling results, so startling in fact that **according to the Times of India of March 6, 2005**, lead researcher Peter Hurd initially called the findings a quote "pile of hooey." Hurd is quick to point out, however, that it is not the finger length that determines aggression. Instead, finger length and aggression are influenced by the same factor – testosterone. The study found that early exposure to testosterone can lead to increased

aggressive tendencies, and that finger lengths will accurately reflect this. Interestingly, the correlation does not hold true for women, and also says nothing about the level of other types of aggression in men, such as verbal and emotional force. **And according to the University of Alberta Express News of March 2, 2005**, Dr. Hurd's research has actually led him to the logical extension of aggression studies – hockey players.

Another, more controversial field of study involves recent findings on the relationship between digit ratios and sexual orientation. **According to the journal Nature of March 30, 2000**, a study of 720 adults conducted in the San Francisco area concluded that men with shorter digit ratios – meaning those whose index fingers are significantly shorter than their ring fingers – are likely to be more fertile and have greater homosexual tendencies than those who don't. Lesbians also showed a correlation, and those with larger digit ratios were more likely to be homosexuals. In case you're a little nervous about casual onlookers learning so much about you by looking at your hands, have no fear – the study found that the digit ratio relationship could only be used to explain, but not predict.

As the 2004 journal of Hormones and Behavior notes, this study set off a flurry of subsequent studies, none without their own controversy. Many lauded the studies as proof that homosexuals are born gay, and that their genetic makeup was the sole determining factor in their sexual orientation. Others criticized the research, noting that the results were inconclusive. It seems that both camps were in part correct.

As the thrilling **journal Psychoneuroendocrinology explains in its January 2005 issue**, there are real links between exposure to testosterone in the womb and one's proclivity to homosexuality. Further studies, such as those conducted in 2002 and 2003 by a Harvard University team, have confirmed these findings. However, the research has its shortcomings and is not as broad in scope as many gay rights advocates had hoped. First, **according to the original BBC news report of March 29, 2000** the study in 2000 only found the digit ratio  correlation in gay men with older brothers. It's theorized that a mother's womb may actually remember having the first child, and thus hormonally adjusts itself for the next one. Also, the study does not account for physical factors that could account for the same result – say, a young teenage girl feeling different from others since she has more masculine hands. Regardless of which side you agree with, the debate over the findings – and subsequent implications – is far from over.

But as you can imagine, the implications for this type of research are many, although the largest impacts will be on the issue of homosexuality and genetic research at birth.

First, at the scientific level, digit ratio studies will continue to have a profound impact on genetics research, especially when it comes to children. **According to the December 2004 issue of the journal of Developmental Psychobiology**, digit ratios have given researchers a rare window into pre-natal development. By understanding the ways in which hormonal changes change our young bodies, scientists are learning more about the hidden factors that shape our hands and our identities.

Finally, the social implications of this research are staggering. **According to the Washington Times of November 28, 2004**, with hot topic issues such as gay marriage and homosexual adoption fresh in our national consciousness, research such as digit ratios studies are likely to raise many eyebrows – but in actuality – solve few problems. Studies such as the 2000 San Francisco project were immediately dissected by those on both sides of the gay issue, and both sides used it to support their agenda. Gay rights advocates pointed to the fact that it showed a genetic cause for homosexuality, while traditional family advocates instead cited the fact that the correlation held true for about 5 percent of survey participants. If a study were to prove that homosexuality is in fact genetically based, many of our national questions could be answered.

Or, they could simply bring up more questions. **As the Seattle Post Intelligencer of September 12, 2004** notes, homosexuality's place in society is not likely to be determined by any amount of scientific research. That understanding must come from each individual, and the science may have little impact on the philosophy.

Digit Ratio research seems to have fingered some pretty interesting information about factors that make up who we are and how we live. For a relatively new field of study, it has made surprising progress, and

it promises to continue challenging our notions on everything from aggression to sexuality. Today, now that we've traced the history of this fascinating research, examined the data, its controversy, and the subsequent implications, it's become clear that hand reading isn't just for psychics anymore. So take and minute and check out your digits – you never know when information like this might come in handy.

Professor: Ok, Sam. What questions do you have of Mr. W. and his topic?

Student in Audience: I don't have any questions!

Professor: Remember, you were assigned the role of audience questioner. Did you not hear anything in the speech warranting further investigation?

Student in Audience: No.

Professor: Nothing? Are you sure? The speech seemed to generate some interesting commentary about science and culture in addition to public policy and sexual orientation.

Student: Well then, why don't you ask the questions? (Student turns red, picks up backpack and leaves.)

Professor: Okay … Anyone else have any questions of this particular speaker regarding Digit Ratio research?

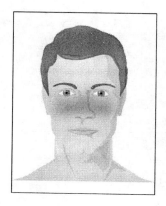

Clearly, the emotional state of the listener was such that he wanted nothing to do with the speaker or topic. Of course, this student may not have been prepared to be an audience member the day he was assigned. Additionally, he may not have been prepared to deal with a strange "sciency" topic or one that challenged notions of sexual orientation. Whatever the case may be, he exhibited physiological signs of discomfort. His flushed face, coupled with some sweating, elevated volume, tensed voice with an increased pitch, and abrupt departure, clearly demonstrated listening apprehension.

While there are any number of things a listener can do to aid his or her listening skill set, Brownell proposes the idea of scopic listening. The "scopic listener," she explains, is a listener who may very well overcome these listening apprehension qualities by seeking out and demonstrating a wide-scope of interests. In other words, how can the information be placed into other contexts for informational use? The student above didn't realize that the speech would easily have fit into a public discussion about sexual preferencing, hormone research, social aggression research and more.

Additional suggestions for working to overcome listening apprehension include slowing speaking patterns often to assess what others are saying, seeking more opportunities to listen to complex, difficult information, and getting physically prepared to concentrate. A 2002 Curriculum Review article adds a few more words of wisdom to students, whose main job is to listen in the context of a classroom. In fact, since we know that so much of our waking hours are devoted to listening, here's some helpful advice:

(1) **Come to class prepared.** Too much time and too many other events and experiences occur between one class and the next to expect yourself to remember specific class content by memory. Spend five minutes reviewing the previous class notes and readings to provide context and continuity for new information.

(2) **Stay organized.** Notes for each class should be dated, with the subject and reading assignments highlighted. This sounds cliché but it works. Trying to review notes that are disheveled and out of place only leads to frustration and confusion. Simply label the date of the notes at the top of your notes and underline the subject.

(3) **Keep your notes legible.** Handwriting should be clear enough to comprehend when studying for midterms and finals weeks down the line. Even better, type your notes in class on a computer (if the professor allows you to do so). If you are going to take notes, old-

school style with pen and paper – skip lines after crucial points so the major points will stand out during review time.

(4) **Load your notes with bullets – bullet points that is.** Complete paragraphs take too long to write and they're a pain to read through. Briefly summarize important material and abbreviate where you can. Come up with your own system of taking shorthand notes that you can discern. Consistency, over the course of a semester, makes a big difference.

(5) **Cue them up.** Teachers almost always give verbal cues when they're making a key point, so listen up. Every professor, let alone every speaker, has particular ticks that should alert you to what is important. In fact, former President Bill Clinton was such a good student because of his ability to anticipate what material would be asked on exams (Maraniss, 1996). Pay special attention to subtle and not-so-subtle red-flag phrases such as, "This is important," "You'll want to know this," "I think this is important," "Without understanding this...", "Keep this in mind," and so forth. And when the instructor writes a fact or phrase on the board, you can bet it'll end up on a test, so copy it down. I clue my students in by saying things like, "If I were you, I'd want to pay particular attention to...". Remember, writing things out is for you, not the professor!

(6) **Offer marginal help.** If you leave a wide margin next to your notes, it'll be easier to add your own observations on the side or highlight important data.

(7) **Give your text a speed-read.** Before closing the book on any lecture, skim the notes to make sure you can read what you wrote and you don't have any pressing questions about the material.

(8) **Get gap coverage.** After class, ask a classmate or the teacher to help you fill in any important facts you couldn't jot down in time. Do it then, right then, after class because if you delay, they won't remember either!

The University of Colorado (1998) asserts that the benefits of actively learning to listen can assist us by forcing us to learn the skill of paying attention (which can be a positive, new learned behavior), avoiding misunderstandings and allowing for people to open us to one another through questioning, commenting or critiquing.

"How to Take Good Notes in Class"

Listening is a Two-Way Street:
Speaker Responsibilities for Effective Listening

Much of this chapter has been devoted to how we, as receivers, can be better listeners. As we know from the discussion of the communication model, we are simultaneously sources and receivers, speakers and listeners. Hence, we are constantly giving and getting communication. Given what we know about how difficult it is to listen, effective speakers keep their audience in mind when constructing their speeches. Moreover, effective listeners realize that to present publically is an opportunity to share, create learnedness and to impart knowledge 'for' the audience members. Public speaking isn't egocentric, rather audience-centric.

Too often, listening is viewed as the receiver's responsibility alone, apart from the speaker. We believe this is a short-sighted view of communication that neglects the speaker-audience relationship. The Ancient Greeks also recognized the importance of helping audience members remember, recall, and encapsulate important points through the use of figures of speech, sometimes called schemes. Schemes are patterns or arrangements of words, often in parallel structures, that aid the audience in helping to remember and recall content. In other words, schemes can be thought of as packaging specially designed for audience members, whereby ideas are presented in such a way as to help audience members comprehend and remember. Schemes are memorable because they are presented in parallel structures that make it easy to remember and recall, and serve to function as a kind of "glue" that helps content stick with a listener in the same way your favorite line from Katy Perry or Taylor Swift may stick in your mind.

Some common schemes that are used by speakers, musicians, lyricists, and poets to help audiences remember include:

(1) **Antithesis** – The juxtaposition of contrasting ideas, usually in parallel structure.
E.g. "That's one small step for man, one giant leap for mankind." Neil Armstrong.
"Many are called, but few are chosen."
"Speech is silver, but silence is golden."

(2) **Antimetabole** – A type of antithesis in which words are repeated in successive clauses, but in reverse grammatical order.
E.g. "Ask not what your country can do for you; ask what you can do for your country." John. F. Kennedy.
E.g. "If a conservative is a liberal who has been mugged, a liberal is a conservative who has been indicted." (Jeffrey Rosen, *The New Yorker*)
E.g. "I, too, was born in the slum. But just because you're born in the slum does not mean the slum is born in you, and you can rise above it if your

mind is made up." (Jesse Jackson, speech at 1984 Democratic National Convention)

"Jesse Jackson 1984 Democratic National Convention Keynote"

(3) **Anaphora** – Repetition of the same word or groups of words at the beginning of successive clauses.
E.g. "We shall fight on the beaches, we shall fight on the landing-grounds, we shall fight in the fields and in the streets, we shall fight in the hills." Winston Churchill.
E.g. "It's **the hope** *of* slaves sitting around a fire singing freedom songs; **the hope** *of* immigrants setting out for distant shores; **the hope** *of* a young naval lieutenant bravely patrolling the Mekong Delta; **the hope** *of* a millworker's son who dares to defy the odds; **the hope** *of* a skinny kid with a funny name who believes that America has a place for him, too." (Barack Obama, "The Audacity of Hope," July 27, 2004, underlined emphasis added)

"Senator Barack Obama: 'The Audacity of Hope' 1 of 2"
"Senator Barack Obama: 'The Audacity of Hope' 2 of 2"

(4) **Epistrophe** – Repetition of same word or group of words at the end of successive clauses.
E.g. "I said you're afraid to bleed. [As] long as the white man sent you to Korea, **you bled**. He sent you to Germany, **you bled**. He sent you to the South Pacific to fight the Japanese, **you bled**. You bleed for white people. But when it comes time to seeing your own churches being bombed and little black girls be[ing] murdered, you haven't got no blood." Malcolm X *Message to the Grassroots*
E.g. "...and that government of **the people**, by **the people**, for **the people** shall not perish from the earth." Abraham Lincoln, *Gettysburg Address* (underlined emphasis added)
"The time for healing of the wounds has come. The moment to bridge the chasms that has divided us has come." Nelson Mandela

(5) **Alliteration** – Repetition of initial or medial consonants in two or more adjacent words.

E.g. "A **m**oist young **m**oon hung above the **m**ist of a neighboring **m**eadow." (Vladimir Nabokov, *Conclusive Evidence*)

E.g. "Was he not unmistakably a little man? A creature of the **p**etty rake-off, **p**ocketed with a **p**etty joke in **p**rivate and denied with the stainless **p**latitudes in his **p**ublic utterances." [C.S. Lewis] *The Screwtape Letters*

"Edgar Allan Poe 'The Raven' Poem Animation Movie"

These are just a few examples of how speakers can use a literary device such as schemes to help audiences remember what is said. We can learn much from the past who have established the cornerstones of public speaking. But speakers and speechwriters are not the only groups that take advantage of these resources? For each of the schemes discussed, can you find examples from contemporary popular musical artists? Think catchy pop songs, and we guarantee you will find plenty of examples of these schemes strategically used by musicians and advertisers alike, to ensure that you won't forget what they say.

Listverse is a unique website that has a top ten list of just about everything one can think of. From the top 10 scandalous Queens in history, to the top 10 bizarre mating rituals of birds. Keeping in line with the top ten theme of this site, we'll end this chapter with our own Top Ten List: *10 Things You Should Keep In Mind When Trying To Keep Other's Attention*:

(10) *Gain their attention* – Start your speech off with something interesting. We often call this the gain and maintain of the speech, but more about this later. In the meantime, recognize that you are always competing for the audience's attention and the first words out of your mouth are the most important. They stage the stage and the tenor for the rest of your speech. Research (Gladwell, 2005) states that, in interview situations, decisions about whether to hire a prospective job candidate are 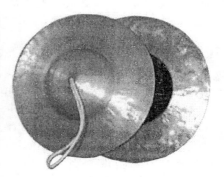 made within the initial seconds of the job interview. Likewise, if you don't "grab" the audience's attention immediately, why would they stick with you as your speech progresses. Moreover, the primacy/recency effect states that audiences remember what is said first and last more than what happens in between. Be very strategic about how you begin your speech.

(9) *Remind them why they are listening* – Let's be honest, audiences listen because they expect to gain something from listening: knowledge, know-how, expertise, secrets to success, entertainment, etc. The number one question all audience members ask themselves, in silence, of course is: "Why is this person speaking to me?" As a speaker, if you don't make this clear to your audience in the first 30 seconds of your speech, you have lost them.

(8) *Repeat* – Remember, your audience only gets to hear what you say once and, on top of that, they have to process what you are saying. Speaking is not like writing. They can't go back and review what you said on their own. After you step away from the podium, so too do your words. Do your audience a favor: (a) Preview what you are going to say. (b) Use signposts, "First," "Second," throughout, as road signs, to help your audience know where they are and where they are going (c) Summarize what you just said. We all benefit from being reminded of important or necessary information.

(7) *Use examples* – Examples make abstract topics personal and compelling. Examples allow audiences to participate in your topic. Specifics, details, vivid imagery and concrete examples induce the most basic form of persuasion: identification (Burke, 1969).

(6) *Speaking in threes or primes* – People tend to remember odd numbers, like, 1, 3, 5, and 7 more than anything else. So, make three points, not four, and five points, not six. In fact, Dlugan extends that repetition by using the rule of threes in your presentation, not only creates attention, but also maintains attention (2009). Consider the following:
"I came, I saw, I conquered." Julius Caesar
"Duty, honor, country." General Douglas MacArthur
"Faster, Higher, Stronger" – Olympic Motto

(5) *Solicit feedback* – In everyday conversation, we seek input, allow others to participate. When you are speaking in public, you still can solicit feedback by gauging the interest level of your audience. Are audience members engaging you in eye contact and nodding their heads? If so, you are probably doing something right. If not, don't panic, but consider adjusting your content and delivery. For example, adapt your nonverbal intonations, like pitch or rate. Variance may very well reengage their attention.

(4) *Tell stories* – Stories that we can identify with and relate to are stories that we can listen to for hours on end. Stories that are logical and have a clear beginning, middle, and end, and ring true with the

audience's own experiences are stories that can compel an audience to want to pay attention (Fisher, 1984).

(3) *Make eye contact* – We feel more obliged to pay attention to speakers who engage us in eye contact. It's a side effect of the law of reciprocity – if you look at someone in their eyes, they will repay you with eye contact and hopefully, their attention too (Cialdini, 2006). Not only this, but Cialdini further reports that reciprocity potentially creates liking, which could be a positive side effect for the speaker and audience.

(2) *Have fun and be passionate* – If you aren't having fun, if the audience believes you are bored, they will follow suit and mimic you. We're not making this up. Communication behavior is contagious. If you are interested in what you are talking about, your audience will more likely be interested as well. Aristotle was a firm advocate of speakers using pathos, or passion, when communicating their objective.

(1) *Repeat* – Repeating is so important it bears repeating. Don't waste people's time: Economy of speech matters. Unnecessary tangents are inattention's best friend. If the audience asks, "why is he/she saying this?" you've lost them. And once you've lost your audience, it's almost impossible to get them back.

Conclusion

In summary, we have learned that listening is difficult. It isn't natural. In fact, it is a skill. One that we can improve upon. Moreover, it is important to remember that when presenting in a public forum, we must remember that listening is difficult for all members at one time or another. As such, there are research techniques that speakers can utilize to vary their presentation as well as engage others. For additional information about listening, visit: https://www.youtube.com/watch?v=eIho2S0Zahl.

References

Beebe, S.A. & Beebe, S.J. (2005). Public speaking: An audience-centered approach (6th ed.). Boston: Allyn & Bacon.

Bell, G. R. (1984). Listen and you shall hear. The Secretary, 47(9), 8-9.

Brownell, J. (2002). Listening: Attitudes, principles, and skills (2nd ed.). Boston: Allyn & Bacon.

Burke, K. (1969). A rhetoric of motives. Berkeley: University of California Press.

Chambers, H.E. (2001). Effective communication skills for scientific and technical professionals. New York: Perseus Publishing.

Cialdini, R. (2006). Influence: The psychology of persuasion. New York: Harper.

Fisher, W. R. (1984). Narration as a human communication paradigm: The case of public moral argument. Communication Monographs, 51, 1-22.

Gitlin, T. (2002). Media unlimited. How the torrent of images and sounds overwhelms our lives. New York: Henry Holt and Company, LLC.

Gladwell, M. (2005). Blink: The power of thinking without thinking. New York: Little, Brown, and Company.

Goleman, D. (1995). Emotional intelligence: Why it can matter more than IQ. New York: Bantam.

Janusik, L.A. (2007). Building listening theory: The validation of the conversational listening span. Communication Studies, 58 (2), 139-151.

Maraniss, D. (1996). First in his class: A biography of Bill Clinton. New York: Simon and Schuster.

Marzana, R.J. (2007). The art and science of teaching: A comprehensive framework for effective introduction. New York: Association for supervision and curriculum development.

Pearson, P. D., & Fielding, L. (1983). Instructional implications of listening comprehension research (Reading Education Report No. 39). Champaign, IL: University of Illinois at Urbana-Champaign. (ERIC Document Reproduction Service No. ED 227 464).

Postman, N. (1985). Amusing ourselves to death: Public discourse in the age of show business. New York: Penguin.

Suggested Websites

Sixminutes.dlugan.com/speaking-rate/ (2012)
Extension.missouri.edu/p/CM150 (2015)
Colorado. Edu/conflict/peace/ treatment/activel.html (1998)
http://sixminutes.dlugan.com/rule-of-three-speeches-public-speaking/ (2009)

Chapter 4
The Importance of Speaking Effectively and Overcoming the Fear of Public Speaking

You may or may not have heard the saying, "one cannot, not communicate". While it's a double negative, a botched grammatical sentence in nature, the point shouldn't be lost due to bad linguistics. The assertion is that everything we do, from any verbal to nonverbal type of behavior, is communicating a message. Indeed it is. Even though sleeping is a nonverbal behavior, it's meant to communicate our desire to others to get some rest, and more than likely, to be left alone. Or perhaps you see the words written, "I love you" on your mirror when you return home in the evening. Our first impression is that the words are an extension of a deep, connected feeling another has for us. The basic fact is this: all actions send meanings to others. Those actions come from either verbal or nonverbal behaviors and cues. Yet, there is more to digest here. Let us consider the spoken word for a moment.

We often erroneously think that the words we speak ARE the essence of a message and that language is static and rule driven. Consider what Makelal asserts here, "The grammatical rules of English language are not determined by the nature of the language itself but the rules of use and the appropriateness of the use are determined by the speech community" (1998). So, in other words, what we often consider effective in terms of speaking, is largely to the norm and acceptance of the community we are surrounded by. While the English language has more exceptions than rules, , we need to dig deeper here and realize a very crucial point of not just language, but how speaking becomes effective: words themselves have no meaning. Words are merely a vehicle, and an important one, that can carry a message. However, it is the speaker that houses the meaning of those words.

It's nearly impossible to distinguish *how* someone says something from what they say. As a child, the meaning of simple, but often heard phrases such as "go to your room" and "you did what?" were almost completely dependent on your parents' tone of voice, volume or pitch. "Go to your room," can be interpreted as a form of punishment or

a simple direction, depending on delivery. And, the utterance, "You did what?", depending on how it is said, can mean the difference between impressing or appalling your parents.

Without the element of the *delivery* of the words, it would be nearly impossible to differentiate between a joke and an order, sarcasm and authentic sentiment. For example, if you had lots of time on your hands and you transcribed a complete episode of the "The Tonight Show" with Jimmy Fallon, the meaning of the show would be completely different versus if you had watched the show, void of Fallon's pauses, facial expressions, tone of voice, and over-the-top gestures. In this example, it becomes clear that his nonverbal delivery of the words themselves gives meaning and life to what he intends to communicate to his audience.

If we venture back into history, the first televised Presidential debate between President Nixon and John F. Kennedy caused quite the uproar. While many Americans had not transitioned to televisions yet or simply couldn't afford them, many settled in to listen to the debate via radio. Receiving a contrary message after the debate, many Americans watched it live, in black and white, on the television. Those that visually watched the nonverbal communication that accompanied the verbals were quick to offer a win to JFK, who was said to have appeared polished and posed. Those that listened to the debate, however, were quick to offer up the win to Nixon, despite not witnessing his nonverbal or knowing the fact that he was quite ill at the time of the debate. Note that the witnessing of one's communication, as well as the mode of delivery, alters the audience's outcome of the debate. Indeed, the ability to authenticate one's verbal and nonverbal communication alters our perception.

Consider this clip from *Family Guy* and the use of sarcasm.

"Sarcasm"

Can you tell when your boss is having a bad day? Do you know when your partner is frustrated or short tempered? What about when a friend speaks confidently to you when retelling a story? For each scenario, what signs do you use to make such conclusions? Most likely, you have a strong sense of others' moods based largely on inferences you are making regarding their nonverbal communication. You may not even be aware that you are doing it, but each of us is constantly taking in information about others. We also always processing.

How a person walks into a room, how close someone stands to you when you are having a conversation, how a speaker stands – upright or slight bent over – the amount and quality of eye contact, breathing rate, the constantly changing array of facial muscles contorting into disgust or joy, the positioning of their arms, where they place their hands and fingers, how often they blink, how they move their head and shoulders in conjunction or in contradiction to what they are saying, and the inflection patterns in their voice, all impact what is said and how it is received and understood. Although disturbing, consider a unique study that was conducted regarding male attackers accosting female victims based upon their nonverbal cues.

"Nonverbal Communication"

In many ways, we read others like we might read a text of words on a page. A major difference between reading a page from your favorite book and 'reading a person' is that the author of the book intentionally and strategically wanted to influence you. However, in everyday communication and public speaking, what is said can't be separated from how it is said because influence and judgments are multi-dimensional, based not simply on what communicators intend to communicate, but also on what their nonverbal communication communicates about them.

Inside The Minds of Audiences – The Attribution Process

As receivers, or audience members, we always try to make sense of what others are saying or not saying, doing or not doing. Trying to ascertain why people do what they do (i.e. motive) is a full time occupation for most of us:

"Is she mad at me?"
"Is the professor disappointed because I haven't attended the last two lectures?"
"She doesn't talk much when I ask her questions – she must not like me."
"Does my employer think I'm management material?"

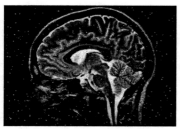
Rarely do people explicitly tell us what they are thinking. Would you find it odd if they did? Most certainly. Oftentimes we assert that some individuals we know don't have enough of a mental "filter". Consequently, we spend much of our time trying to figure out what we believe others are thinking based on an analysis of their nonverbal communication. In the traditional public speaking situation, nonverbal communication influences both audiences and speakers alike.

"What Makes a Great Speaker? Put the Audience First"

From Audience to Speaker

"Wow, the speaker isn't even standing behind the podium. He must not really want to be there."

"What's the deal with her Che Guevara t-shirt? Does she just like the color of the shirt or is she making a political statement?"

"I can barely hear him speak. He keeps mumbling, and even worse, at the end of his sentences, his voice really drifts off. He must not be sure of what he is saying."

"The speaker's eyes are glued to the note cards. He hasn't even looked up once and he's been speaking for four minutes. He must not care about what we think."

"The speaker raised his hand to volunteer to lead off today's presentation. I wish I had that kind of confidence."

"She keeps on pounding on the podium. She must be passionate about what she's talking about."

"Her voice is cracking. She must be nervous."

"His face and neck are turning red. He must not like to speak in front of people."

"The speaker is smiling while speaking. Wow! She must really be having fun."

In each of these examples, audiences attempt to make sense of a speaker based on nonverbal communication. Unfortunately, attributing motive to a speaker based simply on nonverbal communication does not mean the conclusions reached are accurate. However, it is impossible for audiences not to be influenced by the speaker's nonverbal communication. Let us not forget that nonverbal communication is the majority of what we use in our daily interactions to send messages to others.

**"Non Verbal Communication for Speakers
Speaking Tips by Topher Morrison"**

From Speaker to Audience

The nonverbal attribution process is a two-way street. Not only are audience members constantly trying to make sense of the speaker, so too does the speaker try to assess his/her performance based on the audience's nonverbal communication.

"Everyone is looking at me – they must really be interested in what I am talking about."

"People keep looking at their watches – they must think my presentation is boring."

"The person in the front row is nodding at what I'm saying – she must agree with my point of view."

"Several people are whispering to the person next to them – am I speaking too fast for them to understand?"

"Someone got up and left – they must not have liked what they're hearing."

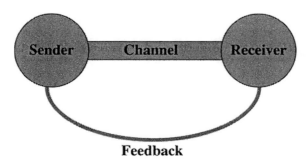

The feedback loop of communication is an ongoing, simultaneous process that connects speaker and audience. Most of the feedback between audiences and speakers is never explicitly stated, but based on conclusions drawn from evidence of which the speaker may or may not be aware.

Speaker Anxiety

When students tell us they have communication anxiety, we usually know they are referring to speaker anxiety. In fact, in all of our years of teaching and training public speakers, we have never been told by a student that they were nervous about sharing ideas. So, let's be clear that for the most part, speaker anxiety means feeling nervous about being *in front of* people. It is a negative anticipation or fear from a real or expected situation of speaking in front of others. The number of people present may or may not affect you. For example, I have had students assert that they are more comfortable presenting to larger audiences versus audiences that are smaller, say 15 or so. Other students report the reverse. Therefore, the anxiety has various factors involved and is individually unique to each of us. So, to be further clear, it happens to **all** of us at some point. This inescapable fact of the public speaking situation – all eyes are on me and all ears are listening to what and how I say what I say – is one of the significant reasons speakers become nervous when speaking in front of others.

Have you ever taken a personal report on communication apprehension (A.K.A. PRCA), or what is more commonly known as a speech anxiety survey? Do you assume you have apprehension but aren't certain? Or perhaps you aren't certain of how mild or intense your apprehension may be? Our public speaking students are continually amazed between the difference of what they 'perceived' themselves to be and what they 'scored' as. If you are interested in assessing your level of apprehension, access the provided link below:

http://www.wadsworth.com/communication_d/templates/student_resour ces/053456223X_hamilton/survey/prca/main_frame.htm

As it pertains to public speaking, communication apprehension refers to both physiological and psychological stressors induced by one or more conditions within a public speaking situation. *Psychological* symptoms of public speaking apprehension include but are not limited to the following:

- Putting off enrolling a public speaking class until the last semester of college.
- Never volunteering to sign up for a speech, only waiting on the instructor to call on you to speak.
- Not being able to sleep night or nights before your actual presentation.
- Skipping class on the day of your assigned speech.
- Convincing yourself that you will 'mess up' and believing that audiences will laugh at you.
- Telling your audience that you don't think you're speech is very good before you even begin your speech; a term used to describe such irrational and catastrophic expected outcomes of behavior is known as 'awfulizing', created by emotive behavioral therapist, Robert Ellis.

Physical symptoms, also known as proprioceptive stimuli, of speaker anxiety usually occur on the day of the speech itself, and include some or all of the following:

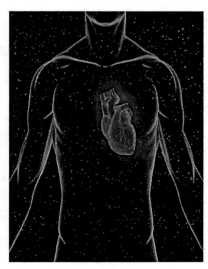

- Increase in heart rate
- Sweaty palms
- Reddened face and neck splotches spontaneously occurring once you stand behind the podium
- Shaky hands or gestures
- Nervous ticks such as running your hand through your hair, knocking on the podium, gripping the podium or clicking a pen

Let's be clear and reiterate before we proceed any further: Everyone experiences speaking anxiety. Rest assured, if you have spoken in public, you will have experienced one or more of the above symptoms of psychological and/or physical symptoms. Speaker anxiety becomes problematic, however when anxiety levels inhibit your willingness or ability to perform.

Too often, speakers who experience high levels of speaking anxiety are more likely to avoid situations that require public speaking. For instance, graduates seeking jobs and students in general have been shown to practice oral communication skills less often even when afforded the opportunity.

In the minds of most students, speaking anxiety is always a negative. This type of thinking is partly a result of modeling. Specifically, the models mostly used as exemplars are great speakers and historic figures who, from the vantage point of beginning speakers, could never have gotten nervous. And so it's no surprise that much of speaker nervousness comes from the fact that we think we shouldn't be nervous. Let's clear up one major misconception: All speakers get nervous. Nervousness is necessary; in fact, it is a physiological phenomenon that you want to learn to manage, not eliminate.

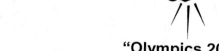

"Olympics 2012:
Michael Phelps has mastered the psychology of speed"

Let's attempt to connect how normal, yet frequent this anxiety can be. World-class sprinters become nervous seconds before the shooting of the starting gun. Michael Phelps reports feeling extremely nervous before each race. Moreoever, were you aware that Barbara Streisand's social nerves were so intense at one time in her life that she refused to sing in public for roughly twenty seven years? This was all due to her forgetting the lyrics of one of her songs during a live performance in the late 60's! What about the great Indiana Jones, Harrison Ford? He admits to a specific fear and nervousness when speaking to others. "It's people I'm afraid of" he states (Bailey, 2008). So why would a public presentation be any different?

Communication anxiety is a symptom of knowing that all eyes and ears will be focused on you, the speaker. Unfortunately, this experience is a rare occasion in our culture. When, if ever, are you the center of attention? We mean the whole you: where you and your body and your ideas and an audience come together in the same place at the same time? Not often, right? Increasingly, much of our communication is via email, word processor, twitter, or cell phone, et cetera, and in each of these channels of communication, the speaker (or sender) is physically separated from the audience. It's no wonder public speaking is such a unique source of anxiety in our technologized world.

"Public Speaking Tips: Practice Speaking"

Sawyer and Behnke (2002) explain that practicing public speaking extends beyond the need to clarify speech content and master other nonverbal features. In fact, it is the additional exposure to public presentation situations that leads to "substantially diminished" speaking inhibition. Like any endeavor, the more we do it, the more comfortable we feel and the more comfortable we feel, the more we can devote our energy and focus to the activity itself rather than mis-directed (and  oftentimes unfounded) anxieties. New public speakers adapt to the pressures of speaking in general by putting themselves in many different types of presentation contexts. Of course, this does not rid speakers of all anxiety. In fact, one study by Michigan State (1968) reported that almost half of the students who identified themselves as moderate to severe apprehension sufferers, dropped from their public speaking course within the first three weeks of the course. So when students or speakers continually allow themselves the opportunity to become acclimated to the natural pressures of specific speaking situations, it will generally reduce public speaking anxiety. This correlates to systematic desensitization by James McCroskey D Ed. (2013) which asserts the classical techniques of conditioning, or reconditioning if you will, a learned behavior. The premise further asserts that what is learned can be unlearned. Based upon ample research, this principle has been effective in the reduction of panic attacks and anxiety in many situations (Corey, 2009). With this in mind, imagine the outcome of practicing early and often and where more mental energy and time can be spent on additional skill sets once public speaking is needed in professional and other practical settings.

Because the act of public speaking is becoming an increasingly unique context of communication, whereby you, your body, your words and ideas, and audiences are rarely at the same place at the same time, it is important to address some common and recurring myths of public speaking that prejudice new speakers from the public speaking situation.

**"Ten Myths of Public Speaking
by Richard L Weaver II, PhD"**

Public Speaking Myths that Create Unnecessary Anxiety

Like any fear-inducing behavior, misconceptions often become the focus of our fears, rather than the realities of the situation itself. Over the years, we have compiled a list of fears students have expressed that reflect what they think about audiences or audience responses rather than what and how audiences actually respond. As you are reading the list, imagine yourself with the idea of some of these myths from a personal perspective. However, don't neglect two areas; 1) these are myths or fallacies (falsehoods) and 2) review the definition of awfulizing and systematic desensitization.

(1) *"What if I make a mistake and mess up?"*

Mistakes are expected in any human endeavor. Unfortunately, most novice speakers magnify the significance of their so-called mistakes. Mistakes are too often a reflection of the speaker's fears, not the audience's expectations. What audiences expect is oftentimes different from what the creators expect of themselves. For example, recently, we were both were having coffee at a local coffee shop while a band was warming up.

The soft rock music sounded good, professional, and beat inspiring to our untrained ears. Once the audience arrived and every seat was full, the band began playing. One song into their set, the lead singer stopped midway and began apologizing. He said there was a problem with the amplifier. What's strange is that, as lay audience members, we were enjoying the music until the lead singer told us, "It didn't sound right." Two more minutes of playing, and the lead singer stopped the music again and apologized for the amplifier. Ironically, because the lead singer pointed out a 'mistake' we didn't notice at first, we could no longer enjoy the music as we originally did because of the singer's hyper awareness.

"Famous Singers: Embarrassing / Funny Moments (On Stage) #1"

Likewise, a mistake in content, missing one step in your outline, mispronouncing a name, not pausing long enough after a transition sentence, or stuttering over a word, is not something a typical audience will notice unless you draw the audience's attention to the so-called mistake. Audiences don't see your speech in parts as you do. You, as  the creator, have spent many hours researching, preparing, and rehearsing your speech. Remember, audiences are hearing your presentation for the first time – their expectations of what *should* occur are vastly different than the speaker's. Lay audiences don't usually recognize what should have happened because they weren't privy to the creation process nor the practice process. No one expects you to be perfect, and moreover, there is no need to draw unnecessary attention with comments like, "Oh my gosh, can I start over?"; "I've never mispronounced this name before'" "Wow, I'm sorry, I totally skipped a step that I went over in practice". This only calls undue attention to the small mistakes.

"How to Recover from Making a Mistake in a Speech"

(2) *"I don't like being judged."*

For the record, we don't either. Who does? But, once again, speakers judge themselves differently than audiences. Think about how you look at yourself in a mirror versus how others view you. In the morning, when you look at yourself in the mirror, you stare at yourself for imperfections partly because you are an expert at your face; you stare at it every morning and evening, and so on. Moreover, you focus on your face is out of context. You look at parts of yourself and obsess. The acne, the new wrinkle, the bruise that becomes more and more prominent the more you stare at it. Fortunately, others don't see you the way you see yourself.

"Using Your Voice Effectively in Presentations and Public Speaking: Paralanguage Roller Coaster"

Speakers who experience high levels of communication anxiety tend to grossly overestimate audience's perceptions. Contrary to what you might believe, audiences don't notice everything. They aren't following every move you make behind the podium and every word you say as closely as you think they are. In fact, this is the great irony of speaker misperceptions. If only audiences followed every move and every word as closely as we thought they did, we'd be much more effective speakers. But audiences never do. They're thinking about themselves. They're thinking about the phone conversation they had the night before. They're worried about the test they have in an hour. Their stomach is growling, and they're fantasizing about the meal they wish they had in front of them.

They're thinking about one word you said that reminds them of a friend they haven't talked to in years. More importantly, the goal of a speech is not to stand behind a podium so the audience can stare at you; rather, you are there because you are providing knowledge, insight, help, inspiration, to an audience. You are not standing behind the podium alone, your research, ideas, evidence, and logic are with you too. YOU have a teachable moment in time!

And FYI – the unending challenge for all speakers: getting audiences to step out of themselves for the few minutes of their lives to focus on you and what you are saying. If you can do that, then yes, you will be a remarkably effective and successful speaker.

(3) "*It seems so awkward standing behind a podium.*"

Novice speakers tend to look more unnatural than experienced speakers behind a podium. Why? Novice speakers, ironically, are less likely to gesture. Experienced speakers gesture. Experienced speakers conceive of their body and nonverbal communication as a means to helping the audience understand what they are discussing. Novice speakers are too focused on themselves rather than on what they are saying. If you care about what you are talking about, gestures will follow. Audiences are suspect of speaker's who don't gesture because it looks so unnatural.

Moreover, experienced speakers gesture because it helps release nervous energy. When was the last time you spoke with someone without using gestures? When was the last time you talked to someone with your hands in your pocket the entire time? When was the last time you spoke to someone without making eye contact? So why would you do any of the above when speaking to an audience?

So do yourself a favor and give your nervous energy somewhere to go – allow yourself the same luxuries you do when speaking in conversation – gesture!

"College & Writing Tips: How to Gesture During a Speech"

(4) ***"I get so embarrassed in front of audiences and turn red every time I speak."***

For some speakers, the more you worry about turning red from embarrassment, the more red your face becomes. A well prepared and powerfully delivered speech always outweighs a red face. Although audiences may recognize the redness in your face or the blotch marks on your neck, it is the job of your speech to re-direct audience attention to what you are saying. If, however, you only concern yourself with the different shades of color on your face, you too will lose your focus and forget why you are speaking. As a speaker, you have something to say. Hopefully, you believe in what you are saying. Audiences quickly forget how red your face turns when you speak once you convince them that what you are talking about is relevant and essential to their everyday lives.

(5) *"Why would anyone listen to me?"*

This is a commonly surprising student concern. As already mentioned, there are few contexts in which you can speak about issues, topics, debates, controversies that are important to you – the speaker. Public speaking is one of the few occasions when you are required to do this. But, this concern is valid – why would anyone want to listen to what you have to say for five, six, seven or even eight uninterrupted minutes? If you, as the speaker, after research and thoughtful preparation, can't answer this – then you're audience won't listen and frankly, you probably shouldn't be speaking! Public speaking should be reason for celebration – opportunities to speak about something you're passionate about, not something you're fear.

(6) *"I don't want my audience to think I'm stupid."*

This myth has a happy conclusion. You can prevent this by preparing well in advance. In our experiences, the only speakers that look stupid are those speakers that haven't prepared. It's nearly impossible to camouflage a lack of preparation. In other classes and other subjects, you might be able to guess right on a multiple choice exam or even bluff your way through an essay. But there is something about the public speaking situation that is revealing. Audiences know. They know when someone hasn't prepared or when a speaker hasn't practiced. There is no way around it: effective speakers prepare and practice. You know when the speaker hasn't thought about how to make the topic relevant or interesting. Unfortunately, we all know these tell-tale signs too well.

"How to Practice for a Speech: Practicing Speeches: Eye Contact"

You Cannot Not Communicate

For the general study of communication, nonverbal behavior is incredibly important because like verbal communication, it provides essential information and context to both the casual and careful audience member. Unlike verbal arguments, however, speakers are often unaware of how important nonverbal communication is to how audience members judge trustworthiness, believability, confidence, and, perhaps most importantly, persuasiveness.

Even barely perceptible nonverbal behaviors can have discernible meaning – for example, we can recognize a person's facial expressions of emotion from as little as a 1/24th-s exposure (Rosenthal, Hall, DiMatteo, Rogers, & Archer, 1979). Research on social intelligence shows that it is possible to interpret people's behavior, feelings, and relationships from something as simple as a photograph (Archer, 1980). Nonverbal cues are often more powerful and reliable than verbal cues (Archer & Akert, 1984). Researchers are also investigating the process of interpretation – how we use nonverbal cues to form impressions and conclusions about others. Correct interpretation is a remarkable feat because, in any interaction, hundreds or thousands of verbal and nonverbal cues stream by us, vanishing in milliseconds How do we discard most of these cues, seizing the few (e.g., a momentary facial expression, a vocal inflection) that tell us what another person means or is feeling?

Making sense of other people's motives, or actions, using nonverbal communication is an ongoing, activity. The adage, "you cannot not communicate" means that audiences use a speaker's nonverbal communication to help make judgments about a speaker's credibility, believability, and persuasiveness. There are several types of nonverbal communication that are particularly pertinent to public presenters. Here is a laundry list that provides a basic understanding of each nonverbal phenomenon.

"Non-Verbal Communication Tools:
Non-Verbal Communication: Silence"

"Non-Verbal Communication Tools:
Non-Verbal Communication: Touch Avoidance"

"Non-Verbal Communication Tools:
Non-Verbal Communication: Eye Contact"

"Non-Verbal Communication Tools:
Non-Verbal Communication: Illustrators"

Paralanguage

As Charles Kriedler explains, "The term paralanguage means 'alongside language,' therefore not part of the language system" (1997, p. 179). Paralanguage is comprised of the nonverbal delivery qualities that can be modified to make words and phrases mean many different things per the necessity of the speaker needs. This may be setting or changing a mood or investing a term, phrase, or idea with a whole new feeling.

In sum, your voice is an instrument. Changing the tune or tone, or playing the music of your words with different emphases, changes the meaning of what you say. Say the words, "I love you" out loud – first with sincerity. Now say them again with sarcasm. Then, with apathy. In a matter of seconds, those three words literally have varied meaning to the listener.

Paralinguistics Exercise: Choose a random article from a newspaper or advertisements from the phone book, or even lyrics from a song.

Using your voice, change the meaning of the words by using your voice. Read the same article, to achieve different effects:

(1) Use your voice to portray sadness.

(2) Use your voice to portray excitement.

(3) Use your voice to portray fear.

(4) Use your voice to portray sarcasm.

Discussion Questions: In each example, how did the speaker's voice change the meaning even though it was the same content?

Tempo

Tempo, or the speed and rhythm with which a speaker speaks, is another tool a speaker can use in changing the meaning of what he/she says. Regional accents are often distinguished by the tempo of speech. The Southern dialect, for example, has a slower tempo than a Northeast accent. When a speaker speaks too slowly, does the audience get bored with a topic? Conversely, if a speaker speaks too quickly, does she lose an audience's attention? Read the following examples, following the instructions, and you be the judge of how tempo changes meaning.

Tempo Exercise: Choose a random article from a newspaper, an advertisement from the phone book, or even lyrics from a song. Using the tempo, or the speed and rhythm with which a speaker speaks, read using the following instructions:

    (1) Read the text as fast as you possibly can.
    (2) Read the text as slowly as possible
    (3) Read the text fast then slow then fast again.
    (4) Read the text, pausing at least 2 seconds after each sentence.

Discussion Question: How does the speed or slowness of speech change the meaning of the text?

Should there be one pace at which a speaker speaks, or should tempo change throughout the speech, at different points, to highlight particular sections of a speech topic? How do you know which tempo to use when speaking to audiences?

Pitch and Inflection

Pitch refers the highs and lows of sound. Inflection is the movement between various pitch peaks and valleys in terms of range of sound. To be as effective as possible, speakers are best advised to employ inflection while speaking. Think of inflection as a type of instruction manual for audiences helping them discern what is most important/less important/least important. When someone speaks without pitch and inflection, audience boredom usually follows. The perfect example of diction void of pitch and inflection is the famous example from *Ferris Bueller's Day Off* (1986) when the teacher monotonously reads each student's name while taking roll, "Bueller, Bueller, Bueller..."

"Bueller..."

"'Anyone, anyone' teacher from Ferris Bueller's Day Off"

Pitch and Inflection Exercise: Choose a random article from a newspaper, an advertisement from the phone book, or even lyrics from a song. Using pitch and inflection, read the text using the following instructions:

(1) Read the text in as monotone voice as possible.
(2) Read the text with as much pitch and inflection as possible (rising and lowering your voice throughout the text).
(3) Raise the pitch at the end of each sentence.
(4) Raise the pitch at the beginning of each sentence.

Discussion Question: How does pitch and inflection change the meaning of the text?

What was gained in translation when you read these lines with pitch and inflection? What was lost in translation when you read the examples in a monotone voice?

The voice is one type of behavior that affects how others interpret what is said, but it is not the only type of nonverbal communication that can be used to enhance a speaker's delivery.

Proxemics

Proxemics is the study and description of variables that aren't vocal or verbal, but is characterized by the distance between people in the course of communicating (Kriedler, 1997). Specifically, proxemics refers to the distance between communicators and other individuals.

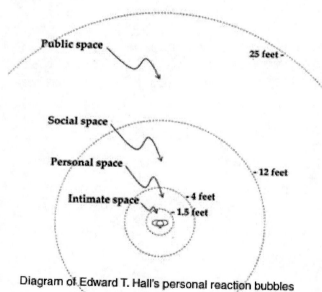

Diagram of Edward T. Hall's personal reaction bubbles

According to Edward Hall, there are four distances of communication in North American culture. These zones range from intimate, being close enough to able to touch the person you are communicating with, to public distance, where the distance between speaker and receiver is 12 feet and beyond and is characterized by a loud voice (Stuart Hall, 1959, The Silent Language by Edward T. Hall).

Although our use and comfort of proxemics is largely dependent upon not only cultural learning and the nature of the connection between the participants, consider the following clip. How might the invasion of one's space affect the way in which one views not only the presenter, but also the message that is being sent?

"Seinfeld's Close Talker"

In public settings, speakers are generally more than a few feet away from an audience. An inescapable reality of the public speaking situation is that speaker and audience are separated by space. At Lincoln's first Inaugural, for example, thousands of people endured rain and cold to catch a glimpse of the new President. However, Lincoln was only as effective as his voice could carry his words because he was without the yet-to-be invented technology of a microphone. And for others who were even farther away, Lincoln was only as effective as his tall frame and gestures allowed.

Exercise: Have two volunteers come to the front of the class and begin talking to each other about their weekend plans at a social distance. Then, while still talking to one another, instruct the two students to continue talking at a personal distance. Then, instruct the two participants to continue talking while at an intimate space. Finally, have the pair continue talking but at a public distance. As a class, discuss how the tenor and content of the conversations changed at each distinct stage of space. How did space affect each participant's feelings, emotions, comfort level, etc.?

While many of your presentations will not be outside, there are specific nonverbal communication delivery techniques you can use to overcome the distance, both physical and psychological, between you and the audience.

Eye Contact

Eye contact may be the most important nonverbal ingredient as it pertains to developing relationships with audiences. After reviewing levels of speaker eye contact and the subsequent perceptions held by their audiences, Stephen Beebe (1974) confirmed previous research that effective speaking relies on this essential skill set. In Western cultures, eye contact is considered a sign of interest and focus. In other words, more is better. Eye contact isn't only helpful for audiences, it is essential in connecting the speaker to the audience.

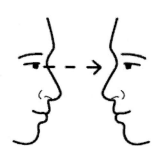

Exercise: To illustrate this point, try speaking to the person sitting next to you about any topic for two minutes. However, while speaking, you CANNOT look at your partner (receiver). Now, this time, try it again, but engage the receiver with eye contact while you impart your message. Was it easier to logically progress from one point to another while engaging your classmate in eye contact? Why? Why not?

Audiences use eye contact to attribute state of mind. Based on eye contact alone, eye contact is important in everyday conversation, as receivers believe:

"Googly Walken"

Prolonged eye contact reveals **interest**.
Wandering eyes – looking at everyone but the speaker – reveals **boredom**.
Raised eyebrows and eye darting back and forth reveals **confusion**.
Rolling of the eyes reveals **disagreement**.

In an earlier chapter, we discussed the importance of ethos, or speaker credibility. Namely, speakers who were perceived as more trustworthy were also more persuasive. Right or wrong, accurate or inaccurate, audiences make judgments about speakers based on eye contact, or the lack thereof.

Exercise: Fill in the blank with your immediate perception. Then discuss why you made this perception.

The speaker looks above the audience, to the clock on the back wall.
Audience Judgment: _____
The speaker stares only at one person in the audience.
Audience Judgment: _____
The speaker only looks to one side of the audience
Audience Judgment: _____
The speaker only stares at her note cards, never once looking up at the audience.
Audience Judgment: _____
The speaker looks at both sides of the room, looking at individuals students for about 2 to 3 seconds at a time.
Audience Judgment: _____
The speaker scans both sides of the room, like a tennis match, only maintaining eye contact with individuals in the audience for a second at a time.
Audience Judgment: _____

Styles of Delivery and Eye Contact:

Eye contact is so essential to the speaker-audience relationship that particular styles of delivery are based on the amount of eye contact established with audience members.

Manuscript

Manuscript style speaking requires the speaker to maintain complete fidelity to the text or note cards. In this speaking approach, each word is carefully crafted in advance and written down word-for-word prior to the speech occasion. In some instances, like a State of the Union Speech, or a Declaration of War Address, each word matters and each misspoken word might mean grave consequences. While some speakers like the comfort of knowing they are fully prepared for their speech, that they will not 'go blank' and forget their words, there are delivery challenges inherent in this approach.

Speakers must attempt to make the manuscript speech sound and look non-rehearsed. This sounds paradoxical because it is. Audiences respond more attentively if eye contact is provided to maintain a necessary connection between speaker and audience. For example, Broadway musicals and plays are manuscript style. That is, each word of dialogue and music is crafted in advance. Yet, after you spend your well-earned money, you want to believe this is the first

and only time the actors have performed. In speaking situations, it is more difficult to achieve this effect, however, because the temptation for speakers to forget about their audience and simply focus on the script at hand, is oftentimes very tempting.

"Improve Your Public Speaking and Communication Skills"

"Manuscript Speech"

Extemporaneous

Most public speaking and business presentations require extemporaneous speaking. This involves preparation in advance of the speech occasion – research, outlining, perhaps even writing out in full the introduction and conclusion – but does not require complete fidelity to the text because a speaker works off an outline or notes instead of a full-sentence speech.

This approach allows for spontaneity with preparation, knowledge of purpose with the possibility of small adjustments in delivery and content to account for the specific and real audience receiving the message. Moreover, extemporaneous delivery allows for more eye contact between speaker and audience. If you have practiced what points you want to get across, the examples you want to use, and the order in which your points will occur, you are freed from the burden of having to get each word exactly right, thereby allowing you to focus on the delivery components that add merit, believability and force to your words.

"Extemporaneous Speech Contest – Finalist #01"

Extemporaneous Exercise: Read an article from a newspaper. Then translate the main points onto notecards using keywords. Before the speaker begins to talk, all members of the audience should raise their hands. The speaker must engage each member of the class with eye contact. After three seconds of eye contact, the audience member will lower his/her hand. The speaker should continue speaking until he/she has engaged all members with eye contact for at least 3 seconds and all hands have been lowered.

Impromptu

The third type of speaking style is referred to as impromptu. In impromptu speeches, there is little or no advanced preparation. Therefore, expectations from audiences are different than they are for manuscript and extemporaneous speaking. If you have little or no time to prepare and research, specific detail cannot be expected. For example, when your teacher calls on you in class, this is an impromptu-like scenario where you may have (hopefully) read the text for class, but did not know which, if any, questions the professor may ask. Without a script or even an outline to work with, eye contact is expected.

"New Video: Impromptu Speech Champion"

Gesticulation and Kinesics

These are the ways in which you use your face, arms, legs, hands and the rest of your body to emphasize and indicate the importance of content within a speech. There are a few important points to keep in mind when trying to overcome the distance between speaker and audience.

Haptics

This is the name given to the study of touch. Although public speakers do not often physically touch audiences in the same way that interpersonal communicators may touch one another (due to different distances, relational differences, and content discussed), touch can play an important role in how a speaker is perceived. Consider, for a moment, how an audience may perceive a political candidate who never shakes any hands before or after speaking to groups. How is this speaker seen differently than a candidate who shakes any and all hands thrust in front of her before and after speeches? Is there a difference in perceived warmth? If so, does that have any affect on overall perception of speakers and the messages they want audiences to ingest?

In addition, while a speaker may not physically touch audience members, there is a psychological equivalent called immediacy. Leaning forward while at the podium can help reduce the physical distance between speaker and audience. Consider moving your podium to the side and placing your notes upon them, glancing over at them over as needed. What does the reduction of the perceived barrier of the podium communicate to the audience? No doubt that it communicates that you are a more open communicator. Audiences assess the psychological intimacy they perceive with speakers based on immediacy, or how they connect with the speaker. In the context of a classroom setting, for example, professors are more highly rated if they step away from the podium and move throughout the class. In this sense, they are achieving physical closeness with students. Moreover, speakers are perceived as more 'immediate' if they engage in eye contact with audience members. Take the context of serving at a restaurant. Studies have shown that tips from patrons increase when touch is initiated. In addition, a server is more likely to receive a bigger tip when they engage in more eye contact with patrons: that is why it is not uncommon for a server to sit next to patrons in the booth or to get eye level with patrons. Once again, the perception of immediacy between speaker and audience is an essential ingredient in the development and maintenance of the speaker-audience relationship (Cialdini, 2006).

IT'S WHAT YOU DON'T SAY THAT COUNTS!

LEARN TO READ AND INFLUENCE PEOPLE THROUGH NONVERBAL COMMUNICATION.

"Public Speaking: Awkward Hand Gestures"

Gestures and Body Movement

Most novice speakers become less animated rather than more animated when in front of an audience. Instead of naturally gesturing as they would in any typical conversational encounter, novice speakers typically exemplify one of the following common gesture-awkward moves when speaking in public:

- Gripping the podium to the point our knuckles become white.
- Putting their hands in their pocket, trying to be naturally smooth and cool only to soon realize that this too, looks awkward and straightjackets their ability to impart their message.
- Fiddling with the note cards, even bending the ears of the note cards.
- Playing with their hair. We're sure many of you have beautiful hair, but watching a speaker groom him/herself can be a bit distracting as we can't help but devote all of our attention to your hair, rather than your speech!

- Playing with a paperclip. We've even seen exotic animals carved out of paperclips while students were giving speeches. Now that's impressive multitasking but ineffective delivery.
- Tapping the podium or table. Based on our experience, we are convinced that the speaker has no knowledge they are doing this, but the audience, unfortunately, can't help but try to tap along with the tune or beat, while ignoring everything else the speaker is saying.
- Clicking a pen. Thank goodness pens can be clicked, because we've seen many a pen clicked while giving a speech. By the end of the speech, we usually know the brand name of the pen, and have memorized the color and style but, of course, remember nothing else.

What should a speaker do, then, if the above gestures distract attention away from the impact of a speaker's ideas? The first rule of speaker delivery is "do no harm". In each of the examples above, harm was done. Attention was divided. The time and dedication the speaker put into his/her speech, was erased by breaking this golden rule of delivery.

"Public Speaking, Movement and Gesture (Highlights) – 1940s"

In public speaking, gestures and body movement can make the difference between effectiveness and awkwardness. Gestures come naturally to us when we speak in everyday conversation. In fact, they help us organize our own thoughts.

<u>**Exercise**</u>*:* A simple example will illustrate the point. Pair up with a fellow student and give the other person directions to your home. After you have completed giving directions, change partners and once again, provide directions, but this time, you can't use any gestures. That's right, no hand gestures to help illustrate how to get to your dorm or apartment. Was it more difficult to give directions without the aid of physical gestures? Why?

According to research, body movement and gestures help clarify thoughts. That might help explain why it was more difficult to give directions when you were not allowed to gesture. Not only can gesturing help speakers remember and articulate their message, they also can add to the impact of one's ideas.

"Chris Rock – Love"

Have you ever watched comedian Chris Rock perform a comedy routine? If you turn the sound down when you watch him perform, you will notice that Rock is constantly moving – almost to the point of making the audience dizzy from his constant left to right stage shifts. While too much movement may be distracting to some audience members, strategic movement can be used to a speaker's advantage.

Novice speakers typically stand behind the podium, hoping to use it as a type of shield or protection from the audience. It feels safer behind the podium, but safer usually translates into ineffectiveness. More advanced speakers, on the other hand, use the podium but are not confined by it. In fact, and as we've noted above, in some forms of debate speakers are encouraged to move strategically away from the podium at particular moments of transition in the speech itself. Thus, moving from the podium to the left side of the class would occur at the first transition point. Then, moving from the left side of the class back to the podium or center of the room would occur at the second main point transition. Then, a shift from the center of the class to the right side of the classroom would occur at the third transition point. Finally, at the conclusion, the speaker would return to the podium to make his/her final comments. In this case, the speaker's movements amplify the different points the speaker is making and helps the audience note the transitions two ways – both through verbal transitions and physical movement.

"Chris Rock – Bigger & Blacker – Aids Test"

The second distinctive characteristic of Chris Rock's performances is his abundant use of gestures. With the microphone in one hand, Rock's whole body amplifies his jokes and amplifies his social critique. Turn down the volume and simply watch. Can you tell what emotion he is trying to reflect in his facial movements and his over-the-top hand gestures? He's reaching you, even without the sound. His whole body is speaking, not just the words. His whole body animates and brings to life his routines, injecting a full dimensional interaction with the audience rather than simply relying on a one dimensional, verbal routine. Because a public speaker and audience are always communicating at a public distance, gestures need to be even more pronounced than they typically would in everyday conversation.

Third, physical gestures are so essential to a presentation that they serve as a form of content in and of themselves. For example, when President Bill Clinton told the American people that in no uncertain terms, "I did not have sexual relations with that woman, Miss Lewinsky," he was believable. Look at the video – his eyes stared straight into the camera, his posture upright, and most importantly, look at his left fist. It rises as he authoritatively says what he says. Sadly, his gestures were more believable than the content of what he was saying. Here, Clinton did not overtly display what we call leakage cues to the untrained eye. Eckman describes these as nonverbal gestures that give away lies or misleading information when one is being deceptive (1968). The example of Bill Clinton shows us the power of gestures – we tend to believe how someone says something as much or more than what they are saying.

**"Bill Clinton:
I Did Not, Have, Sexual, Relations, with THAT Woman, Miss Lewinsky"**

Finally, gestures bring life to ideas. Ideas without the life of the speaker's gestures are easily discarded and quickly forgotten. It is no surprise that many famous evangelical speakers highlight gestures to accentuate their message. For example, Reverend Jeremiah Wright, who became a prominent figure in the 2008 presidential campaign, exemplifies the unity of delivery and message. Wright's delivery – an all-body experience – so conveyed his message that it's impossible to separate his delivery from the message or the message from the delivery. Those same words, conveyed in a different manner, perhaps even in written form, might not have created such a controversy.

"Barack Obama Pastor Jeremiah Wright Anti-American and Racist"

Similarly, speakers whose message does not coincide with their delivery pose conflicting messages to audiences. In these situations whereby the delivery does not match the message or the message does not match the delivery, audience members will more likely defer to gestures rather than what someone is saying.

Speaking and One's Use of an Ethical Character

Before exiting this chapter, let us briefly look at the importance of 'you' and 'your speaking' as a tool in public presentations. In the above sections of this chapter, we have focused upon effective speaking and delivery, as well as how to understand your delivery from a psychological and physiological perspective. But, it would be unwise to leave this section without briefly investigating *Aristotelian phronesis* as a means for practicing what is known as ethical communication. More simplistically, let's begin by understanding Aristotelian phronesis.

Artistotle eloquently advises speakers on how to speak more effectively through the use of his artistic proofs. Each one, ethos, pathos and logos, is separate in nature, distinct, yet connected as one so as to aid the presenter in the 'how' of public speaking., *Phronesis* translated from the Greek definition, alludes to intelligence or one's sense of wisdom. And as one would expect, the topic of phronesis is often debated in most ethics courses. Yet Aristotle took the term of *phronesis* and deepened it when connecting it to *ethos* and public speaking. He asserted that there are three types of appeals to one's character; ethics being one and virtue and goodwill being the other two. The role of ethics was of great concern to him when instructing others on public speaking.

Briefly reference back to the previous clip which highlights President Clinton's power of gestures. However, for this purpose, think about the content of his speech and the outcome that followed. According to Aristotle, we as public speakers have a charge to present the most ethical assertions and are to provide clear communication whenever possible. In fact, Aristotle found it necessary and sufficient in order to be virtuous. We are to use speech and action as 'right' or as ethical as possible (Garsten, 2006). Therefore, *Aristotelian phronesis* defines intelligence from a more thoughtful, mature and wise perspective. Let's face it, we all know an 18 year old who seems and perhaps acts mature, or a 40 year old who seems and perhaps acts immature. But regardless of age, Aristotle is asserting here that it is our job as a presenter to use better judgement; one that chooses more mature actions and speech as necessary. Why you may ask? Let the question reverse itself for one moment. How did NOT using such *phronesis* work out for Clinton in the long run? Or for anyone who has not perhaps utilized speech or action that is inherently ethical? Simple. The perception of the audience and/or audience members matters. To be seen as virtuous and to be perceived as having an ethical character, Aristotle believed that using practical thought and wisdom when addressing others was a vital key to appealing to the character of ethics. So, as we leave this chapter, ask yourself, 'what is my role in presenting the most 'right' or ethical speech and action and how can I go about doing that'? In answering such questions and then implementing the action, we are then using *Aristotelian phronesis*; using practical, wise communication and discerning the most effective means with which to communicate our purpose.

In summary, delivery is to speaking as scary music is to horror films. Have you ever watched a scary movie without the sound? If so, you know the movie appears almost comical when the sound is turned down. However, when the sound is up, the accompanying music sets the tone, creates the backdrop, creates expectations for fear, and helps the audience suspend disbelief and enter into the world of fear. Likewise, a speaker who takes advantage of his body as an instrument sets the tone and climate for the interpretation of his message.

What audiences think of speakers can't be separated from how they say what they say and how they act when speaking. Communication apprehension reflects our fears about what and how others think of us while speaking. Nonverbal communication is an essential tool speakers can use when trying to impact and impress their audience. Likewise, particularly distracting nonverbal communicating can betray a speaker's message and sidetrack audience attention. Also, as a presenter, our use of action and speech directly connects to our ethical character. This chapter has detailed particular forms of speaker delivery that can enhance speaker effectiveness. For more on effective speaking, refer to the following:

"Barack Obama's 3 Best Public Speaking Tips"

For more on communication apprehension, refer to the following:

"Communication Apprehension"
References

Archer, D., & Akert, R. M. (1984). *Nonverbal factors in person perception*. In M. Cook (Ed.), *Issues in person perception* (pp. 114-144). New York: Methuen.

Bailey, Eileen (2008). *Celebrities with Anxiety.* In References: "In Normal Conversation," 2000, Feb 28, Bob Thomas, Associated Press.

Beaver, D. (2006). Warning: Humor can be hazardous. ABA Banking Journal, 98.

Beebe, S. A. (1974). Eye contact: A nonverbal determinant of speaker credibility. Speech Teacher, 23 (1), 21-25.

Burke, K. (1959). Attitudes toward history. Los Altos, CA: Hermes Publications.

Carlson, A. C. (1986). Gandhi and the comic frame: "Ad bellum purificandum." Quarterly Journal of Speech, 72, 446-455.

Carlson, A. C. (1988). Limitations of the comic frame: Some witty American women of the nineteenth century. Quarterly Journal of Speech, 74, 310-322.

Cialdini, R. (2006). Influence: The psychology of persuasion. New York: William Morrow and Company

Corey, Gerald. (2009). Theory and practice of counseling and psychotherapy. Belmont, CA: Thomson Brooks/Cole.Costanzo, M. (1991). Methods and techniques: A method for teaching about verbal and nonverbal communication. Teaching of Psychology, 18, 223-227.

Costanzo, M., & Archer, D. (1989). *Interpreting the expressive behavior of others: The Interpersonal Perception Task. Journal of Nonverbal Behavior*, 13, 225-245.

Fordham, D.R. & Gabbin, A. L. (1996). Skills versus apprehension: Empirical evidence on oral communication. Business Communication, 59,

Garsten, B. (2006) *Saving Persuasion: A Defense of Rhetoric and Judgment*. Harvard Univ. Press,

Hall, J. A. (1985). *Nonverbal sex differences: Communication accuracy and expressive style*. Baltimore: Johns Hopkins University Press.

Hickson, M. L., & Stacks, D. W. (1985). *Nonverbal communication: Studies and applications*. Dubuque, IA: Brown.

Kerr, W. (1967). Tragedy and comedy. New York: Simon and Schuster.

Knapp, M. L. (1978). *Nonverbal communication in human interaction*. New York: Holt, Rinehart & Winston.

Kreidler, C. W. (1997). Describing spoken English: An introduction. New York: Routledge.

Lakoff, G. & Johnson, M. (1980). Metaphors we live by. Chicago: University of Chicago Press.

Lund, N. (2003). Language and thought. New York: Routledge.

McCroskey, J. C. (1977). Oral communication apprehension: A summary of recent theory and research. Human Communication Research, 3, 269-277.

Mineka, S., & Thomas, C. (1999). Mechanisms of change in exposure therapy for anxiety disorders. In T. Dalgleish & M. J. Power (Eds.), Handbook of cognition and emotion (pp. 747-764). Chichester, UK: Wiley.

Patterson, M. L. (1983). *Nonverbal behavior: A functional perspective*. New York: Springer-Verlag.

Rosenthal, R., Hall, J. A., DiMatteo, M. R., Rogers, P., & Archer, D. (1979). *Sensitivity to nonverbal communication: A profile approach to the measurement of differential abilities*. Baltimore: Johns Hopkins University Press.

Sawyer, C.R. & Behnke, R.R. (2002). Behavioral inhibition and the communication of public speaking state anxiety. Western Journal of Communication, 66.

Smith, C. & Voth, B. (2002). The role of humor in political argument: How "strategery" and "lockboxes" changed a political campaign. Argumentation and Advocacy, 29.

Chapter 5
The Importance of How to Research, Finding Evidence and the Elements of Argumentation and Debate

As a speaker making public arguments, you will need to know how to research speech topics and translate your research into logical, clear, and compelling supportive evidence. This chapter is of particular relevance for informational, argumentative and persuasive speeches as audiences will expect nothing less than reasoned, researched, and riveting speeches. And, as the presenter to the audience, it is your job to make this happen.

How Do I Research?

Like anything else that one expects to have a sense of credibility that sits upon a foundation of ethics and believability, speechmaking requires gathering the information necessary to provide an informed and compelling presentation. After deciding upon a topic, effective speakers should assess the basic framework for the speech.

"How to Research a Paper"

From Wide to Focused

After determining the general purpose of the speech – informative, persuasive, ceremonial – then speakers should decide upon the specific goal of their speech. Once the general topic is known, a specific purpose and thesis is decided, and an organizational structure is hypothesized, the search and research process can continue. At this point, think of a pail of water that you will pour into a large, empty container until the container is full. This is the same process you will go through as you search for material that may or may not be useful to your speech. Initially, you search for information that pertains to your topic, then, you determine which information and material is relevant to your specific purpose and thesis. Then and finally, you must find and create the most relevant and appropriate material for your specific audience. Not an easy process for sure, but one that will assist you in establishing credibility and assist in engaging the audience.

Hint: Copy and paste all electronic documents into folders listed under subtopics you come across. Or, favorite all links that you find so you have easy access to the source.

The last thing you want to do is find a great resource and then forget where you found it. Keep copious notes and records of your research as you proceed! As you find hard print materials, take extensive notes and keep those notes (written or electronic) in a file folder named for your topic. It's better to be over-organized than it is to lose a source as you're researching.

A cold, hard fact of the research process is this: Once you begin, it never ends. The process begins the moment you have your topic, but expands after the purpose/thesis of your speech is known. The research process will allow you to gather materials used to support explanative and persuasive points throughout your speech. However, the mistake most ineffective speakers make is arbitrarily ending the search process the moment a certain number of sources are found. We understand the reality of meeting the minimum sources necessary. However, consider this: Would an instructor and/or audience view you more positively if you went above and beyond the minimum required? Chances are – YES! Doing more is much more effective and productive than doing less.

Considering the wide array of sources that may be used in a given presentation, it only makes sense to keep the search process going even after a speech has been outlined. Essentially, the research process, especially the evidence search sequence, never ends – thanks to the never-before access to online documents and resources. Your audience is expecting you to become a mini-expert on your speech topic – and if you don't exhaust research resources, they will know. It's hard to camouflage inadequate, outdated, and irrelevant sources and evidence.

"Basic Research Skills: Evaluating Sources"

Begin as Early as Possible!

This is a very important rule of thumb that we know rarely, if ever, occurs. Procrastination may be possible in other endeavors. But beginning speech preparation the day before delivery makes it nearly impossible to gather, assimilate, edit, and incorporate the material into an effective outline, let alone leave any time for delivery preparation. Once again, we've seen what happens when students wait too long to begin the research process. It's not a pretty sight. Simply put: the earlier you start the process of reading and gathering materials widely, the more time you will have select the most appropriate and

helpful supporting material from what is found. Bottom line is this – there is no substitute for proper preparation.

Take Extensive Notes & Compare Sources

The search process is not enough to warrant a "finalized" presentation. It is necessary to read and interpret the found material as much as possible. In addition to this sense-making function of searching – finding out what sources and information are available and how the material might be relevant to your topic – effective speakers should also take detailed notes of found materials so that those materials can be easily accessed. Once a researching speaker understands the content of found support materials, it is important to run a comparison between sources. For instance, when a researcher appears to support research findings by a larger medical entity, you will be more likely to accept those findings than a random piece of research you found on a bogus-looking website. I always remind my students that eminent and primary sources are crucial to establish and maintain effective credibility. For more on primary sources, review the following site: Primary Sources at Yale.

Keep Track of References & Craft a Bibliography

Effective speakers seek efficiency in the process of source searching and support. If you know that you need to use a certain style (such as MLA or APA), go ahead and keep a running list of sources you come across already organized and listed using your required style. In fact, it may be helpful to generate a working works cited or references list already in alphabetical order and updated as you find new material useful to your project. Again, if you don't, your omissions will catch up with you in the end. In addition to this list, you may as well craft what's called a bibliography as a form of source note taking. A bibliography matches a works cited or references list notation with an abstract of each source comprised in about one paragraph. The contents of this abstract usually provide the basic details of each source, including any original research questions and findings. By keeping track of your sources through an organized list, not only will it take you less time to structure your outline, the quality of your overall presentation will improve as well.

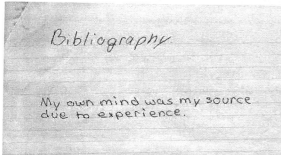

Bibliography

My own mind was my source due to experience.

Where Do I Research?

"Where do I go to do research?" That is the universal question. It's a daunting question too because with so many resources available, knowing where to find good research and how to avoid stumbling upon bad research can save you lots of time and needless frustration.

Online Research: Most students already know how to get online and use the internet. In fact, many students are so adept at using Web 1.0 (Greater World of Web Pages) and Web 2.0 (Social Media), that it seems anything is fair game to be included as support for research papers or public speaking engagements. However, this is not the case. In fact, consider the top five most frequented websites online: Google, Yahoo, Facebook, YouTube and Microsoft's Windows Live. Three of these are search engines providing advertising dollars to clever webdesigners who optimize their wares for people to "happen upon" their websites. One of these is a

social media site devoted to talking to friends. The last is a video support site where anyone, and we do mean anyone, can upload video for world-wide exposure. Who, in all of these instances, guarantees you quality material as you search for materials? None of these most popular sites provide researchers a disclaimer that you will find anything useful. This holds true for the quality as well, even if you do luck into some good information. Don't worry, because there is life online beyond Google and Facebook where you can find useful, higher quality information.

Databases: Databases tend to aggregate and catalogue specific types of information in terms of publication venues. For instance, if you were to use a paid-service database such as Lexis-Nexis through your local university or school, you would note that it is a database cataloging information from newspapers, news wires, newsletters, federal legal code and law journals. In essence, this database provides an online collection and exposure to researched, legitimate sources generated in both print and online forums. Communication and Mass Media Complete is another database used by many students to find research and information related to the study of communication across contexts such as public, interpersonal, organizational, small group and more. Many universities also subscribe to some level of the Ebscohost and Project Muse databases which provide access to research journals and trade publications within the humanities and social sciences. There are similar databases used for the hard sciences and business.

Across all of these databases, research communities review the material before publication in hard and soft forms. Hence, these databases carry with them the legitimacy of their various, affiliated disciplines. As a result, you should feel more comfort with accessing and using resources from these databases than from a general search engine request.

Search Engines & Webpages

Surf carefully when barreling through webpages because sharks often are lurking beneath the water's edge. Make sure you get the right information from webpages including authors, date last updated, and date posted. Additionally, always seek to know the qualifications of those who author webpages. If it helps, the University of California provides some guidelines for assessing the quality and reliability of webpages. They ask researchers to assess the URL (link) to see if the domain type is .edu, .gov or .org, assess the name in the link to see if it matches the name on the page, and look for anything unusual in the link. On the page proper, can you find information "about" the authoring entity or the mission of the page? What are the author's credentials, if any are to be found? Is the page up to date? Is information provided on the page linked to additional resources, researched and referenced itself, or reproduced as partial?

Students may also visit the library pages of

Johns Hopkins University:
http://www.library.jhu.edu/researchhelp/general/evaluating/

Franklin and Marshall College:
http://library.fandm.edu/howto/websites.html

When in doubt, don't hesitate to go to your college's learning resource center and ask for assistance from the librarian. They are trained professionals who specialize in the researching of not only the databases, webpages and search engines, but also how to teach students to research correctly and efficiently.

Carefully Consider the Legitimacy of Online Sources

To put it simply, database and hard print source research are the safest bets. In most instances, the authority of a research community reviewing and placing a stamp of approval on publications requires a certain amount of rigor and ethical acuity on the part of authors. When webpages must be used, however, triangulate the legitimacy of the page, page author, and material published (using the California, Berkeley system).

Library: Believe it or not, books – yes, those very hard things that collect dust – still provide a very large and significant amount of information when it comes to research. Using a website such as Amazon.com or Barnes and Noble online may provide an introduction to writers and researchers discussing your topic, but you will still have to get the full text from your library to assess the complete details and information in the text, in most cases. Even Google books' provision of some books' texts is

incomplete such that researchers often cannot get all of a book's text without paying a subscription fee. And even then, not all books are provided on that website. In many cases, these online points of information provide good starting places in tandem with libraries' website search interfaces. After the initial searchers however, researchers will still have to get the full text to assess the usefulness of the material. When this cannot be obtained online, a hard copy should be found either in libraries, or through library exchange programs such as interlibrary loan.

One last note on books. It is, as always, still very important to check the writing and research credentials of authors. This includes both achievements as well as organizational and institutional affiliations. The efficiency of the internet allows for verification of credentials often times. Finally, it is almost always helpful to investigate how the material in books compares to material you find in research journals. Are the two in agreement? Is the book material an anomaly in comparison to an outstanding amount of information provided in research journals? Is the opposite true? Knowing that the information you use, even hard copy research, is legitimate helps both your research and presentation confidence and adds to the overall legitimacy of your presentation's content!

Interviews: Testimonials may be obtained by going directly to (or telephoning or skyping) sources of information and interviewing them. Gathering information in this way often provides more robust testimonials including an opportunity for more pathos, adds legitimacy to you as a researcher, and extends, clarifies, or negates research you have exhumed from other sources. It is, however, always important to utilize the most credible of participants, if possible, when you are assigned and/or choose to interview an individual as a source. For more on successful source interviewing, please refer to the following site: Journalist's Resource: Interviewing a source. The legitimacy of this type of research depends both on the qualifications of the person/entity interviews, and on the research veracity and personal qualifications of the speaker.

Surveys: Generally speaking, a survey refers to compiling a series of questions to ask a segment of a population questions in order to deduce a presentation of that particular population. However, surveys can be varied in nature in that one can be asking individuals specific questions about themselves or asking questions that are specific to intangible concepts such as opinions or behaviors. Consider compiling a questionnaire in your sociology course where you are asked to measure the opinions of your fellow classmates regarding the upcoming Presidential candidates. Questions may include asking about the opinion they may have of one candidate versus the other. But, note that questions may also vary to include surveying fellow students about which candidate they see has more foreign policy knowledge, or asking questions about which candidate they believe to have more charisma. Or, consider a questionnaire for a nutrition class that surveys fellow students on their nutritional intake. This may include polling the students about a daily food log, but also include questions about exercise and the intake of alcohol or other substances. Notice that in the former survey one would be creating more questions based upon opinions and subjectivity, whereas in the latter survey, questions would be compiled that sought out a student's behavioral pattern. As one can assess from this example, it is always important to identify the targeted population so specificity can be given to the questions. It is imperative to remember that the manner in which a question is not only phrased, but also asked, can greatly affect the results of the response, which will in turn affect the results of the survey. For more specifics on the vast world of surveys, review the linked information regarding how to properly conduct effective surveys: What is a Survey?

The research process is always cumbersome, intense, frustrating, and like anything good for you, somewhat painful. However, it is necessary as the quality of your evidence is a byproduct of your original source research.

Evidence

A few semesters ago, a very environmentally conscious student decided to educate her peers about a new class of vehicle with which she believed we would all become familiar: Electric Cars. Here's how she started her presentation:

> It's something none of us look forward to. Those dreadful few minutes of standing at the gas pump, painfully watching the price of your purchase climb higher and higher. Face it; everyone's wallet takes a beating at the pump today. Even my small, "fuel-efficient" car costs upward of $30 to fill. Now imagine you could fill your vehicle for only a dollar. Yes, a dollar. The good news is you don't even need to use your imagination, because according to a 2007 article published in Popular Science, the cost to refuel a Xebra is only about one dollar.

After reading the excerpt from her speech, are you aware you have just experienced the use of evidence? In fact, you have just witnessed multiple types of evidence and a source citation. For many students, gathering and employing effective evidence is one of the more difficult aspects of the speech construction process. In reality, evidence, used appropriately and strategically, can be one of your most effective tools in informing and persuading audiences. In this chapter, we will discuss the different types of evidence you can use to most effectively impact your audience and provide some helpful tips about when best to use each type of tool.

Stories

We are storytelling creatures (Fisher, 1984). Each of us is a storyteller in our everyday lives. Stories are narratives we provide for the enjoyment of others, and/or to connect our experiences to the lives of others. Stories have a beginning, middle and end. They invite the audience to identify with the plot, characters, climax, resolution, etc. As Rukmini Bhaya Nair (2003) explains, a narrative is:

> a dynamic structure that converts 'talk' into 'text'…A 'good story' is one that can be 'taken away' by listeners and/or tellers and repeated in other conversations, other contexts, other cultures. It may also undergo further structural conversion into other media such as written text, film, drawings, and back again.

The general notion of an effective storytelling includes features such as coherence (does a story hang together appropriately?) and audience salience (does a story make sense to the listeners?) (Fisher, 1984).

Effective Stories:
(1) Provide a narrative with a clear beginning, middle and end that logically fits together as whole.
(2) Communicate using everyday language and experiences known by an audience.
(3) Allows/invite audiences to "see themselves" in the story.
(4) Personalize an issue in language anyone can understand.
(4) Are believable – i.e., the story did happen or could happen.
(5) Are the appropriate length given the time constraints of the speech.
(6) Support your overall point or argument.

Example:
In 1996, Vice President Al Gore, when speaking at the Democratic National Convention, used a very personal story about his sister to draw attention to protect children from smoking and from tobacco advertising, he said.

Some of the most powerful forces that do the most harm are often hard to see and even harder to understand. When I was a child, my family was attacked by an invisible force that was then considered harmless. My sister Nancy was older than me. There were only the two of us and I loved her more than life itself. She started smoking when she was 13 years old. The connection between smoking and lung cancer had not yet been established but years later the cigarettes had taken their toll.

It hurt very badly to watch her savaged by that terrible disease. Her husband, Frank, and all of us who loved her so much, tried to get her to stop smoking. Of course she should have, but she couldn't.

When she was 45, she had a lung removed. A year later, the disease had come back and she returned to the hospital. We all took turns staying with her. One day I was called to come quickly because things had taken a turn for the worse.

By then, her pain was nearly unbearable, and as a result, they used very powerful painkillers. And eventually it got so bad they had to use such heavy doses that she could barely retain consciousness. We sometimes didn't know if she could hear what we were saying or recognize us.

But when I responded to that call and walked into the hospital room that day, as soon as I turned the corner – someone said, "Al's here" – she looked up, and from out of that haze her eyes focused intensely right at me. She couldn't speak, but I felt clearly I knew she was forming a question: "Do you bring me hope?"

All of us had tried to find whatever new treatment or new approach might help, but all I could do was to say back to her with all the gentleness in my heart, "I love you." And then I knelt by her bed and held her hand. And in a very short time her breathing became labored and then she breathed her last breath.

Tomorrow morning another 13-year-old girl will start smoking. I love her, too. Three thousand young people in America will start smoking tomorrow. One thousand of them will die a death not unlike my sister's, and that is why, until I draw my last breath, I will pour my heart and soul into the cause of protecting our children from the dangers of smoking.

And that is also why I was intensely proud last week when President Clinton stood up for American families by standing up to tobacco advertising aimed at getting our children addicted. He proposed - he proposed the first-ever comprehensive plan to protect children from smoking; to ban tobacco advertising aimed at our children, and to ban it for good.

It took courage for Bill Clinton to take on the tobacco companies. I promise you it is no accident that no president has ever been willing to do it before. (http://www.pbs.org/newshour/convention96/floor_sp eeches/gore_8-28.html)

Perhaps before reading this sample from Gore's speech, you'd never heard of him. Perhaps you never knew he had a sister. Nonetheless, do you believe Gore's story was effective? Why or why not? Did his story make you think of someone you know who died of a tobacco-related illness? Did you find yourself sympathizing with Nancy or with Al Gore himself even though you've never met them nor perhaps have never heard of them until now?

Stories can transform a relatively abstract topic into a very intimate issue that has a name, a family, a background, and a history. Famed former talk-show host Oprah Winfrey knows the power of stories. Winfrey gave the commencement address to the 2009 Duke University graduating class. In her speech, she used a story to make her point...

I just finished taping a show this week with so many powerful lessons that I wanted to weep, and I want to share some of those lessons with you today. As a matter of fact, there were so many lessons in the show that I taped just last week, that's going to air next week, you'll see it, I did weep. It was about some tough guys in prison for murder, for manslaughter, armed robbery, guys full of anger and violence. And they're involved in this program where dogs, little puppies, are taken from shelters and the eight-week-old puppies are given to the prisoners, eight-week-old puppies that would have otherwise been euthanized. The puppies live right in the prison cells with the prisoners 24 hours a day. And I forgot to ask them ... how they housebreak them, because it's not like you can say, "I need to take the dog out."

But the prisoners train these puppies to then be service dogs to help our soldiers in Iraq who come back with traumatic brain injuries and post-traumatic stress, and then send them to the veterans from Iraq. Some of these inmates had never known love or responsibility. They'd never taken care of anybody, nor knew what it felt like to have somebody love you back when you take care of them.

But one of the things they teach the dogs is how to kiss the soldier's face. A lot of the soldiers come back with post-traumatic stress and have terrible experiences, and if the soldier is starting to go to a bad place in his mind, the dogs lick and kiss the soldier's face to bring him back to reality. So this means that the  prisoners themselves also had to get the kisses from the puppies they were training. It's clear the kisses were also bringing the prisoners back from a hard, cold place, and to see these criminals, who had never, many of them, experienced love themselves, cry on camera, in front of each other, cry in redemption, their voices quivering as they talk about the chance to do something good, to do something kind and unselfish, by helping the wounded soldiers in Iraq and teaching the dogs, was so moving.

And when the severely injured soldier – what we did was we went and found one of the soldiers who had received a dog and brought him back to the prison so that he could meet the prisoner who – who trained the dog. And when they met, I tell you, the audience and I were a puddle of tears. And what I learned from that I want to share with you, graduates. If you can find a way to give back just as these felons are giving from behind bars, you will be a huge success, because for sure one of the things I've learned is that the best way to enhance your own life is to contribute to somebody else's.

http://news.duke.edu/2009/05/winfrey_address.html

What's so strikingly powerful about stories as evidence is that they are hard to disagree with. How can you argue against the story Winfrey provided? Can you? What would you say? Stories seem to defy the typical claim-evidence relationship as they touch the listener both emotionally and rationally. Consequently, when a speaker recounts an effective story, the audience is often left admiring what has been said rather than questioning the merits, accuracy, validity or relevance of the story itself.

"Effective/Ineffective Stories"

Not all stories are made alike. Like all things, there are good stories and bad stories, or more specifically, effective stories and ineffective stories. Some stories are so unique  that it is very hard for audiences to connect immediately. Talking about return on investment (ROI), for instance, may not make much sense to a group of ministers. At least, not initially. However, talking about ROI as a metaphor for investing in outreach programs will probably make a great deal of sense to a nonprofit organization comprised primarily of ex-financiers. Add in a story about how you used ROI as a concept to invest in student/camp leadership with the outcome of improved learning and better student enjoyment and you will most likely gain some connection with both groups.

However, note the importance of the audience in predicting the level of connection. For an audience of ministers, the ROI concept is professionally foreign, meaning that the personal story would help provide context for how ROI may be used in a non-economic manner. In addition, the personal example would also remind the audience how ROI can be used beyond the realm of business.

Remember, the audience is key in determining how you should go about using certain types of stories, language, and concepts. This is where audience analysis and understanding your demographic will assist you in choosing the most effective story. If you spend most of your time in this particular speech telling a story about ROI as a spiritual investment, the unique thesis may very well enforce a mental "sticky note" such that this audience hangs onto the idea and uses it again the future. On the flip side, audiences may very well forget an idea if it falls too far outside of their vocabulary or experiences. Stories that are too far-fetched or appear to be more creations of a Hollywood scriptwriter rather than a real experience may backfire.

Examples

Examples illustrate a point by drawing attention to a specific instance or case. Public presenters often benefit from the use of examples because it allows the audience members to make visual connection in their minds with your content. While examples may be lengthy or not so lengthy depending upon the need for explanation and a speaker's time constraints, examples can also be real or hypothetical. However, real or hypothetical, examples must be believable.

Examine the examples used in the following three speech excerpts:

According to Susan L Ray in 2006, the main ethical dilemma of whistleblowing is the "clash of values" – for example loyalty to one's own integrity…or loyalty to self- versus loyalty to an organization one works in. "The tension between the need to prevent abuses and preserve trust is an important tension point in whistleblowing and a major source of ambiguity."

Finally, there is the notion of an immutable god. If Hume and other empiricists are correct and people establish morality through some sort of hypothetical imperative, then god cannot share a common moral system with humanity. In the hypothetical imperative man establishes morality through empirics, experience, and tradition. If god is unchanging, he has no experience.

However, even though all of us cell phone users pay a monthly surcharge for E911 services, many local counties don't have the equipment necessary to locate callers. A good example of this is Greene County, right here where you live. Because it is imperative that we all receive the emergency services we're paying for…and the safety we deserve, we must first understand the consequences of missing e911 services, then we will examine the causes, so that we can finally enact some solutions to increase public and personal safety.

Notice that each use of an example draws from different experiences. In the first instance, the speaker draws an example from another source. In the second, a short example is used to help explain difficult philosophical concepts. In the third, a localized example demonstrates how the audience members in the room are living a shared experience and, likewise, the presentation is justified as important. Notice, and as mentioned above, the use of these examples allows for the audience members to clarify and make connections between the speaker's content and their own understanding. Creating imagery in the audiences' mind through the use of examples is a powerful tool.

The actor Daniel Day Lewis, upon receiving a Screen Actors Guild Award (SAG), dedicated his Screen Actors Guild Award to Heath Ledger. He said, "Heath Ledger gave it (regeneration/inspiration) to me". To prove or establish his point, Daniel Day Lewis went on to cite two specific examples, or instances in which Ledger inspired him: namely, he cited Ledger's roles in the movies *Monster's Ball* and *Brokeback Mountain* to illustrate his point.

"Daniel Day-Lewis Sag Speech (Heath Ledger)"

Otherwise stated, an example is the speaker's way of answering the audience question "Really? Then show me."

In sum, effective examples:

(1) Make difficult ideas or concepts clear and salient.
(2) Are simple and clear.
(3) Provide justification for topics.
(4) Extend ideas so that an audience better comprehends a topic of discussion.
(5) Help audiences remember by focusing their attention on specifics.

Statistics

Dr. Seuss stated, "I like nonsense. It brings the brain cells to life." What a fun, and perhaps true enough, quote. But the use of statistics is anything but nonsense. Statistics are mathematical proof demonstrating quantities and connections between various phenomena. Some researchers have recently suggested that statistics provide a very powerful boost in supporting claims and legitimating speakers, hence knowing about statistics in general is a very important feature of strategic and effective presentations. Here are a few of the statistical concepts a presenter should know:

Mean:	This is the average of a set of numbers. Add up all the numbers you are evaluating, divide by the number of numbers and you get the average or mean.
Median:	This is the middle number of a set of numbers.
Mode:	This is the number that appears most often within a set of numbers.
Range:	This is the numerical difference between the smallest and largest numbers in a set of numbers.
Frequency:	This is the assessment of each number such that it is known how often that number occurs within a set of numbers.
Dark Figure:	Statisticians have used this name to reference any implied number used to hype occurrences that are unobserved. For instance, when someone says that crime is very high around a high school because the rates of stolen items has shifted slightly higher but those are only the "reported cases," that person is relying on the assumption that many people have experienced crime but have not reported it within a certain distance of the high school.

Let's briefly examine an excerpt from a student's speech on 911 to highlight the differences between "good" and "bad" statistics:

According to ABC's Primetime Live of August 25, 2005, only two thirds of the nation's 25 largest cities have upgraded their equipment to be able to trace calls from cell phones. And, the state of non-metropolitan e911 is much worse. But it's not due to a lack of payment. Mobile Radio Technology reported on April 1, 2005 that all but 3 states – Hawaii, Missouri, and Wyoming – collect wireless 911 surcharges ranging from 50 cents to

2 dollars per phone each month. This adds up to hundreds of millions of dollars annually. But the 911 surcharge we 190 million U.S. cell users pay monthly isn't being used for 911 services.

This excerpt demonstrates both the good and the bad of statistical evidence. The statement that only seventeen, or "two thirds," of our largest cities being prepared is a critical concern. The speaker could also have said "two out of every three" or "sixty six percent." This is a clear use of statistics to demonstrate relationships between 911 have and have nots. However, the implied negative of "non-metropolitan e911" being more critical relies on no presentation of statistical evidence. This is a dark figure in use and encourages the audience to envision just how bad the experiences must be for everyone not living in one of the seventeen largest U.S. cities. Are all of these examples persuasive? Perhaps, but the use of statistics is for empirical proof. Effective and ethical statistical use requires the watchwords of honesty, clarity and correctness. For more information on the use of statistics in presentations, review the following site: Presentation Skills: Bring Statistics to Life.

Testimony

Testimony can be a very effective type of evidence used by presenters. Essentially, testimony is any example derived straight from the mouth of someone about whom you are talking or someone with expertise or experience with your presentation topic. Consider this student speech example:

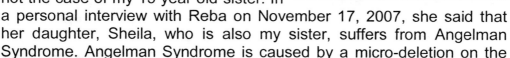

Most fifteen year olds are excited about things like being able to drive. This is not the case of my 15 year old sister. In a personal interview with Reba on November 17, 2007, she said that her daughter, Sheila, who is also my sister, suffers from Angelman Syndrome. Angelman Syndrome is caused by a micro-deletion on the maternal side of one's fifteenth chromosome. As a result of the micro-deletion, Sheila is physically and mentally about the age of one. She can't talk and communicates by whining and crying when she doesn't like something. She also can't walk, and instead scoots around on her behind. Due to her condition, Sheila is tough to take in public. She has no concept of personal space. On numerous occasions, Sheila has grabbed food off of others' plates during a meal. "She thinks what's yours is mine and what's mine is yours" said Reba. "She's used to being fed by other people so much that when other people have food in their hands, to her, it's her food. Sheila has no

concept of personal space. She loves to be close, but for someone who doesn't understand her well, her being right up in their face is creepy." Sheila also tends to make a lot of loud noises when the surroundings are either too loud or quiet. Said Reba, "National anthems before sporting events are always a coin flip whether Sheila will be quiet or not. On occasion during our contemporary worship service at church, the music will become loud, and Sheila will start screaming and flailing her arms because it's too much for her to handle." Because Sheila doesn't get to go in public frequently, she treasures it when she gets to go on an outing. Sheila loves nothing more than going on a car ride. She shows this to others by grabbing her coat off the coat rack and bringing it to mom and dad, as well as bringing her shoes to others when she is ready to leave. When others leave the home and Sheila doesn't get to go, she sits at the front door and cries. When riding in the car on the way home, Sheila often begins to cry. "When we're about five minutes away from home with Sheila in the car, she lets you know she doesn't want to go back home. She's a smart girl. When we pull into McDonalds, she sees the golden arches and knows it's the place with tasty hamburgers, and when we're a couple minutes away from home, she can tell"

Compare the too-lengthy student examples above with the shorter testimonial provided below and keep in mind that both testimonials were selected from eight-minute persuasive presentations.

Rozanne Weissman in the August 28, 2003 Christian Science Monitor, explains that "the very term 'energy conservation' elicits negative images in the minds of American consumers…images like smaller cars… and Jimmy Carter telling us to simply turn down the thermostat." But, she adds, Americans do like to be told they're smart. So, as enlightened consumers, we have an obligation to change some of the negative social impression of energy conservation.

The primary difference between these two testimonials is length. The second example provides more time for the current speaker to use the rest of the speech to examine energy conservation while the first example may well overwhelm the speaker's point by reducing the ability to talk more about solutions to Angelman Syndrome.

Effective testimonials:
(1) Help audiences understand the emotional and human aspect of an argument.

(2) Help audiences see how other experts agree with the presenter, thereby taking advantage of social proof.

(3) Allow for the argument to be introduced with the credentials of the expert providing the testimonial, thereby adding to the credibility of the overall argument.

Ineffective testimonials:

(1) Take up too much time, add unnecessary emotion levels to a presentation

(2) Go completely off topic, prompting the audience to ask themselves why this person was being quoted for this topic

To watch how using testimony as speeches work, review the following YouTube clip:

"15 Year-Old Girl Leaves Anti-gun Politicians Speechless"
Definition

Providing definitions can be quite helpful in explaining components of a phenomenon, or explaining the phenomenon itself. An instance in one of our recent speaking courses included defining SEO (Search Engine Optimization) as a way for internet users to become more marketable. SEO was defined according to the general idea that a webpage should "meet" those content criteria that search engines "look for" when assessing all available webpages during an internet search.

Finding definitions can involve technical expert sources or general reference sources. The example mentioned above matched the general SEO definition from a generic dictionary (such as Webster's or American Heritage) with an additional expert source taken from "industry standard bearer" such as a book written by an SEO professional. The more specific definition provided details such as the methods that search engines use to scrape information from websites, "crawl sites" with analytic "spiders," and value webpages with social media behavior. For each of these criteria, the speaker also explained his/her meaning by using a technical source such as a book on web analysis and search engine construction.

Another type of definition that can be helpful to speakers when attempting to explain components of a phenomenon is through the use of an _operational definition_. The definitions described above are often very helpful, however, sometimes the best definition is a definition of the phenomenon in action or use. For example, when you try and explain to your partner how much you love him/her, it would seem silly to explain your love in the form of a dictionary or technical definition. Thus, an operational definitional is probably the best way you can effectively express the depth and specifics of your care. For example, you might say you love the sound of your partner's laugh, sense of humor, and overall intelligence. In this way, you are defining your love in the real context of your relationship rather than providing a generic, decontextualized definition.

Analogy

Analogies can be a very effective tool when helping explain a difficult concept or process to an audience. In essence, an analogy compares an idea/concept/thing the audience is already familiar with to an idea/concept/thing the audience is unfamiliar with.

There are two types of analogies – *literal* and *figurative*, that each compare the known to the unknown, typically using the word "like."

Literal analogies involve a comparison between idea/concept/objects from similar classes. Cars to cars, hotels to hotels, universities to universities professors to professors, et cetera.

Example: Professor Mendez is like Professor Router, except you actually have to attend Professor Mendez's class.

Example: Like the United States war in Vietnam, our conflict in Afghanistan is a never-ending war that is costly in terms of American lives and treasure.

Figurative analogies involve a comparison between ideas/concepts/objects from different classes. Figurative analogies are helpful when trying to provide new or unique insight into ambiguous or difficult-to-grasp concepts.

Example: "My momma always said, 'Life was like a box of chocolates. You never know what you're gonna get.'" Forrest Gump (1994)

Example: Writing a speech is like running a marathon. Both involve lots of self-doubt and a whole lot of sweat.

<u>Effective analogies</u>:

(1) Are clear and compelling.

(2) Help the audience make connections that add to the understanding of relevant subject matter.

(3) Add interest, creativity and even humor to arguments.
(4) Humanize a subject matter by making comparisons to references the audience is familiar with.

Ineffective analogies:

(1) Are too complex and difficult to grasp.

(2) Compare two unfamiliar ideas/concepts/objects.

(3) Depend on comparisons with obscure and out-of-date references the audience may be unfamiliar with.

"Figurative Analogies vs Literal Analogies"

Rhetorical Applications: From Logic to Enthymemes

Regardless of whether you're a fan of Aristotle or action films, one thing is for sure: we live in an age where scientists hold great influence. And while we may be traumatized by that fifth grade biology class, science provides us so much of our intellectual drive and economic output. Without scientists we would have neither the capacity to listen for survivors through concrete and steel when earthquakes hit nor the ability to dig for them. Without scientists we would not understand the full complexity of our ecosystem. Without scientists we wouldn't be able to visit a Trader Joe's to buy our favorite natural and organic foods. In today's day and age, that would truly be seen as tragic for some.

Scientists have also contributed a great deal in terms of intellectual life. In terms of their methods to generate more knowledge about the world, they rely on inductive and deductive methods of testing and reasoning through their application of the scientific method. Induction is the process of collecting information about ideas and objects to learn more about them. Deduction is a process of using known premises to conclude with a sound and valid thought. Of course the soundness and validity tests of this form of reasoning are very important in terms of logical thinking, but for our purposes we wish only to demonstrate an example (that is, by the way, considered sound and valid):

All Men are Mortal

President Obama is a Man

Hence, President Obama is Mortal.

Note that this form of thinking relies on premises (the first two well-known claims) to infer a concluding thought. Unlike inductive necessity, this syllogism (three part deductive reasoning chain) does not rely upon further observations regarding the President's health or his manhood because the premises are already known.

In terms of persuasive reason patterns used by public speakers, the enthymeme has come to represent a very useful version of deductive reasoning. As Aristotle made clear, there is something energizing for audiences when speakers don't verbalize all of the premises or when speakers, perhaps, verbalize only one premise but neither the conclusion nor the other premise. So, in other words, leaving part of the picture unspoken, but can be implied by the listener. This rhetorical flourish encourages the mind of the audience to help spell out the whole argument.

Let's assume we were speaking to a group of colleagues about which florist to use to buy flowers for an acquaintance's birthday. We might say, "We cannot trust florist X because she has overcharged before." The conclusion is that we cannot trust her. The one explicitly stated premise is her previous overcharge. The implied premise that overcharging requires mistrust is absent. Or rather, the implied premise is activated in the mind of the audience. The colleagues, for instance, probably thought, "Yeah, we shouldn't trust someone who overcharges!" In any event, the use of the enthymeme is often considered persuasive primarily because it gets listeners involved in the inference process making them feel as if they are helping to construct arguments. The important point is that inducing participation by the audience to complete the "missing" premise or conclusion leads to self-persuasion, perhaps the most complete and most effective type of persuasion. Think about it personally – to convince ones' self and answer ones' own questions is personally and cognitively very rewarding. Pride and egoism may be somewhat involved here, but nonetheless, it can be effective in self-persuasion.

In general, most users of argument are cautious to not engage in fallacious reasoning as a means of persuasion. While this would be bad form in terms of formal logic, it would also most certainly give way to unethical behavior. When an audience perceives such unethical behavior on the part of the speaker, it makes sense to also assert that those audience members would lose trust in the speaker's ethics, therefore resulting in an inability to be persuaded As Stephen Toulmin, the logician, designed it to be the case, the use of the argument form is intended to provide a clear structure both for competent assembly as well as disassembly and comprehension. When irrational arguments are used, confusion, distrust and uninformed behavior become the result. Here are a few fallacies that should be avoided as a speaker and fallacies that you should be alert to as an audience member:

(1) **Ad Hominem:** This is an attack claim made against a speaker or author rather than against the content of what a speaker author has said or written. For example, "It is said he cheated on his wife, so how could we trust him to present the facts in an ethical manner to the committee."

(2) **Straw Person:** This is an attack on a person's argument by focusing on something else rather than the original argument. In other words, the speaker's words are manipulated or twisted so an easier argument can be made. For example, "My opponent is saying he wants to put more monies into healthcare. I'm shocked and disappointed that he cares so little about our military and the defense of our country".

(3) **Post Hoc Ergo Propter Hoc:** This is the faulty reasoning that because something occurs before another thing the original thing causes the latter. Note that this type of faulty reasoning is often referred to as false cause.
For example, Charlene shows a chart that the temperatures have been steadily rising for the past decade every summer. She also notes that ice cream sales have been decreasing in the summer months. Therefore, ice cream helps to cool the world and global warming isn't a reality.

(4) **Appeal to Authority:** Claiming something is true or relevant merely because someone of authority has said that it is so. For example, "The Mayor of the city claims Mama Jean's has the best chicken around. Must be true."

(5) **Red Herring:** This is the fallacy committed whenever an arguer uses a distraction to divert attention away from the original content of the discussion. For example, "We may have lost track of some of the donations, but let's not forget the thousands of dollars we have poured into the community service programs for our local youth. We care about our kids".

(6) **Slippery Slope:** This is the faulty argument that because one thing will happen, another thing will happen. This argument assumes the intervening steps between the outcomes without articulation. For example, "If we allow football teams to pray before games, then before we know it those teams will be having car washes, bake sales and candy drives for extra monies".

(7) **Hasty Generalization:** This occurs when someone draws example from a small sample instead of researching into a larger possibility. The fallacy forms when the sample is too small to be indicative of the whole. For example, "My grandfather smoked cigarettes since he was 15 and lived until he was 82. Therefore, cigarette smoking can't be harmful for you".

(8) *False Dilemma:* This is the fallacy committed when only two choices are presented, but more exist. More of an "either or" option. For example, "Either you are with our President or you are against him". Of course, if both claims are false or cannot happen, then the either/or logic cannot hold.

(9) *Guilt by Association:* This is an attack against a claim merely because one person dislikes another person, and the person they dislike accepts the claim. For example, "Sam supports an increase in the minimum wage. This is the same stance that our local politically extremist group supports. Politically extreme people like Sam shouldn't be taken seriously".

"Word Play and Reasoning"

Clearly, it is the ethical responsibility of speakers to avoid purposeful use of fallacies and it is equally the obligation of audience members to be able to recognize others' use of fallacies. For those interested in the fine points of public argument, where arguments and evidence are analyzed, dissected and retorted, the public forum of debate is the perfect laboratory.

From One, Many: Building Arguments into Debate

Ok, so where do we go from here? Well, learning to craft arguments takes time and precision. Crafting a claim carefully warranted by way of competent grounding is the first step. Including competent arguments in public presentations is the next step.

If you want to go beyond basic presentation skills, you may become interested in debating. If this is the case, it is important to realize that debate tends towards selecting a winner and loser. While public speaking provides a forum for individuals to add voice to ideas, concepts and information within the public sphere. Regardless of the tendency of the idea of 'my win is your loss', it is still worth exploring the conceptual and practical features of debate given its pervasiveness in numerous professional arenas as well as its potential for improving critical thinking.

"SNL Spoofs Biden-Ryan Debate"

So what does it take to debate? Well, here are a few of the basics:

- Debate is generally a discussion whereby two parties disagree. Arguments are used to demonstrate the quality and quantity of the disagreement.

- Topic: Each debate has a topic and the opposing speakers deal with the same topic, from two different sides. While there may be other sides, it is imperative the debaters understand how they differ in perspective on the topic. Consider two individuals debating the merits of vanilla and chocolate ice cream. Either could change his or her mind in the debate and start advocating for pistachio, but it would still be a debate of pistachio versus vanilla or pistachio versus chocolate. If both debaters agree, there is no point of contention and, hence, no reason for a debate.

- Resolutions: Based on general topics, resolutions provide a more specific focus for topics. Rather than debating generic concepts like ice cream flavors, for example, a resolution provides a starting place for the debaters and entitles the advocacy of one of the debaters. For example, Resolved: Vanilla Ice Cream is the best. Note that this resolution provides specificity for the opening of the debate. Whoever affirms this resolution speaks first and should, according to competent argument skill, provides reasons and evidence as to why vanilla is best.

Resolutions tend to range across a myriad of types, lengths, contexts, vernaculars and professions. Some debate theorists have indicated that academic debates tend to use mainly resolutions of fact, value and policy.

- A fact resolution claims the definition and/or ontology of a thing is appropriate.

- A value resolution claims either that a thing be valued a certain way, that one value be placed over another, or that a certain value be held in higher or lower regard.

- A policy resolution calls for some kind of policy action regarding a particular object, person, nation, behavior, or situation.

"The Art of Debate: Never Lose an Argument Again"

Argument theory holds that the affirmative speaker is the person who takes on the responsibility of the Burden of Proof, meaning they have the task of proving the resolution (i.e. vanilla ice cream is best ice cream). Because the claim – ice cream is the best ice cream – is uttered as a new way of thinking, valuing, or behaving, the burden is on the first speaker to provide clear reasons as proof that this claim is legitimate. The opposing speaker then has the burden of rejoinder in that she must provide counterclaims with countergrounds as a way of maintaining legitimacy in the debate.

In academic contexts, debates tend to refer to early, lengthier speeches as constructives because affirmative and negative theses (the overarching arguments) are still being constructed through the processes of articulating evidence, assessing warrants, and when necessary defending warrants with backing. Toward the end of most debates, smaller speeches referred to as rebuttals tend to occur. Often these speeches are summaries of earlier speeches, but these speeches also give individuals last chances to bolster their arguments in addition to last chances to critique opponents' cases.

Most debaters consider a number of theoretical underpinnings to guide their work as competent debaters. *Debate-ability* refers to the amount of "ground" each debater has. The more room to make an argument, the more ground. The more ground on both sides in a debate, the more debateability.

Topicality tends to refer to how much an affirmative speaker is "in support of" the specificity of a resolution. The language of the resolution is generally scrutinized to demonstrate the topical or untopical nature of the affirmative debater.

Inherency is a term used in policy debates to assess the likelihood that an advocated policy isn't going to occur in the status quo anyway. After all, if something hasn't happened yet but it is immanent, why does it require unique advocacy?

Debaters often use *hypothesis testing* as a form of argument analysis within debates. For instance, if we are debating health care funding we may offer up a tax revenue generating-plan for testing. Assessing the "cons" may include pointing out tax exhaustion. Providing "pro" arguments may include implications such as reducing long term care issues with preventative measures and solving underinsured persons. In the end, the test occurs largely through the process of arguing the relative merits of suggested policies and values in contrast to one another.

Individuals engaged in academic debates may suggest numerous ways to assess debates for those who are listening. This is usually called *framing the debate* and the framework for a debate tends to indicate how an audience should assess the arguments. While the Toulmin model is often an assumed model for assessing the legitimacy of arguments within the debate, the framework provides a score card to show what kinds of arguments "count" the most. This is particularly important for many public communicators engaged in debate because some arguments conclude with tacit assumptions about quality and quantity. At the college level, a fairly wide-spread framework assumed by many debaters is a *cost-benefit framework* whereby affirmative debaters and negative debaters argue the costs of affirmative and negative cases over against the potential benefits such cases might accrue. Additionally, the impact of the advantages compared to the impact of the disadvantages has become particularly important given that it mirrors pro/con analysis used by many other individuals while purporting to analyze advantage and disadvantage arguments with a great deal more scrutiny in terms of structure.

Of course this very brief overview is intended only as primer. There are many very good books on the subject of academic debate. These books cover numerous types of debate and provide depth of analysis and discussion for those interested in the practice of debate. And, given that folks as varied as Jane Pauley, Oprah Winfrey, and Vernon Jordan refer to their time in public speaking and debate as a participating reason for their success, it is probably in your best interest to consider learning the skills of public debate. If for no other reason, practicing critical thinking skills surely justifies such work. For more information on how to construct a debate for a public speaking course, review the following: Debate Writing.

References

Fisher, W. R. (1984). Narration as a human communication paradigm: The case of public moral argument. Communication Monographs, 51, 1-22.

Hitchcock, D. & Verheij, B. (2007). Arguing on the Toulmin model: New essays in argument analysis and evaluation (Argumentation Library). New York: Springer.

Nair, R. B. (2003). Narrative gravity: Conversation, cognition, culture. New York: Routledge.

Ray, S. (2006). Whistleblowing and organizational ethics. *Nursing Ethics*, *13*(4), 438-445.

Toulmin, S. (1969). *The Uses of Argument*, Cambridge, England: Cambridge University Press.

Suggested Websites

http://wps.pearsoned.com/wps/media/objects/6524/6681325/Debate_writing.pdf

Chapter 6
The Specifics of Organization

Research that serves the speech well, as you know, takes a great deal of commitment and work. However, all of that hard work would go to waste if one doesn't work on the organization of the speech itself. Face it: as a college student you know that organization isn't easy because you have so many elements in your life to juggle as you're professing in your educational journey. Yet, you also know that priorities need to come first when you organize any element in your life if you want a professional and positive outcome. So, how does one go about organizing all of the research that has been unearthed? In many ways, organizing evidence into a structured fashion can be compared to baking. Individual ingredients have no function or purpose until they are put together in a particular way to achieve a desired end – a great dessert. But note the preciseness that is needed. One cannot just decide to disregard the measurements required because if that were the case, the cake may not rise or the cookies may fall flat. Specifics are required to be an effective baker. Likewise, evidence and research becomes a speech, rather than a diatribe, a conversation, or a mere rant, because the evidence and research are organized and ideas are coalesced for audience consumption. At its most basic level, all creative works have a beginning, middle, and end. This structure serves two purposes: (1) it helps creators construct works of art and (2) it helps audiences easily digest material. If done right, the audience can't imagine your speech, or good meal, being served or prepared any other way.

Organization Gone Wrong

Perhaps the best way to highlight the importance of organization is to remind you of what happens when speeches or presentations are organizationally challenged. In other words, the following are telltale signs of organization-less presentations:

- When you can't tell *why* the speaker is speaking to you (no thesis of intent).

- When you *don't care* why the speaker is speaking to you (no relation to the audience).

- When the speaker tells you she's going to speak about the dangers of second-hand smoking, but spends her entire speech talking about why she doesn't smoke (misguided organization and research with no ability to stick to the thesis).

- You listen attentively to the entire speech, only to be surprised when the speaker prematurely ends his speech, sitting down with no notice he was finished (missing the crucial element of the conclusion with the structure).

- You wanted the speaker to continue developing her first point, but she covered four additional points, none of which was as interesting or compelling as the first point (inability to provide a coherent foreshadowing and not developing points equally within the body).

- The speech doesn't have an introduction. As a result, you have no idea what the speaker is going to talk about or even why you should listen (lack of introductory structure providing intent and clarity of what is to come).

- In one breath, the speaker is talking about health care and in the next breath she is talking about economic policy. You wonder what the real topic of the speech is and can't figure out how the two points fit together (inability to structure an appropriate outline and follow it as needed).

- Five minutes into the speech, you find yourself forgetting what the speaker's original point was and wished the speaker had provided some kind of reminder (inability to connect relations and input reinforcements into the organization of the speech).

Each of these brief examples illustrates that organization is more than simply arranging ideas. Rather, organization is one significant way you can demonstrate ethos to your audience. In fact, the organizational choices you make in the speech construction process reveal the extent to which you understand your audience, how well you understand how much or little the human mind can process and remember at any one time, and perhaps most importantly, shows the audience that you have done the diligent work of distinguishing between what must be in the speech and what doesn't need to be in the speech.

"What is Character (Ethos)? / How to Craft an Argument"

Organizing 101: The Philosophy of Organizing Creation

According to literary critic Kenneth Burke, speeches, like all artistic creations, must keep in mind the importance of form, or organization: "the creation of an appetite in the mind of an auditor and the adequate satisfaction of that appetite" (Burke, 1953). Simply put, just like in any good movie or in any well-remembered song, every speech must create a reason and a need for an audience to want to listen. And, once this 'appetite' has been created, the remainder of the speech must keep the promise of fulfillment so that by the end of the speech, the audience should be intellectually full and their curiosity satisfied! The University of Pittsburgh also reports that an effective organization aides the audiences in remembering crucial elements, as well as offering credibility to the speaker (2007).

Basic Organizing Structure

The basic organizing structure is made in the image of the body. Plato, the Greek philosopher, used the body as the metaphor to explain organizational structure (Hackforth, 1952). The head, in his metaphor, is the introduction. Introductions create an appetite, set the scene, provide necessary backdrop, and prepare the audience for what is to follow.

The body is the skeletal structure that holds up the head. This is the "meat" of your speech and includes the content of your presentation, including all points you want to make with requisite supporting evidence and citations.

And finally, the feet stand for the conclusion. The conclusion wraps up the speech, reminds the audience how their appetite was satisfied, and leaves the audience with something to remember. Penn State recommends that the conclusion constantly includes three things – 1) review 2) final appeal and 3) an ending with an impact (2015). For a review of the structure, as well as video examples, review the following site: Effective Presentations in Engineering and Science.

Organizing Purpose

This section is probably the most difficult. That's the way it should be. Right now, you have ideas but no clear point. You have all kinds of research, but you may not know how to organize these points together, let alone know which evidence supports which points you want to make. And, you may even be feeling that the original purpose of your speech isn't exactly what you wanted to talk about now that you've actually done the research.

Don't panic. These are normal and expected states of mind. In fact, if you don't question yourself a bit in the organizing process, our experience would lead us to believe that you're missing something. Frustration in this part of the process is a good sign that you will eventually end up with a quality speech.

Organization is the ultimate editor. This part of the speech construction process is always messy. It needs to be because you are doing the hard work for the audience – in advance of the audience, for the audience, and by the audience. A well-organized speech looks natural to the audience, yet it is the most difficult part of the process for you as the speaker due to the fact that you, and you alone, must determine what is to be included and/or excluded within the content of your speech.

General Purpose

Let's start at the beginning and not get ahead of ourselves. I often instruct my students to take one 'stressor' at a time so as not to overwhelm themselves. In order to determine what should be included/excluded the content, we have some questions for you that will help you clarify what you're doing and what you're trying to achieve:

(1) What is your overall goal?
(2) Is it to inform the audience?
(3) Is it to persuade the audience?
(4) Is it to entertain the audience?

Knowing your general purpose is an important first step in determining what kind of research is necessary, what kind of evidence will be appropriate, and how to organize the details of your speech. Oftentimes, your instructor will provide you with direction on the general purpose as speech assignments are typically distinguished by their general purpose: informative speech, persuasive speech, and entertainment speech. In each, however, the intent is to let the audience clearly understand the overall intent.

Although these general-purpose categories appear distinct, they are not mutually exclusive. Because your purpose is informational does not preclude you from persuading your audience about the relevance and importance of your topic. The mere act of choosing to include some information and exclude other information means you are directing the attention of your audience, or persuading them because you are

providing the audience with a partial picture your topic and what they need to know about your topic. Full disclosure and complete representation of your subject matter is impossible: hence, persuasion in an essential component in each of the categories. In addition, information is an essential ingredient in both speeches to persuade and speeches to entertain. Finally, entertainment should be an essential ingredient in the informational speeches and persuasive speeches. So, in regard to these three major classificatory themes, read them as guides or emphases, not as mutually exclusive categories. In all speeches and presentations, information, persuasion and entertainment are present, thus, the general purpose is simply a matter of emphasis, not exclusion.

Let's assume your general purpose is to inform. This delineation is helpful because it will guide your decision making process as to what to include and exclude in the body of your speech. First, your main purpose is to inform your audience on or about a particular subject matter. Second, with the burden of informing your audience, you must provide evidence. Finally, you know that your audience will judge you based on how well you informed or enlightened them about a particular subject matter.

If your general purpose is to persuade, your focus changes. The burden is persuasion, thus, the information you choose to include in your speech must be carefully selected to both inform and persuade (i.e. you are not trying to be completely objective, but selectively objective). Consequently, you will be expected to take sides, and advocate a particular perspective or change in behavior. Moreover, with the general purpose of persuasion, you know that you are not expected to be even-handed and provide both sides of an issue (unless strategically advantageous – see chapter on persuasion). Finally, with a general purpose to persuade, the effectiveness of your speech will be judged on how well you persuade your audience, or the degree to which you change, reinforce or convert your audience.

The third type of general purpose is to entertain. With the general purpose of entertainment, your burden is to entertain and enliven the audience through laughter or through admiration. Second, you need not provide information unless it is entertaining nor do you have the burden to change behavior, as much as to help the audience rejoice, celebrate, or pay attention to a subject matter in a unique manner. Finally, the effectiveness of your speech will be judged not on the quality of your 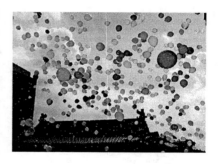 evidence or the extent to which you changed minds, but on how well you entertain your audience, or the degree to which you help them forget about their everyday worries, troubles, and more.

"Special Occasion Speeches – By Richard L. Weaver II, PhD"

Consider the following two speech introductions and see if you can tell which one is informative and which one is persuasive:

(#1)
At 14 years old, Blake Ross called himself the ultimate nerd. Having conquered several of the world's most complicated computer

programming languages, Blake decided it was time to get a job. And according to Wired News of January 23, 2005, he didn't have to look far. Having spent most of his young life tinkering with programs and working on web pages, Blake was actually offered a job – not at the local grocery store, but as one of the chief programmers for America Online. Though he didn't know it then, Blake Ross would be at the forefront of the biggest news to hit the internet since Paris Hilton. It's called Firefox, a web browser with the potential to forever change the way that we surf the net.

To see why the **Chicago Tribune of July 18, 2004** believes that Firefox is nothing short of a revolution in the making, we'll first hit the "back" button and take a look at the history of the web and web browsers we've come to know, love…and occasionally hate. We'll then explore the phenomenon known as Firefox and discover why it's been drawing some not-so-friendly-fire from Microsoft, before finally discussing – in some peer-to-peer fashion – the implications of this new world wide wonder. Even if you've already heard of Firefox or even downloaded it, stayed logged in – you might just learn something from this, a "People's history" of the web.

(#2)

According to the July 24, 2006 edition of the Ottawa Citizen computers nowadays generally go obsolete after only two years of use. Every year more and more tons of obsolete technologies are sent to less developed nations like India, China, and Africa. And why not? For US retailers and manufacturers it is justified by the powerful trinity; cheap,  easy and effective. Yet, much like sweeping dust under the rug, exporting e-waste, or electronic waste, to other countries is solving one problem, at the cost of creating many more. When e-waste is shipped to these countries monumental health and environmental problems abound. The February 10, 2006 edition of the University Wire reports that the central nervous system is what's at risk the most since extreme exposure to e-waste toxins like lead, mercury, and cadmium cause intestinal cramps, birth defects, and irreversible brain damage. Given the impact to millions of poor who live in or close to the dumps where e-waste is reposited and/or reprocessed AND given that children are the most affected physically, mentally and emotionally, we must put an end to e-waste abuse. To do so, we will surf the World Wide Web overseas and see how horrible e-waste is. Then we'll upgrade our intel to find out how this problem was created, before we crash the system with solutions to help us stem the e-waste problem.

As is obvious in both cases, the general purpose of speech example #1 is informative and the general purpose of speech #2 is persuasive. Did you also notice in the preview of each of these speeches (itself a structural component of outlining) that speech #1 sought to enlighten you on the subject matter while speech #2 sought to move you to action?

Specific Purpose and Thesis

After determining the general purpose, you can begin to focus on the specific purpose – that is what you will inform, persuade or entertain the audience about. Otherwise stated, the subject matter of the speech and/or what you want the audience to know about your topic. This is a major editorial choice on your part because out of all the things/subjects/topics in the world to inform your audience about, you choose x (and not y, z, etc.).

General Purpose: To inform.
Specific Purpose: To inform my audience about the Xebra, all-electric car.

In this example, the specific purpose narrows the purpose and solidifies the goal of your speech. It is important to choose a subject that can be thoroughly addressed in a speech. Notice that the specific purpose seeks not to inform audiences about all-electric cars, but the Xebra, all-electric car. In contemplating what to include/exclude from your speech, you will need to decide whether one main point needs to be devoted to informing the audience about all-electric cars in general before informing them about the specifics of the Xebra car. Regardless, the specific purpose is as helpful to you as it is to the audience, because one of the greatest challenges in the construction process is knowing where to begin, how much information you need to provide, and of course, when enough is enough. Hence, a thesis is born:

Thesis: In order to be more knowledgeable about the Xebra, it is important to understand what the Xebra is, how the Xebra differs from traditional vehicles, and some of its advantages and disadvantages.

General Purpose: To persuade.
Specific Purpose: To persuade my audience that you should buy the Xebra, all-electric car.

To achieve the specific purpose as articulated, you must persuade the audience about the following issues: (1) how their current car is unfit; (2) why electric cars are a better alternative; (3) of all the types of electric cars available, why the Xebra is the best choice.

Consequently, the specific purpose not only stipulates what you are going to talk about or what you are going to address in your speech, it also requires something of you. That is, the specific purpose can help you clarify what topics must be addressed in order to achieve your goal. Hence, a thesis is born:

Thesis: In order to persuade my audience to buy the Xebra, it is important to understand how their current car is unfit, why an electric car is a better alternative, and finally, how the Xebra is the best electric car on the market.
General Purpose: To inform
Specific Purpose: To inform my audience about the Xebra, all-electric car.
Thesis Statement: To inform my audience about how an all-electric car works, how it is different than fuel-based cars, and finally, explain why the Xebra is different than most other electric cars.

In summary, a general purpose helps you better understand your goal and your burden as a speaker. The specific purpose outlines what specifically you will discuss and the thesis statement specifies how you will go about accomplishing that goal.

Organizational Patterns

If you are still unsure as to how best address your specific topic (i.e. what your thesis is), there are specific organizational patterns that fit particular subject matter and will help you, once again, determine what is necessary to include in your speech and what can and should be excluded from your speech. The three major organizational patterns for informational speeches are: (1) Chronological (2) Topical and (3) Spatial patterns.

"How to Write a Speech: Organizational Speech Patterns"

Chronological: The speech body is comprised of past, present and future.
   Example: Beehive Construction starts with site selection, then wax footings are developed, and finally the comb chambers are added.

Topical: The speech body is organized in terms of thematic topics.
   Ex: Homeland Security is Conceptual, Organizational and Physically-Structured.

Spatial: The speech body is organized in terms of space.
 Ex: To better understand maze building we will assess first the entire plot of land, then we will examine the outside of the maze pre and post cut, before examining the final work inside of the maze rows.

Exercise: Use the same informational speech topic to organize the same subject using different organizational patterns to highlight how the organizing pattern dictates what is addressed/omitted in the speech.

General Purpose: To inform.

Specific Purpose: To inform my audience about the Xebra, all-electric car.

Structure: Topical

Thesis Statement: In order to be more knowledgeable about the Xebra, it is important to understand what the Xebra is, how the Xebra differs from traditional vehicles, and some of its advantages and disadvantages.

Structure: Spatial

Thesis Statement:

Structure: Chronological

Thesis Statement:

For more informational, persuasive and chronological patterns, review the following link: Patterns of Organization: Informative, Persuasive, and Commemorative.

Body Types

To this point, the organizing choices you have made are made to help you, the speechmaker, in the organizing process. Now, let's consider some specific organizing practices that you can use in the speech to help maximize the impact of your ideas when presented to your audience.

The first piece of advice is to break the order. That is, don't begin the speech construction process with the introduction. First, devote your time and energy to the body of your speech. Then, you can more effectively work on the introduction and conclusion once you have a better idea of what is included in the body of the speech. Analogize it to deciding what to barbeque for dinner. Once you decide to make hamburgers, you know that you need to make the patties and of less importance are the hamburger buns. The buns, while important for keeping all of the contents 'in', are one of the less crucial elements to the juicy barbequed burgers – the main item that needs the most attention.

Main Points

Main points emerge from your thesis as they are the appetite you create that must be satisfied by properly addressing in the body of the speech.

Thesis Statement: In order to be more knowledgeable about the Xebra, it is important to understand what the Xebra is, how the Xebra differs from traditional vehicles, and some of its advantages and disadvantages.

Main Point #1: What is the Xebra?

Body

I. The Xebra is one of the first all-electric cars to be marketed in the United States.
- A. According to a 2007 article in the Chicago Tribune, the all-electric Xebra is produced by Shandong Jindalu, a taxi maker in China (Chicago Tribune 2007).
   1. In 2006, ZAP (which stands for Zero Air Pollution) became the first company to sell Xebras in the United States.
   2. A 2007 Inside Bay Area article revealed that Xebra dealers are now scattered throughout the nation at specialized dealerships, with locations as close as Columbia, MO (Inside Bay Area 2007).

Main Point #2: How is the Xebra different from traditional vehicles?

II. There are two Xebra models available for consumers to choose from.
- A. The first model is a four-door car. (VA, Picture of Car)
   1. According to the previously cited Inside Bay Area article, the car model is about ten foot in length and comes in a variety of bright colors, as well as zebra strips (Insider Bay Area 2007).
   2. The previously cited Chicago Tribune article lists the retail price of the Xebra car at around $10,000 (Chicago Tribune 2007).
- B. The second model option is the two-door truck. (VA, Picture of Truck)
   1. According to the previously cited Chicago Tribune article, the Xebra truck is approximately the same length as the car and features short 4 foot bed with sides that fold flat (Chicago Tribune 2007).
   2. The truck model sells for around $11,000.
   3. The previously cited Inside Bay Area article revealed that paint options for the truck model include a bright blue and tamer white (Inside Bay Area 2007).

Main Point #3: Advantages and disadvantages of the Xebra.

III. The Xebra has both advantages and disadvantages. (VA, Chart of Advantages v. Disadvantages)
- A. There are 2 major advantages to the Xebra.
   1. The first advantage of the Xebra is that is saves owners money both in their purchase of the vehicle and at the pump.

a. According to a previously cited Inside Bay Area article, the selling price of a Xebra vehicle is between $10,000 and $11,000; this is about $15,000 cheaper than the average vehicle (Inside Bay Area 2007).

b. Because the Xebra runs entirely off rechargeable batteries, it also saves drivers from paying high gasoline prices.

2. The second major advantage of the Xebra is that is very eco-friendly.

a. According to the previously cited Inside Bay Area article, because it is run entirely on batteries, the Xebra emits almost zero air pollutants (Inside Bay Area 2007).

b. It also reduces gasoline usage.

B. Although the Xebra has advantages, it also has 3 disadvantages.

1. The Xebra's first disadvantage is its lack of amenities.

a. According to the previously cited Chicago Tribune article, all Xebra models have no air conditioning (Chicago Tribune 2007).

b. In addition, the car model does not have a trunk.

c. Finally, all models have only crank windows because any additional power items would drain the vehicle's batteries.

2. The second disadvantage of the Xebra is its size.

a. Because the Xebra is technically classified as a motorcycle it is not required to meet same the standards as a typical car, and as a result, is not built with 5 mile per hour bumpers or air bags (Chicago Tribune 2007).

b. The previously cited McClathy-Tribune Regional News article also describes how the Xebra's light weight makes driving in snowy and windy weather a hazard (McClatchy-Tribune Regional News-The Bellingham Herald 2007).

3. The Xebra's third disadvantage is its short battery life.

a. According to the previously cited Chicago Tribune article, recharging the Xebra requires plugging the car in for 8 hours (Chicago Tribune 2007).

b. In addition, the vehicles can only go about 22-25 miles before requiring charging.

Number of Points

Notice that there are three main points. There is no magic number in terms of how many main points to include in a speech as time constraints and topic subject matter play a role in determining the exact number. However, there are important guidelines to follow, or at least think about when constructing main points:

(1) Always have more than 1 main point. If you devote your entire speech to one main point, you are, in a sense, putting all of your eggs in one basket. Having more than one main point demonstrates to your audience that you have fully explored the topic and are providing more than a one-dimensional perspective on the subject matter. In addition, it doesn't appear to the audience that you have one 'big' speech or body. Breaking it down into more than one supportive point also allows for a positive shift of the attention for the audience members.

(2) Limit your main points to 2-4. Having too many main points in your speech can be confusing and usually means you don't fully explore each point in enough detail. If you have more than four main points, there should be a clear and overriding purpose. More often than not, speeches that contain more than 4 main points are messy, confusing, and hard to follow. Remember, it is your job to decide what should be included and excluded. Namely, editing is your responsibility and shows that you understand what is most important for your audience to know given your specific purpose.

(3) Put your most important or compelling points first or last. Too often, the most important or powerful point is lost in the middle. Audiences remember what comes first or last. Don't allow your point to be lost in the middle. Try an example: ask a friend to remember 13 numbers. More than likely they will recall the beginning or the end of the number pattern. This is an example of primacy and recency – what we recall in the beginning of patterns and at the end. In most cases, those elements in the middle will be forgotten.

Connecting the Dots

Having clear and compelling main points is an essential element of any good speech. However, main points alone won't suffice. Remember, this is the first and only time your audience will hear your speech. Audience members can't reread your comments if there is a little understanding or a lack of clarity as when they are reading a written document. So, in order to maximize the audiences" understanding, it is helpful to your audience members by connecting the dots. After countless hours in the preparation process, going from general purpose to specific purpose, creating a thesis statement, researching and finding evidence, you may find yourself committing a sin of creation: assuming that what you have created makes intuitive sense. By now, it all makes sense to you. The three main points about your speech topic appear logical, natural, maybe even preordained. However, don't forget how much time and effort it took you to get to that point. Don't forget how confusing it all was in the beginning of the process. So, give your audience some help by showing them: a) how your points fit together and b) how they relate to the topic. In so doing, you will maximize clarity and help your audience follow the logic of your topic and your own thinking, thereby increasing ethos and keeping your audience happy!

Transitions

Have you ever been on a long road trip with your family or friends? Imagine going on a road trip where you know your destination, but you had no idea how long it would take you to drive, you didn't know where you might stop for breaks and food along the way, and you were never reminded about the purpose of the entire trip. Audiences want to be led. They, we, want to know where we are going and where we have been. They, we, like to know when the next break will be. Transitions are linkage, or segways between points, revealing the logic of your speech and helping the audience follow along with your thinking pattern.

Transition #1 between Main Point #1 and Main Point #2:

"Now that I have discussed what the Xebra is, next let's take a look at how it differs from traditional gasoline-powered vehicles."

Transition #2 between Main Point #2 and Main Point #3:

"Now that we have looked at how the Xebra differs from gasoline-powered vehicles, next let's examine some of its advantages and disadvantages."

For more clear examples of effective transition statements, review the following link: Use of Transitions for Public Speaking – Examples.

Internal Reviews and Previews

Internal reviews and previews occur within the body of the speech. The purpose of internal reviews and previews is to keep the audience's attention where you want it: on what you are talking about rather than getting lost. If you've ever been lost while driving, you know it's almost impossible to pay attention to anything else other than getting un-lost. Likewise, to keep your audience focused by 'pointing' – 'we were there,' 'here is where we are', and look there, 'that's where we are going.'

Informational speech

"Having talked about what the Xebra is **(internal review)**, let's now talk about how Xebra differs from traditional vehicles." **(internal preview)**

Persuasive Speech

"As I've just discussed, all-electric cars are already here **(internal review).** The car you currently drive – that's a thing from the past." **(internal preview)**

Entertainment Speech

"Now that you know a Xebra doesn't always have to have black and white stripes **(internal review)**, what separates it from the car you currently drive." **(internal preview)**

Depending on your purpose, internal reviews and previews keep the audience focused, remind them of where you have been and prepare them for what is to come. Also, they also help connect the dots for the audience, an important feat in transitioning the audience's attention from one point to another, and one aspect of your subject area to another.

Introductions and Conclusions

Organizing the Introduction

After you have developed the body of your speech, it is time to begin the process of constructing the introduction. As the head of your speech, this is your first, and oftentimes, only, opportunity to achieve what every good speech does: make a good impression. Think of yourself not just as the speaker, but also the impression manager to the audience. Too often, the audience is lost only seconds into a speaker's speech. As a result, all the hard work and attention put into researching, gathering, and organizing the body of your speech falls on inattentive ears.

In order to escape the fate of being forgotten, introductions should include the following:

(1) **Attention Getter:** First and foremost, get the audience's attention! In my course I call the attention getter the 'gain and maintain'. The purpose is to provide the audience with an attention getter, which will draw them in and hopefully, desire to maintain interest. The good news is that the audience is willing to give you the benefit of the doubt in the first fifteen to thirty seconds of your presentation. After that, however, if you haven't provided them a compelling reason to want to pay attention (i.e. created an appetite), they will think about everything in the world but your speech (i.e. how many dots are inside of each ceiling square, what they had for lunch yesterday, and if your introduction is really lousy, their very existence itself). Here are some strategies you can begin your speech that will gain the attention of the audience:

   a. *Stories:* Tell a story. Audiences are familiar with stories. We relate to the world through stories. Stories will make your topic more personal and invite the audience to see the human side of your subject. They provide a visualization in their minds. Moreover, stories are effective tools for gaining the attention of audiences because we identify inductively – that is, if your grandmother died of cancer, then you are more likely to pay attention than if a general statement is given about the dangers of cancer. Audiences identify with specifics, not abstractions. For this reason, the story is a powerful tool to orient the audience and draw them into your topic. Consider the following stories used to bring attention to these speakers' speeches:

(#1)

Too busy trying to play with family and friends, young Philipino Ian Castro hasn't heard about the "friendly fire" and "collateral damage" that our American public has come to fear since the start of the Afghanistan conflict. But even if Ian had heard our fears translated into his native Spanish, he wouldn't understand. See, Ian is incapable of hearing, let alone comprehending, almost any message. Like thousands of other children and adults around the world working and playing in their own back yards, his young body and mind suffer the impairments of toxic pollution – pollution that's been spilling from almost ALL of OUR military bases for over 50 years. What's more, **The Ecologist of April 2002** explains that we have failed to see these problems, even though they are virtually everywhere.

(#2)

Take for instance Jeff Ferguson, a North Carolina high school teacher who, in 2004, asked his science class to volunteer to participate in an experiment to test our body's inability to deal with the acid in milk. Many of his students drank until their bodies began purging. Though Jeff was reprimanded then his contract cancelled by administrators the following year, due to the endangering of students' lives – volunteers merely drinking milk mind you – it's pretty clear that people continue to discount the problems of milk. Jeff broke no school policy, but his simple demonstration of milk's unhealthy qualities does just that. It demonstrates the negative consequences of milk as well as our inattentiveness to the impact of too much dairy.

Discussion Questions: Which story was the most compelling attention getter? Why? For what reasons? Would you have added/deleted anything to make either attention getter even more compelling?

> * *Note – It can also be an effective strategy to open up with a dramatic or mysterious story which will quickly grab their attention. Yet, as a twist, stop the attention grabbing tale at a crucial point and save the remainder of the story for the concluding gain and maintain.*

b. **_Provocative statistics:_** Statistics work. Audiences give credence to statistics because they appear to be more objective, and more "scientific" than an anecdote or specific instance. Understand that by your inclusion of statistics, you are establishing your own credibility in the sense that you are invested in the topic bur conducting outside research, oftentimes of information that is not your own. Audiences appreciate this level of commitment. However, not just any statistic will work in the introduction. For a statistic to gain the attention of the audience, it must be both startling and relevant. It must be a surprising statistic, a statistic that is so high or so low that breaks through the clutter of other statistic. Remember, it is incumbent upon you to grab the audiences' attention. And, note that the statistic must be relevant. Too many times, we've witnessed students and professionals use statistics that were in fact startling, but had nothing at all to do with the topic at hand. Consider the following examples:

(#1)
A University of Pittsburgh Medical Center study from June of found in an analysis, testing 133 women with multiple sclerosis, 61 percent had problems with bladder control that could interfere with sex and 47 percent said neurological problems inhibited their sex lives.

(#2)
Today, we've introduced ... the 5th Ocean, its significant relationship with the environment, and its policy & rhetorical implications. It may not have seemed like a big deal to explore a body of water that has always existed. But given that the National Science board reported in 2002 that only 15% of Americans know anything about scientific issues, it's pretty important we get this oceanic understanding right the first time.

(#3)
The FCC reported on September 22, 2005 that 30% of 911 calls, about 50 million calls annually, are placed by people using wireless phones, and that percentage is increasing every year.

Discussion Questions: Which statistic was the most compelling? Why? For what reasons? Would you have added/deleted anything to make either attention getter even more compelling?

c. **_Quotation:_** Quotations work, especially when the audience is familiar with the quotation. Once again, the quote must have something to do with your topic and it must create appetite in some sense. The effective use of quotations can also show your audience that you share common reference points. For example, quoting a line from "Friends" or from some other relevant popular culture text might work in showing your audience that you understand them, and that the topic you will be addressing has implications. However, finding a quote from a 13th century monk that has nothing to do with the topic under consideration only shows your audience that you know how to find quotes on Google. While it may sound good, that kind of quote finding won't work. Consider the following quotation examples:

(#1)
Regarding the crescendo qualities of some television salespersons' hyperactive, on-air presences, one recent blogger stated: "The norm has become the over-bearing, fast-talking, cocaine-like persona of the infamous Billy Mays."

(#2)
For owners, the best protection, as Thomas Jefferson once noted, is simply to remain "eternally vigilant." According to an October 7, 2004 Congressional testimony by HUD Assistant Secretary John Weicher, the first line of protection against real estate fraud is an informed consumer. Ring, cocaine-like, Billy Mays-like quality of the loud, fast talking pitchmen."

Discussion Questions: Which quotation was the most compelling? Why? For what reasons? Would you have added/deleted anything to make either attention getter even more compelling?

d. **Jokes:** Although your job as a presenter is more than likely to not engage in stand-up comedy during your speech, it is often helpful to open with an attention grabber that lightens the mood and sets a positive communication climate in the opening. However, note that much like the use of statistics in your introduction, a joke needs to be relevant to the topic. If you are discussing the effects of pollution in the oceans, to open up with an unclean joke about Snow White and the seven Dwarfs would be unprofessional. Not only does it not connect with the topic, but it would set a tone of ineffectual structure from the get-go. As a general rule, the use of jokes are: 1) relevant to the topic, 2) generally clean (here, note that in most cases we do not know the specific breakdown of morals, values and beliefs in audience members. It is better to be safe than sorry in terms of accidentally offending audience members). And , 3) the joke is seen as 'humorous' to the majority of individuals you test it upon. We all have different and varying senses of humor and what one finds humorous may not be perceived as humorous at all to another. Since jokes don't translate well into written form (as we lose intonations, fluctuations, etc. ...), review the following clip or an example of the use of humor in the attention grabbing portion of a speech.

"Using Humor in Speeches"

Sample Introduction:

Attention Getter: It's something none of us look forward to. Those dreadful few minutes of standing at the gas pump, painfully watching the price of your purchase climb higher and higher. Face it; everyone's wallet takes a beating at the pump today. Even my small, "fuel-efficient" car costs upward of $30 to fill. Now imagine you could fill your vehicle for only a dollar. Yes, a dollar. The good news is you don't even need to use your imagination, because according to a 2007 article published in Popular Science, the cost to refuel a Xebra is only about one dollar **(Popular Science, 2007)**.

Discussion Questions: Which type of attention-gaining strategy was used in this introduction? Did it gain your attention? If so, why? If not, why not? How could this attention gaining aspect of the introduction be improved? Be specific.

(2) **Thesis**

The thesis, simply stated, is what your speech is about. The thesis is sometimes hard to construct because you are, in effect, reducing your whole speech to one sentence. Imagine you are standing in line at the grocery store, and the person in front of you is Steven Spielberg. You've been writing a screenplay for the last year, and alas, as luck would have it, here is your opportunity. You say, "Excuse me, Mr. Spielberg, nice to meet you. I've been writing a screenplay for the last year." While Mr. Spielberg is unloading his shopping cart, he responds, "oh yeah, what is it about." What you say is the thesis or main point of your screenplay. Mr. Spielberg, like your audience, doesn't have the patience to endure you explaining every single detail. He wants the whole screenplay, or in your case, the whole speech, summarized in one nice and tidy line. If you can't reduce your speech to one compact and succinct sentence (i.e. if you go on and on and on and on), audiences will stop listening.

When creating your thesis, think hard about the essence or goal of your speech. In other words, if you had to reduce your speech to one line, what it would be?

"Patrick's Guide to a Speech Thesis"

Sample Thesis: Today I will tell you about the Xebra all-electric car.

3) **Relevancy (Relations statement)**

After you have gained the attention of the audience, you have to do something with it. Gaining attention is only the first step, but by no means the last. Perhaps an even worse sin than not attempting to gain the attention of the audience is to gain audience attention and then not direct their attention to your speech topic. Once you have the audience's attention, you must convince the audience that what you will talk about in your speech matters *to them.* More specifically, it is your job to convince the audience of the benefit of listening to your speech.

SO WHAT? Too many times, we've witnessed students who have compelled the audience's attention, only to completely overlook the fact that, each speaker has the solemn responsibility of answering the "So What?" question. No, your audience won't ask this question out loud, but the question will pop into their head at about the 12-second mark (no, this is not scientifically proven, but empirically tested after witnessing thousands of speeches as a communication professor).

The good news is that we are all audience members, and thus, who better to anticipate this question but you! Not every speech needs to change the audience's lives. In fact, if you promise that the speech will make them rich, or help them live to 100 years of age, you have created quite the appetite. And, there is nothing worse for your own credibility and for the audience than to promise them more than you can deliver!

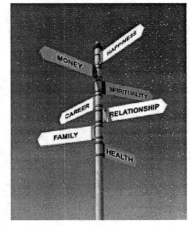

Relevancy is not preordained. It must be created and demonstrated to your audience. A couple of quick and easy questions that might help you make the case for relevancy:

a) In what aspect of your audience's life does your speech address? Economically? Physically? Emotionally? Spiritually?

b) How will the speech affect their future? What might it prevent? What might it correct? What might it allow?

Sample Audience Relevance: In my in-class survey five out of six of you said you own a car and drive regularly, and four out of six indicated that most of your

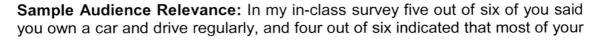

driving is short distance and in the city. Therefore, this presentation matters to the majority of you in this class who not only need to utilize transportation on a daily basis for the purpose of coming and going to college, but also because as a college student, the research indicates that to most college students, being financially conservative is important.

4) **Preview – the Forecast Statement**

The preview is your first explicit promise to your audience. Thus far, you've gained the attention of the audience, succinctly stated the point of the speech, convinced the audience as to the relevance of your topic to their lives, and now, in the preview, you explain *how* you will achieve your goal (i.e. of informing or persuading your audience) and in what order you will accomplish this goal.

The preview demonstrates that you have clearly defined and delineated what is most important for the audience to know. Specifically, in the articulation of the preview you demonstrate to the audience that you've narrowed the important and relevant subject matter concerning the topic for the audience.

Sample Preview Statement: In order to be more knowledgeable about the Xebra, it is important to understand what the Xebra is, how the Xebra differs from traditional vehicles, and some of its advantages and disadvantages.

The Conclusion

You've done so much work up to this point. You've introduced the audience to a topic of interest and importance, you've delved into the main points and now, after all that hard work, you need to conclude the speech. Unfortunately, the conclusion is oftentimes the most neglected part of the speech process. Yes, it occurs at the end, and by the time you get to preparing the conclusion, exhaustion may have set in as well as the apprehension associated with a looming deadline. However, slighting the end of the speech has drastic consequences.

Remember the appetite you created in the introduction? The conclusion is the section of the speech in which you must remind the audience of how the speech satisfied the appetite you created in the introduction. Moreover, the conclusion allows the audience to know that speech is almost over. This is an important shift. Up to this point, you've provided the audience new information, new research, new ideas, and the conclusion is important because it alerts the audience to the move from what they have heard to what you want them to remember.

In the conclusion, you need to do the following:

a) **Signal the imminent end to the speech.** It's taxing on any mind to listen to anything, uninterrupted. At this point, after you've been speaking for six, seven, or eight minutes, you want to make a clear break. Ironically, telling the audience you are going to soon end your speech means that they will pay more attention to what follows. Running without a finish line is exhausting. However, even after a 26-mile marathon, runners are able to sprint because they see the finish line and they know there will be a quick end to their physical and mental exhaustion. Likewise, by informing your audience that your speech will be over, you help them see the finish line and provide motivation to listen more intently for the final part of the speech. Sample concluding phrases are as follows:

> *In conclusion,*
> *To summarize,*
> *In this speech, I have discussed…*
> *Today, we have explored…*

b) **Briefly summarize what the speech was about.** Repetition matters, especially at the end. Remind the audience what you told them by shifting their attention from what they have heard to what you want them to remember.

> **Summary Statement:** Today I have explained to you what the Xebra is, how it differs from traditional gasoline-powered vehicles, and some of its advantages and disadvantages.

c) **End strong.** Movies that end with a whimper are disappointing, right? Dates that end on a sour note are viewed as a disappointment – despite what might have transpired before the final goodbye. Likewise, ending your speech on a strong point is essential. These are the last words the audience will hear from you because the conclusion is the last opportunity to control the message. After your final words, what your speech was about is in their complete control. Make certain your job is done in an effective and impactful manner.

One way to help your speech continue long after you finish talking is by giving the audience something to talk about. Give them talking points that they can use to answer the question, "Hey, what was Maya's speech about?"

d) **Closure.** A good closure statement should make the audience feel like the speech was a completed whole. You fulfilled your promise and informed the audience about what you introduced in the introduction.

> **End Strong/Closure:** Think back to the last time you had to refuel your vehicle. When gas prices are high, most likely you are not overjoyed when it comes time to pay. Today consumers not only have the opportunity to save money at the pump, but help save the environment as well, and it's all possible with a Xebra.

"How to Write a Speech Conclusion"

Sample Speech in Full

Electric Gasoline

General Purpose: To inform
Specific Purpose: To inform my audience about the Xebra, all-electric car.
Thesis Statement: In order to be more knowledgeable about the Xebra, it is important to understand what the Xebra is, how the Xebra differs from traditional vehicles, and some of its advantages and disadvantages.
Organizational Pattern: Topical

Introduction

I. **Attention Getter:** It's something none of us look forward to. Those dreadful few minutes of standing at the gas pump, painfully watching the price of your purchase climb higher and higher. Face it; everyone's wallet takes a beating at the pump today. Even my small, "fuel-efficient" car costs upward of $30 to fill. Now imagine you could fill your vehicle for only a dollar. Yes, a dollar. The good news is you don't even need to use your imagination, because according to a 2007 article published in Popular Science, the cost to refuel a Xebra is only about one dollar **(Popular Science, 2007)**.

II. **Thesis:** Today I will tell you about the Xebra all-electric car.

III. **Audience Relevance (relation):** In my in-class survey five out of six of you said you own a car and drive regularly, and four out of six indicated that most of your driving is short distance and in the city.

IV. **Preview Statement (foreshadow) :** In order to be more knowledgeable about the Xebra, it is important to understand what the Xebra is, how the Xebra differs from traditional vehicles, and some of its advantages and disadvantages.

Transition: First, I will discuss what the Xebra is.

Body

I. The Xebra is one of the first all-electric cars to be marketed in the United States.
  A. According to a 2007 article in the Chicago Tribune, the all-electric Xebra is produced by Shandong Jindalu, a taxi maker in China **(Chicago Tribune 2007)**.
    1. In 2006, ZAP (which stands for Zero Air Pollution) became the first company to sell Xebras in the United States.
    2. A 2007 Inside Bay Area article revealed that Xebra dealers are now scattered throughout the nation at specialized dealerships, with locations as close as Columbia, MO **(Inside Bay Area 2007)**.
  B. There are two Xebra models available for consumers to choose from.
    1. The first model is a four-door car. (VA, Picture of Car)
      a. According to the previously cited Inside Bay Area article, the car model is about ten foot in length and comes in a variety of bright colors, as well as zebra strips **(Insider Bay Area 2007)**.
      b. The previously cited Chicago Tribune article lists the retail price of the Xebra car at around $10,000 **(Chicago Tribune 2007)**.
    2. The second model option is the two-door truck. (VA, Picture of Truck)
      a. According to the previously cited Chicago Tribune article, the Xebra truck is approximately the same length as the car and features short 4 foot bed with sides that fold flat **(Chicago Tribune 2007)**.
      b. The truck model sells for around $11,000.
      c. The previously cited Inside Bay Area article revealed that paint options for the truck model include a bright blue and tamer white **(Inside Bay Area 2007)**.

Transition: Now that I have discussed what the Xebra is, next let's take a look at how it differs from traditional gasoline-powered vehicles.

II. The Xebra differs from traditional gasoline-powered cars in 2 ways.
  A. The first major difference is the Xebra's vehicle type.
    1. According to a 2007 Seattle Times article, the Xebra is technically classified as a 3-wheeled motorcycle and features one wheel in the front and two in the back **(Seattle Times 2007)**.
    2. The Xebra's simplicity and single front wheel is the secret to keeping the selling price low.

B. The second major difference between the Xebra and traditional gasoline-powered vehicles is its battery.
   1. According to the previously cited Chicago Tribune article, the Xebra runs entirely off six rechargeable, lead-acid batteries **(Chicago Tribune 2007)**.
   2. An article in a 2007 issue of the McClatchy-Tribune Regional News reveals that the Xebra's plug fits into a standard household outlet for charging **(McClatchy-Tribune Regional News-The Bellingham Herald 2007)**.
   3. A single charge will allow the car to reach top speeds of 40 mph and travel for up to 25 miles, according to the previously cited Seattle Time article **(Seattle Times 2007)**.

Transition: Now that we have looked at how the Xebra differs from gasoline-powered vehicles, finally let's examine some of its advantages and disadvantages.

III. The Xebra has both advantages and disadvantages. (VA, Chart of Advantages v. Disadvantages)
   A. There are 2 major advantages to the Xebra.
      1. The first advantage of the Xebra is that is saves owners money both in their purchase of the vehicle and at the pump.
         a. According to a previously cited Inside Bay Area article, the selling price of a Xebra vehicle is between $10,000 and $11,000; this is about $15,000 cheaper than the average vehicle **(Inside Bay Area 2007)**.
         b. Because the Xebra runs entirely off rechargeable batteries, it also saves drivers from paying high gasoline prices.
      2. The second major advantage of the Xebra is that is very eco-friendly.
         a. According to the previously cited Inside Bay Area article, because it is run entirely on batteries, the Xebra emits almost zero air pollutants **(Inside Bay Area 2007)**.
         b. It also reduces gasoline usage.
   B. Although the Xebra has advantages, it also has 3 disadvantages.
      1. The Xebra's first disadvantage is its lack of amenities.
         a. According to the previously cited Chicago Tribune article, all Xebra models have no air conditioning **(Chicago Tribune 2007)**.
         b. In addition, the car model does not have a trunk.
         c. Finally, all models have only crank windows because any additional power items would drain the vehicle's batteries.

2. The second disadvantage of the Xebra is its size.
   a. Because the Xebra is technically classified as a motorcycle it is not required to meet same the standards as a typical car, and as a result, is not built with 5 mile per hour bumpers or air bags **(Chicago Tribune 2007)**.
   b. The previously cited McClathy-Tribune Regional News article also describes how the Xebra's light weight makes driving in snowy and windy weather a hazard **(McClatchy-Tribune Regional News-The Bellingham Herald 2007)**.
3. The Xebra's third disadvantage is its short battery life.
   a. According to the previously cited Chicago Tribune article, recharging the Xebra requires plugging the car in for 8 hours **(Chicago Tribune 2007)**.
   b. In addition, the vehicles can only go about 22-25 miles before requiring charging.

Conclusion

I. **Summary Statement**: Today I have explained to you what the Xebra is, how it differs from traditional gasoline-powered vehicles, and some of its advantages and disadvantages.
II. **Closure**: Think back to the last time you had to refuel your vehicle. With the high gas prices, most likely you were not overjoyed when it came time to pay. Today consumers not only have the opportunity to save money at the pump, but help save the environment as well, and it's all possible with a Xebra.

Exercise

Take a famous speech found at www.americanrhetoric.com and outline it according to an introduction, body, and conclusion. Sometimes, a speech's organization is so well done that you don't know how it is organized until you dig deeper. For additional visual examples on the structure of presentations, please review the following site: 6 Steps to Effective Public Speaking.

References

Burke, K. (1953). Counterstatement. Los Altos: Humes Press Company.
Electric cars charge ahead. (2007, June 15). *The Seattle Times*, p. F1.
Hackforth, R. (1952). Plato's Phaedrus. New York: Bobbs-Merrill Company.
New Xebra sparks interest all over Bay Area. (2007, January 27). *Inside Bay Area*.
Plug in and drive with electric car. (2007, June 10). *McClatchy-Tribune Regional News-The Bellingham Herald*.
Who killed the gas guzzler. (2007, March). *Popular Science*.
Xebra's lack of amenities could be a jolt. (2007, February 8). *Chicago Tribune*.

Suggested Websites

http://www.speaking.pitt.edu/student/public-speaking/organization.html
http://www.engr.psu.edu/speaking
https://www.boundless.com/communications/textbooks/boundless-communications-textbook/organizing-and-outlining-the-speech-10/principles-of-organization-51/patterns-of-organization-informative-persuasive-and-commemorative-205-10678/

Chapter 7
Effective Speaking and the Use of Ethos

Most of us can testify that public speaking is a potentially nerve wracking experience. But, like many other stressors, they can be worked out, and in many cases, conquered, through exposure and experience. It certainly isn't easy, yet becoming more effective at public speaking is very possible. Consider this quote – "Communication is a skill that you can learn. It's like riding a bike or typing. If you're willing to work at it, you can rapidly improve every part of your life." Brian Tracy. Furthermore, Plato, the moralist and philosopher, asserted that the good man doing right to achieve a happy life. His student, Aristotle, provided a template for public communication that incorporated the notion of the "good" speaker as an essential means of persuasion.

The tools of persuasion Aristotle discussed, oftentimes referred to as artistic proofs because they are within the control of the speaker, may be over two thousand years old but they are essentially the very tools we still attempt to use today. They include: (1) ethos, or ethical qualities and appropriate character; (2) pathos, or emotional capacity, and (3) logos, or words and analysis. While we've already addressed each of these forms of persuasion in the chapter on persuasion, ethos is such an integral but undervalued means of persuasion we believe it merits further investigation.

"The Art of Persuasion"

According to Aristotle's *On Rhetoric*, speakers may be persuasive beyond the use of specific and overt strategies like language use and organization. Otherwise stated, the effectiveness of a speech cannot be reduced to a series of strategies, rather it must take into account the perceived wisdom, virtue and goodwill of the speaker. Consequently, *who* speaks to an audience and *how* the speaker is perceived are essential elements that cannot be overlooked when attempting to ascertain speaker impact and success.

Audiences attempt to determine the ethical character of speakers using two modes of speaker preparation: moral character and dramatic role creation.

Moral Character

In general, a good speaker is someone who is well-received according to the public values of the time and place, widely liked, and fits the public ideal of what the good speaker speaking well should look, sound and act like.

For example, contemplate the definition of the word 'moral' – 1. of, pertaining to, or concerned with the principles or rules of right conduct or the distinction between right and wrong; ethical: *moral attitude.* Of equal importance is the second definition of the term – **2.** expressing or conveying truths or counsel as to right conduct, as a speaker or a literary work (dictionary.com). In a nutshell, the audience is looking to a person's fundamental principles which include ethical conduct and accuracy. More important to consider is *what* the audience will then gift the speaker if he or she perceives the correctness of one's moral character, that being *trust.* If the audiences trusts the speaker based upon their morality, she or she will more than likely be open to being persuaded. Consider the following:

"President Clinton Apologizes to the Nation"

Former President Bill Clinton, while touted during his tenure to be viewed as one of the most effective president's in U.S. history, significantly lost much of this support because of the above scandal. As indicated from the definition of moral, his principles of 'right' conduct and 'truth' were called into question. We can but only wonder what would mark his Presidency had his choices been different. Regardless, as indicated by research, once trust is broken, it is often one of the hardest elements in any kind of relationship to regain due to the mistrust of future immoral choices. Jones and others claim that the normative expectation that the trustee *ought* to do what one trusts him or her to do, rather than optimism that s/he *will* do it (Jones 1996, 12).

Now, in opposition, consider the following excerpt taken from Martin Luther King Jr's 1968 speech, "I have been to the mountaintop." As you read part of King's speech, ask yourself: Does this speech excerpt sound like the good speaker speaking well? Does King fit the idea of what the good speaker should sound and act like?

We aren't going to let any mace stop us. We are masters in our nonviolent movement in disarming police forces; they don't know what to do. I've seen them so often. I remember in Birmingham, Alabama, when we were in that majestic struggle there, we would move out of the 16th Street Baptist Church day after day; by the hundreds we would move out. And Bull Connor would tell them to send the dogs forth, and they did come; but we just went before the dogs singing, "Ain't gonna let nobody turn me around."

Bull Connor next would say, "Turn the fire hoses on." And as I said to you the other night, Bull Connor didn't know history. He knew a kind of physics that somehow didn't relate to the transphysics that we knew about. And that was the fact that there was a certain kind of fire that no water could put out. And we went before the fire hoses; we had known water. If we were Baptist or some other denominations, we had been immersed. If we were Methodist, and some others, we had been sprinkled, but we knew water. That couldn't stop us.

And we just went on before the dogs and we would look at them; and we'd go on before the water hoses and we would look at it, and we'd just go on singing "Over my head I see freedom in the air." And then we would be thrown in the paddy wagons, and sometimes we were stacked in there like sardines in a can. And they would throw us in, and old Bull would say, "Take 'em off," and they did; and we would just go in the paddy wagon singing, "We Shall Overcome." And every now and then we'd get in jail, and we'd see the jailers looking through the windows being moved by our prayers, and being moved by our words and our songs. And there was a power there which Bull Connor couldn't adjust to; and so we ended up transforming Bull into a steer, and we won our struggle in Birmingham. Now we've got to go on in Memphis just like that. I call upon you to be with us when we go out Monday.

"Martin Luther King, Jr. 'Mountaintop'"

Clearly, King's urging of his audience to go to Memphis is a plea drawn from his own personal experiences – "I remember in Birmingham"; "but we just went before the dogs singing;" "And we went before the fire hoses"; "And then we would be thrown in the paddy wagons", "And every now and then we'd get in jail". In short, King is not asking his audience to do something that he himself hasn't or wouldn't do.

Moreover, King's ethos, or character, is evident in this excerpt because he demonstrates that he understands the needs, concerns, and fears of his audience. Specifically, his speech references underscore a common and shared knowledge. For example, not only does his audience know who Bull Connor is, but they also understand the reference to the bull-to-steer metaphor, where the traditional authority of power is rendered powerless by the will of the righteous many.

In summary, King's individual speech cannot be interpreted and evaluated apart from his many years of important humanitarian and civil rights work prior to the 1968 speech. When King used the inclusive language of "we", he spoke from experience, not from the safe distance of history, but from the earned struggle he, along with his audience, endured together.

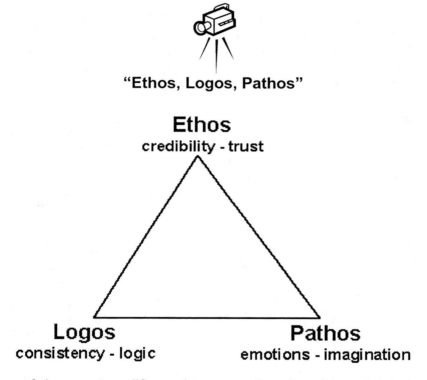

"Ethos, Logos, Pathos"

Ethos
credibility - trust

Logos
consistency - logic

Pathos
emotions - imagination

Perhaps one of the most prolific authors on ethos has been Aristotle, who believed and asserted that such a characteristic is at the very core of being a correct person, therefore leading to what contributes to making an effective and persuasive presenter. He further touted that lively a well-balanced life came from having a center of values. Aristotle viewed more of an extreme between two states, one involving something in excess and the other being in depletion or deficiency. His belief was that one's chosen virtues were to be viewed as no different from having a specialized ability or skill. Think of this in terms of a technical specialist knowing the correct balance of something in order to produce the correct product he or she is crafting. Too much or too little of something will throw off the desired end result. Another example is to think of a Blacksmith or perhaps a glass blower. The exact degree of heat, working of the material and tools all need to be precisely balanced in order for the end result to be the desired shape or object. So for Aristotle, the courageous person, for example, judges that some dangers are worth facing and others not, and experiences fear to a degree that is appropriate to his circumstances. He lies between the coward, who flees every danger and experiences excessive fear, and the rash person, who judges every danger worth facing and experiences little or no fear. Aristotle holds that this same topography applies to every ethical virtue: all are located on a map that places the virtues between states of excess and deficiency. He is careful to add, however, that the mean is to be determined in a way that takes into account the particular circumstances of the individual (1106a36-b7). Like Plato, he regards the ethical virtues (justice, courage, temperance and so on) as complex rational, emotional and social skills…what we need, in order to live well, is a proper appreciation of the way in which such goods as friendship, pleasure, virtue, honor and wealth fit together as a whole. In order to apply that general understanding to particular cases, we must acquire, through proper upbringing and habits, the ability to see, on each occasion, which course of action is best supported by reasons. Therefore practical wisdom, as he conceives it, cannot be acquired solely by learning general rules. We must also acquire, through practice, those deliberative, emotional, and social skills that enable us to put our general understanding of well-being into practice in ways that are suitable to each occasion (Stanford Encyclopedia of Philosophy 2010).

Aristotle was not alone in his concern with ethos, or public character. Cicero, the famous Roman lawyer, statesman, and philosopher, drew from previous teachings of Greek thinkers such as Plato and Aristotle to articulate his notion of ethos. Cicero spoke about the importance of gaining politically positioned "pull" before speakers assumed they were worthy to speak in certain social circles or about specific topics. Cicero's notion would be similar to experience of a student page in Washington D.C. feeling the pressure not to speak to senior congressional leaders (i.e. for fear of embarrassment, because it would be against tradition, or because of differences in knowledge level on important policy matters) until introduced by someone already in congress. The norms of social hierarchy Cicero alluded to meant that social norms dictated who was "allowed" to speak in the public forum or who had "earned" the right to speak to audiences based on their previous experiences, accomplishments, and social standing.

**"ABC World News Now:
Election 2012: Social Media Effect"**

Of course while social networking is still important in our modern world (think Twitter and Instagram driving commerce and helping a presidential candidate win an election), times have changed and the political nature of the U.S. Republic is much different than that of ancient Rome. We have not experienced centuries of tyrannical rule nor have we endured a military regime imposing itself on our homeland. However, as audiences, we are still influenced by a speaker's reputation and the power of endorsements. Consider the following two speeches of endorsement given by political "patrons" regarding prospective candidates-for-office.

In 2004, then Democrat Congressperson Zell Miller endorsed Republican incumbent President George Bush in the 2004 election:

> I first got to know George W. Bush when we served as governors together. I admire this man. I am moved by the respect he shows the First Lady, his unabashed love for his parents and his daughters, and the fact that he is unashamed of his belief that God is not indifferent to America. I can identify with someone who has lived that line in "Amazing Grace," "Was blind, but now I see," and I like the fact that he's the same man on Saturday night that he is on Sunday morning. He is not a slick talker but he is a straight shooter, and where I come from deeds mean a lot more than words. I have knocked on the door of this man's soul and found someone home, a God-fearing man with a good heart and a spine of tempered steel – the man I trust to protect my most precious possession: my family.

This election will change forever the course of history, and that's not any history. It's our family's history. The only question is how. The answer lies with each of us. And like many generations before us, we've got some hard choosing to do.

"Zell Miller 2004 RNC Speech"

Of presidential candidate, Barack Obama, former President Bill Clinton said at the 2009 Democratic National Convention:

I am here – first – to support Barack Obama. And second – And second, I'm here to warm up the crowd for Joe Biden, though as you will soon see, he doesn't need any help from me. I love Joe Biden, and America will too.

What a year we Democrats have had. The primary began with an all-star line up and it came down to two remarkable Americans locked in a hard fought contest right to the very end. That campaign generated so much heat it increased global warming.

Now, in the end, my candidate didn't win. But I'm really proud of the campaign she ran. I am proud that she never quit on the people she stood up for, on the changes she pushed for, on the future she wanted for all our children. And I'm grateful for the chance Chelsea and I had to go all over America to tell people about the person we know and love. Now, I am not so grateful for the chance to speak in the wake of Hillary's magnificent speech last night. But I'll do the best I can.

Last night, Hillary told us in no uncertain terms that she is going to do everything she can to elect Barack Obama. That makes two of us. Actually, that makes 18 million of us – because, like Hillary, I want all of you who supported her to vote for Barack Obama in November. And here's why. And I have the privilege of speaking here, thanks to you, from a perspective that no other American Democrat, except President

Carter, can offer…Clearly, the job of the next President is to rebuild the American dream and to restore American leadership in the world. And here's what I have to say about that: Everything I learned in my eight years as President, and in the work I have done since in America and across the globe, has convinced me that Barack Obama is the man for this job.

"Bill Clinton Democratic Convention Speech"

Did you notice how both of the endorsers used their personal experiences as the foundation for their support of Bush and Obama respectively? Zell Miller supported the Republican George Bush, not the Democratic presidential candidate John Kerry. Likewise, Bill Clinton, even though he acknowledged "his candidate (wife, Hillary Candidate) didn't win" he also said he was "convinced" that Barack Obama was the right person for the job.

From the audiences' perspective, each of these endorsements were of particular importance and legitimacy because each endorser seemingly supported a candidate against their own particular interests – crossing party lines and supporting a candidate who ran against his wife – to advocate a candidate they believed was best for the country's interest.

Did Bill Clinton supporting Barack Obama make Obama a better candidate? Did Congressman Miller's endorsement of Bush mean he would make a better candidate than John Kerry? Not necessarily. However, each endorsement provided insight into the character of Obama and Bush, prompting the audiences to ask themselves: If someone I respect respects this candidate, then why shouldn't I?

"Bill Clinton calls for four more Obama years"

Dramatic Role Creation

Ethos is not simply about who supports you. Speakers can take ownership of their own ethos through a carefully constructed persona. For example, in a June 23, 2009 Press Briefing, President Obama responded to a question about the merits of health care reform:

Well, let's talk first of all about health care reform more broadly.

I think in this debate there's been some notion that if we just stand pat we're okay. And that's just not true. You know, there are polls out that show that 70 or 80 percent of Americans are satisfied with the health insurance that they currently have. The only problem is that premiums have been doubling every nine years, going up three times faster than wages. The U.S. government is not going to be able to afford Medicare and Medicaid on its current trajectory. Businesses have to make very tough decisions about whether we drop coverage or we further restrict coverage.

So the notion that somehow we can just keep on doing what we're doing and that's okay, that's just not true. We have a longstanding critical problem in our health care system that is pulling down our economy, its burdening families, its burdening businesses, and it is the primary driver of our federal deficits. All right?

So if we start from the premise that the status quo is unacceptable, then that means we're going to have to bring about some serious changes. What I've said is, our top priority has to be to control costs. And that means not just tinkering around the edges. It doesn't mean just lopping off reimbursements for doctors in any given year because we're trying to fix our budget. It means that we look at the kinds of incentives that exist, what our delivery system is like, why it is that some communities are spending 30 percent less than other communities but getting better health care outcomes, and figuring out how can we make sure that everybody is benefiting from lower costs and better quality by improving practices. It means health IT. It means prevention.

So all these things are the starting point, I think, for reform. And I've said very clearly: If any bill arrives from Congress that is not controlling costs, that's not a bill I can support. It's going to have to control costs. It's going to have to be paid for. So there's been a lot of talk about, well, a trillion-dollar price tag. What I've said is, if we're going to spend that much money, then it's going to be largely funded through reallocating dollars that are already in the health care system but aren't being spent well. If we're spending $177 billion over 10 years to subsidize insurance companies under Medicare Advantage, when there's no showing that people are healthier using that program than the regular Medicare program, well, that's not a good deal for taxpayers. And we're going to take that money and we're going to use it to provide better care at a cheaper cost to the American people. So that's point number one.

Number two, while we are in the process of dealing with the cost issue, I think it's also wise policy and the right thing to do to start providing coverage for people who don't have health insurance or are underinsured, are paying a lot of money for high deductibles. I get letters – two, three letters a day – that I read of families who don't have health insurance, are going bankrupt, are on the brink of losing their insurance; have deductibles that are so high that even with insurance they end up with $50,000, $100,000 worth of debt; are at risk of losing their homes.

And that has to be part of reform, making sure that even if you've got health insurance now, you are not worried that when you lose your job or your employer decides to change policies that somehow you're going to be out of luck. I think about the woman who was in Wisconsin that I was with, who introduced me up in Green Bay – 36 years old, double mastectomy; breast cancer has now moved to her bones and she's got two little kids, a husband with a job. They had health insurance, but they're still $50,000 in debt, and she's thinking, my main legacy, if I don't survive this thing, is going to be leaving $100,000 worth of debt. So those are the things that I'm prioritizing.

Now, the public plan I think is an important tool to discipline insurance companies. What we've said is, under our proposal, let's have a system the same way that federal employees do, same way that members of Congress do, where – we call it an "exchange," or you can call it a "marketplace" – where essentially you've got a whole bunch of different plans. If you like your plan and you like your doctor, you won't have to do a thing. You keep your plan. You keep your doctor. If your employer is providing you good health insurance, terrific, we're not going to mess with it.

But if you're a small business person, if the insurance that's being offered is something you can't afford, if you want to shop for a better price, then you can go to this exchange, this marketplace, and you can look: Okay, this is how much this plan costs, this is how much that plan costs, this is what the coverage is like, this is what fits for my family. As one of those options, for us to be able to say, here's a public option that's not profit-driven, that can keep down administrative costs and that provides you good, quality care for a reasonable price – as one of the options for you to choose, I think that makes sense.

"White House Press Briefing with President Obama"

In this example, President Obama was not simply responding to a question. He was also – and perhaps more importantly – responding to a question that allowed the American people to assess his ethos on this important and hotly-contested topic.

In his rather long answer, President Obama is attempting to demonstrate a grasp of the situation, the complex topic of health care, and highlight his understanding of his audience's worries. First, he uses a linear, numbered structure to guide his comments and order his specific responses to a reporter's question regarding health care. Additionally, he speaks to his understanding of the issue by articulating the scope of the problem, the scope of the spending issues involved, and the diversity of individuals affected by health care reform. Finally, Obama relies on evidence and personal stories drawn from those with whom he has spoken and from whom he has received letters.

"Presidential Debate 2012 on Health Care:
Mitt Romney Says 'Expensive' 'Obamacare' Hurts Job Growth"

By crafting his answer using these forms of organization, evidence and reasoning, President Obama attempted to build and maintain the persona of a knowledgeable executive, capable of understanding the gravity of the discussion, and competently versed in the details of the issue to discuss it in a way toward which Americans could understand and relate. These methods of role construction took place against a backdrop of an ongoing "health care debate" that clearly embattled senators and stirred up the ire of town hall meeting attendants over the course of the late spring and summer of 2009. A clear and competent executive speaker, then, stands apart from the clamor of a non-polished speaker in a larger discussion – a protagonist worthy of championing important issues by talking rationally, using evidence, and speaking honestly and empathetically with the American people.

Ethos is not miraculously attributed to speakers. It is much like the adage of trust – it must be earned. In fact, audiences oftentimes determine a speaker's ethos based on a sentence-by- sentence and paragraph-by-paragraph analysis (consciously or unconsciously) of a speaker's competencies during the communication encounter itself (Eckhouse, 1998).

Audiences simultaneously judge the whole of a speech to make sense of the person speaking (i.e. does the speaker understand me, does she have a grasp of the topic, are the examples used relevant to my life) and make sense of the parts of a speech (i.e. grammar, logic, evidence, reasoning) to judge the person speaking. Consider, for instance, two different approaches a speaker could take if she wanted to deliver this speech on computational origami:

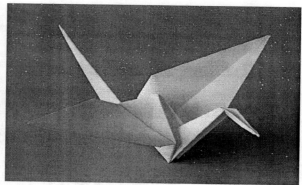

Example #1:

It is important for people to have hobbies since, sometimes, hobbies help us retain our sanity. Just ask Erik Demaine … he turned a math hobby into a professorship at MIT and a Macarthur fellowship – a financial grant awarded to promising scientists. Demaine's hobby is one of the math world's most promising applications for everyday science, though it's far from ordinary.

According to the January 18, 2003 edition of the *Nova Scotia New Scientist*, Demaine talked his way into Dalhousie University at the age of 12, despite having no grades to speak of. Then, as a math major he attended Waterloo University. Eight years and a PhD later, he is the youngest professor at MIT, when most people his age would be satisfied with no debt. The theory that got him there: Computational Origami, the geometry of paper folding.

Example #2

Hobbies, they're fun. I like to skateboard. Erik Demaine, he doesn't. He likes hobbies, just not skateboarding. But his hobby is pretty weird. He turned a math hobby into teaching at MIT. He's also been given a pretty cool scientific award. His hobby is one of the math world's most promising applications for everyday science, though it's far from ordinary.

In the January 18, 2003 edition, wait, January 21st I think, of the *Nova Scotia New Scientist*, Professor Demaine provides his biography of working at Dalhousie University at the age of 12, wow, that's young – I don't even remember what I was doing at 12 – then joining Waterloo University as a math major later. Eight years and a PhD later, wow, that's a long time to go to school, huh, he has a theory: Computational Origami, the geometry of paper folding. Pretty cool stuff.

Both speech introductions demonstrate some stylistic problems, however, the second example is less complete than the first given the lack of narrative information (hobbies connection, theory development, how hobbies and theory are connected, what he teaches, et cetera.), unclear explanations for his award, unclear timelines, and the informal and awkward use of contractions, sloppy grammar and well, too much informality.

Even though the second introduction sounds like it may have been delivered in front of a less formal audience, it still reveals that the speaker worried little about her ethos. After only reading the introduction, you have already begun (and you can't help yourself even if you didn't want to) making judgments based both on the speaker and the whole speech, including assessments like:

(1) Does the speaker really know about his/her topic?
(2) Does the speaker really care about his/her topic?
(3) How skilled is the speaker in helping me care about computational origami?
(4) How credible or believable is the speaker?

Likewise, when audiences listen to your speech, they are simultaneously making judgments about the content of what you are saying – how well do you know the topic

and material – and you, as a communicator – how much should I believe what this person is saying? Whenever a communicator and an audience are involved, questions of ethos inevitably will emerge, often making the crucial difference between how your content is received, conceived, and interpreted. Thus the importance of ethos is not limited to speeches alone, but is an essential variable in all communication encounters.

In many ways, you are your words and your speech is you. You are your email and your email is you. And, you are the paper you turn into your professor and the paper represents you. Audiences look to these everyday means of communication – speeches, email, papers, and business interviews – to assess you and your ethos. Small choices can sometimes make big differences in how you are perceived. This supports the communication principle that 'one cannot not communicate', thus leading us to understand we are always communicating and always being perceived by others. This should make you deeply consider your role of ethics when you are speaking to others. Keep in mind that the following list of seemingly minor content-related choices in all forms of communication can sometimes be very important factors in helping audiences determine who you are and whether you should be believed:

- **Be concise:** Work not to be redundant. Efficiency in terms of word and phrase choice will win the day. Say more with less.

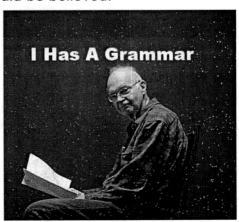

- **Choose words carefully:** Make sure you understand the widely received understandings of terms. Misuse of terms can lose the attention of your audience.

- **Pay attention to syntax:** Word order is important. When possible, use active construction – Susan walks her dog – rather than passive construction – The dog was walked by Carolyn.

- **Punctuate appropriately:** Remember: less is more. Make sure you never miss terminal punctuation (i.e. periods, question marks). Always double check all commas and apostrophes.

- **Follow the rules of grammar:** Make sure there is agreement between nouns and verbs, between nouns and pronouns, and between multiple verbs within a sentence.

- **Closely revise electronic communication:** Before you send your email, make sure you reread it. Remember, you can't take back mistakes – even small ones like typing "there" for "their" – as you never know how those mistakes will influence the receiver's perception of you. Fair or not, right or wrong, editing is the quickest way many people use to assess ethos (Eckhouse, 1999, 131-225).

Student Presentations and Ethos

One inevitable question that conscientious students ask us all of the time is: what can I do to make sure my speech goes well? The answer, not surprisingly, lies within the realm of ethos.

Let's examine the introductions from two student speeches to learn how to better enact ethos as a strategy. The first speech is an informative speech regarding an environment pest in Africa:

Example #1:

There are stories of hope, stories of love, charity, and sacrifice, stories in which people lay down their own lives for others. This isn't one of those stories. Think cynical. Think dark. Think ungodly awful. How twisted is this tale? It so astonished Oscar nominated filmmaker Hubert Sauper that he tromped around Africa in disguise for three years to document it. He explained in an interview with The New York Times on Feb 23, 2006 that he would watch cargo planes fly into rural areas with donated food supplies such as American peas for local, starving townships…while cargo planes filled with locally caught fish

would fly out to Europe…and other world markets. The setting is Mwanza, Tanzania – a fetid shantytown on the shores of Africa's Lake Victoria, the world's second-largest freshwater lake, and a place some call "birthplace of man." This story is of the fight for survival by its people, who catch Nile Perch (gigantic fish ranging up to 6 feet long and 400 lbs. – insert VA), who then process the fish, and then see their pale pink fillets flown to first world consumers in surplus Soviet military cargo planes. According to The UTNE Reader of October 12, 2005, the problem surrounding this artificially introduced predator has been brought into public view by Hubert Sauper's documentary Darwin's Nightmare. Yet, while Darwin's Theory of Natural Selection illuminates the idea that bigger and stronger will often out-compete the smaller, weaker for resources – and, in the end, for life itself…examining the introduction of the Nile Perch reveals an unvarnished, brutal narrative on how globalization has torn apart local communities and ecosystems all over the world. So…in an effort to survey humanity's collision with the environment…we will first follow the course of…the Nile perch…and its introduction into Lake Victoria, before moving to our current state and the implications of this "scientific" experiment on the people of Africa.

"Darwin's Nightmare"

The second excerpt is from the introduction of a persuasive speech dealing with the overconsumption of milk:

Example #2:

Long Island dentist Alexis Gersten never thought about what she poured over her cereal until her son turned one. "Having a new milk drinker, I sort of wanted to start him off on the right foot," she said. But according to the New York Times November 9th, 2005, Ms. Gersten grew worried about reports she started finding – Reports dealing with synthetic growth hormones, pesticides and antibiotics in milk…and what they might do to her child and to the environment. She also grew increasingly concerned about the health of the cows and the survival of local farmers. So, she joined a host of new mothers who are making milk the fastest growing slice of the organic market. States Gersten, "some of my friends who don't really think about feeding their children organic food will feed them organic milk." Well while the choice of organic or non-organic is a noble one, a more telling question is: should milk be a major part of our diet in the first place? Because the evidence makes clear that the answer is "no," we will take the next few minutes to assess why it is we "got Milk" when it presents clear problems to our health in myriad ways. Then, we'll examine the utterly ridiculous causes of our dairy epidemic. And finally, we'll move the carton to the trash as we develop a few solutions to curb our appetite for milk.

How do these two very different speech introductions demonstrate ethos for their respective speakers? It is clear that the informative speech (Example #1) – relies on an additional source and an award-winning filmmaker. In addition, the persuasive speech (Example #2) begins with a testimonial excerpt to develop the human-interest story of one mother's concern for her child.

In both examples, there are strategic uses of support materials to back up the claims being made. In both cases, we can also see the beginning of organizational structure as the body of each speech is outlined and the introductions follow the recipe of attention getter, thesis or topic, warrant, and main point preview.

As discussed in multiple chapters throughout this book, evidence matters. It is necessary in constructing proof, in moving from assertion to an argument. But that's not its only function. Student speaker credibility is both initiated and further developed by the effective use and citation of evidence (Grice & Skinner, 2004).

The sources you choose to cite for your evidence and the types of evidence you deem worthy of supporting your arguments, helps the audience learn about you and your topic (Morgan, 2007). What would you think of a speaker whose only source is from Wikipedia? What would you think of a speaker's grasp of a topic if she addresses the topic of immigration while citing evidence that is over twenty years old? How credible is a speaker who quotes the same expert over and over again throughout the speech, even when it doesn't seem the quotations appear out of context and randomly chosen?

"Preparing for Public Speaking"

Given that support selection and organizational structure can add to speaker ethos, here are some specific guidelines that will help you strategically use ethos to become a more effective and persuasive speaker:

- **Prepare, prepare, prepare:** The character you portray in delivery will be much better served by the fact that your presentations are clear, supported, delivered efficiently, and with the appropriate structure and paralanguage.

- **Do your research:** Know what you are saying by doing your homework…and then support your speech with well-researched and well-articulated sources. Unprepared speakers can't hide. Audiences can tell very quickly whether a speaker is prepared or 'faking it.'

- **Include well-known sources:** The inclusion of well-recognized sources means the audience is more likely to believe the rest of your speech is of equally high quality. Don't give your audience a reason to doubt the quality of your entire speech because of questionable sources and or inappropriate (i.e. unclear, irrelevant) and irrelevant evidence.

- **Demonstrate the basics of clarity and source transparency:** Ethos affiliated with the use of evidence is always bolstered when the audience has access and can practice researching your sources. One simple way for an audience to judge you is to judge where you go to gather information, and evidence, etc. Your parents were right, you are who you hang out with, or for our purposes, you are who you cite.

- **Make every attempt to communicate truthfully:** similar to the above mentioned area; your audience is seeking truth. Are you providing that truth for them and not misleading them with half-truths and fallacies? Remember again, when an audience member believes they have been deceived or manipulated, it may greatly reduce their inherent trust of your credibility, thus severely reducing your desire to have them follow or support you. Trust is one of the greatest obstacles to overcome in a relationship if it has been broken (Lewiki, 2003).

- **Audiences remember:** Providing carefully constructed, well researched, and interesting public presentations will impact later presentations. If you prepare, research, structure your speech, practice a great deal in early-semester presentations, your audience is more likely to view later speeches in a positive light. What you did in the last speech does influence how others will view your upcoming speech. Fair? Maybe not, but there is no reset button.

- **Be a good audience member:** If you are not a good audience member for your peers' speeches – if you fall asleep, text, or talk during others' speeches – expect that behavior or lack of care for others to catch up with you. On the other hand, there will be nothing but positive perceptions when you show courtesy to a fellow speaker. Things have a way of coming full circle. As well, included in being a good audience member is being an ethical listener. Do not forget that if you desire and expect others to tune into you, you should also return the same behavior. Epictetus, a Greek philosopher who was connected with the Stoics, quoted, "**we have two ears and one mouth so we can listen as much as we speak**". Audiences have memories too, 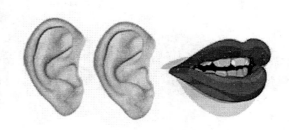 and if your behavior provides them a reason to disbelieve you, they will.

- **When possible, fit presentations and presentation topics into larger goals and interests:** Adele Scheele (2005) explains the importance of using the college experience both as a learning laboratory as much as a microcosm for learning about the world beyond academe. We always advise students to take advantage of their speaking opportunities. Speak about what you are interested in or would like to learn more about. If you don't speak on topics that are of interest to you, why would the audience be interested? The first demonstration of speaker ethos is the choice of speech topic or how a speaker conceives of a topic. Speaker interest (or lack thereof) is contagious (also known as emotional contagion): if you have interest in your topic, so too will your audience. If you don't care about your topic, don't expect your audience too either. Simply put, what feelings you have towards your topic comes through if your presentation. Think of your tone, your inflections, your rates, your volume, etc.... All of these are delivered with more commitment when one has 'buy-in' to their topic. As the old saying goes, "build it and they will come". So offer them the passion for your subject matter and watch in return as your audience connects to you and your content matter more in-depthly.

We gave this very advice to a student a few years ago and, as a budding scientist who also wanted to improve her speaking skills, she came up with a fascinating topic for her informative speech that combined her interests, career goals, ethos from evidence, and structure. Here is an excerpt from that speech:

"An Honest Liar: The Amazing Randi Story"

Enter James Randi, the scientist most well-known for deploying skepticism in almost a cult-like following. *The Skeptic's Dictionary* (last updated July 15, 2005) lists five international skeptical organizations extending a monetary prize to anyone who can demonstrate any kind of paranormal activity…and it just so happens that the organization currently offering the largest sum is the James Randi Educational Foundation based in Fort Lauderdale, Florida. The Amazing James Randi is a professional magician who considers it his job to "debunk" and expose frauds. The self-proclaimed Guru of Anti-WooWoo said in an April 14th 1998 interview with the *St. Petersburg Times* that with magic, the performer and his audience agree that what's happening is an illusion, but scam artists would have their audience believe that what they're doing is real. As a professional magician, he knows the tricks used by scammers to fool their audiences and can easily discover the fraud.

Though his non-profit foundation wasn't officially founded until 1996, the challenge has been going on since 1964, when according to the JREF website last updated Oct. 28th, 2005, Randi was challenged by a parapsychologist on a live radio program to "put his money where his mouth is," prompting Randi to immediately offer $1,000 of his own money to the first person who demonstrated a paranormal power under satisfactory observational conditions. Since then, the prize has increased to $1 million, still having yet to be claimed by anyone. But there are many who've started the application process and failed the tests.

According to the foundation's online documentation, the James Randi Educational Foundation received over 650 applications between 1964 and 1982, and between 1997 and February 2005 there had been a total of 360 official, notarized applications. The process of applying is simple: the applicant must compose a two paragraph description of his or her ability, sign it, get it notarized, and mail it to the foundation so a test date can be agreed upon.

On July 1, 2005, James Randi reported to the *Skeptical Inquirer* that about 80 percent of all applications to his million dollar challenge claim to be dowsers or diviners, meaning that they claim to find water, gold, lost children, or anything using a forked stick or a pendulum. One man told Randi that he had the ability to locate lost hunting dogs by placing a piece of the dog's hair on the end of his dowsing stick...a process, he claimed, that tuned in on the dog's DNA. The man also claimed he could locate bullets by tuning in to their DNA. Obviously, the prize works to unveil ignorance even in its application process since cases like this require no tests. Bullets, it seems, don't have DNA. But most of the cases Randi's Foundation handles require tests to prove or disprove the paranormal claims of the person entering the challenge. To do so, the foundation simply uses passive observation and the scientific method to prove that these people are merely normal.

"James Randi Debunking on Tonight Show"

Notice that the speech fits the bill for her training as an empiricist. She is talking about a topic that is of interest to her while being accessible and interesting to general audiences. Her topic, the Randi Foundation, celebrates skepticism by debunking the paranormal. Notice that she used sources from the topic itself (the website), from the professional magazine publication of skeptics, and from a newspaper. We should also note that this speech followed a string of presentations that consistently relied on diversified, verifiable sources that audience members could "check" when the speech was over. On all counts, her presentational content and structure demonstrate the ethos she wanted to maintain as a user of facts – an empirical scientist cum turned presenter.

Just as important, did you notice that her speech tells a story that her audience could become involved in, whether or not they considered themselves future scientists? Like traditional narratives, the speech had a protagonist and any number of antagonists that may need to be vanquished through the scientific philosophy of the lead character. Long story short, this speaker followed both our suggestions for strategically demonstrating ethos, and thus, as a result, was a more effective speaker.

Conclusion

Persuasion cannot occur without the important element of ethos. The two areas rely on one another. Ethos is reflected in a speaker's speech and the speech is a reflection of speakers. The intention of your speech will come through in your delivery. As it pertains to the artistic proof of ethos, speakers can enhance their credibility in the minds of audiences by making good judgments about: (1) what should be included/excluded in their speech; (2) the types of sources and evidence used to support their arguments; and finally, (3) the careful attention given to the style, grammar, and clarity of their presentations. For more on the purpose of ethos, review the following article: http://www.european-rhetoric.com/ethos-pathos-logos-modes-persuasion-aristotle/ethos/.

References

Kennedy, G. A. (Ed.) (1991). Aristotle's On rhetoric: A theory of civic discourse. New York: Oxford.

Eckhouse, B. (1999). Competitive communication: A rhetoric or modern business. New York: Oxford.

Fisher, W. (1999). Narration as human communication paradigm. In Lucaites, J.L., Condit, C.M., & Caudill, S. (Eds.), Contemporary rhetorical theory: A reader (265-287). New York: Guilford Press.

Grice, G.L., & Skinner, J.F. (2004). Mastering public speaking (5th ed.). Boston: Pearson.

Jones, K., 1996. "Trust as an Affective Attitude," *Ethics*, 107: 4–25

Lewicki, Roy J. and Edward C. Tomlinson. "Trust and Trust Building." *Beyond Intractability*. Eds. Guy Burgess and Heidi Burgess. Conflict Information Consortium, University of Colorado, Boulder. Posted: December 2003.

May, J.M. (1988). Trials of character: The eloquence of Ciceronian ethos. Chapel Hill: North Carolina Press.

Natali, Carlo (ed.). *Aristotle's Nicomachean Ethics, Book VII*. Oxford: Oxford University Press, 2009

Scheel, A. M. (2005). Launch your career in college: Strategies for students, educators, and parents. Westport, CT: Praeger.

Chapter 8
Strategies – The Varieties of Speaking

"A few mistakes does not a fiasco make. Professionals will throw them off actually but then file them away to reinvent as an anecdote in later presentations. Make them part in later presentations! Put them behind you and keep going."
– Ruth Bonetti

The old adage, "It's not what you say, but how you say it" speaks volumes in the world of public speaking. Just as you can work on structure and learn to improve upon it, you can also improve your delivery through learning and applying new strategies, skills and techniques. Hence, just as there are different types of speeches (i.e. speeches to entertain, speeches to inform, speeches to persuade), there are also many different ways to deliver speeches. This chapter explores different delivery strategies and provides specific tips to maximize audience impact for each specific style of delivery.

Manuscript

As discussed in a previous chapter, manuscript style speaking requires speakers to maintain complete fidelity to the text or note cards. In this speaking approach, each word is carefully crafted in advance and written down word-for-word prior to the speech occasion. In particular, for policy-laden speeches, the speech typically endures a vetting process whereby different departments or interest groups read, examine, and edit the speech to ensure accuracy.

Even though manuscripted speeches are written word for word, manuscript speeches are different than the delivery copy a speaker brings to the podium to speak from. While the content of the manuscript speech and manuscript delivery copy is the same, the manuscript delivery copy ensures accurate delivery and maximum speaker effectiveness. Read the following manuscript speech and then compare and contrast it with the manuscript delivery copy.

"Choosing a Speech Delivery Method"

Manuscript Speech

Everyday trucks filled with delicious, fresh, produce pass by Lisa Ortega's home in the Bronx in New York City. Too bad she'll never taste them. Lisa, like millions of other low-

income, inner-city, inhabitants, will only be able to buy half-rotten produce – tomatoes you can sink a finger into, carrots with mold growing on them, oranges shriveled and covered in bruises. Why can't Lisa get her hands on decent food? Simply put she is too poor and she lives in the wrong part of town. If Lisa were to make triple her current salary AND live ten miles south, she would be able to get not only fresh produce, but organic as well. As it stands, Lisa is happy to get partially decayed food.

Inner city residents can't get access to quality groceries primarily because many Supermarket chains believe they can turn a better profit in wealthier suburbs. According to the Business Wire of August 10, 2004 there are three times more supermarkets in wealthy neighborhoods and four times as many supermarkets in neighborhoods that are predominately white. Many inner city residents can't afford to own a car and taking a taxi to better suburban supermarkets isn't an affordable option either. So millions, like Lisa, settle for rotten groceries. To better understand how to stop this nutritional travesty, we must first examine why people are not given equal access to a basic necessity of life – quality food. Then we will reveal that the primary justifications of making more money are myths. And finally, we will examine some feasible solutions we can use to enact some change.

So what do most inner city residents eat? Well, as we stated, supermarkets hardly exist in the inner city. But another food provider has filled the void left behind. Dr. Maya Rokeymoore, vice president of the Congressional Black Caucus Foundation, explained in her public address to the National Urban League on April 11, 2004, "It's easier to get a fatty piece of fried chicken that it is to get an apple," Junk food and fast food are often better economic options … or the ONLY options for inner city residents. When it's easier to get to a fast food restaurant than it is a supermarket there can be disastrous effects on a population. The Daily News Tribune of August 22, 2004 emphasizes that 23% of lower-income Americans are  obese, compared to 16% of the middle and upper class. This is something Lisa Ortega can attest to when she looks at her sixteen year old daughter who at barely five feet tall is 170 pounds. Lisa makes nearly twice the amount of money her neighbors make, yet she can only spend $110 a month on food. Hence, it makes greater economic sense for Lisa to buy off brand frozen pizzas than high priced produce that will rot within a day of purchase.

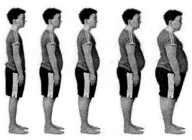

And, according to Dr. James O. Hill, director of the Center for Human Nutrition at the University of Colorado in a PBS interview of April 8, 2004, obesity in lower-income communities is shown to cause diabetes, heart disease, stroke, and cancer. For a population that typically can't afford health care this is disastrous ... for them ... and for a country who will ultimately pay for the health needs of the poor. All of these unnecessary health risks when research – has shown that if given access to healthy produce the poor will buy it! A 2002 University of Southhampton study showed that lower income neighborhood in Leeds ate 18% more fruits and vegetables once a supermarket opened in their area. Even those in Leeds with the worst diets, doubled their produce consumption after the supermarket opened.

So now that we have realized the problem plaguing our poorer citizens, let's bust the 2 myths used to legitimate, thus facilitate, this caloric injustice: "demand for the supply," and "inability to lower cost." MYTH #1: supermarkets claim that demand for produce has left the inner-cities ... and they blame the white flight that started in the mid-sixties. The

Los Angeles Daily News of March 18, 2004 explains that supermarkets in inner city Los Angeles, like most large U.S. cities, experienced a 30% reduction between 1975 and 1991. Many supermarket owners claim they moved to suburbs for purely economic reasons. But, citizens of the inner-city do want good produce. And, if a supply is made available, demand has already indicated that it will rise. The Preventative Cardiology Conference of September 7 2004 reveals that the average inner-city family spends about $2,200 a year on groceries compared to

$4,600 a year for the typical suburban family. But if suburban shoppers spend more on groceries, why is it that some of the most profitable supermarkets are located in inner cities? A 1998 report by non-profit Initiative for a Competitive Inner City, found that of all the Stop & Shop grocery stores in the country, the most profitable were located in inner-city Boston. A similar report in 1996 showed that a quarter of the overall profits of the Pathmark supermarket chain were brought in by the mere 22% of their stores located in inner-cities. Obviously, urban dwellers want good produce, and when presented with the option to buy it, they will. It seems urban shoppers make up in population what they lack in income. And, apparently, more people spending less money individually still makes for a bigger profit in the inner cities than in the suburbs. (5:36)

MYTH #2: It's impossible to lower prices on inner city food. Since the quality of the produce in the inner cities is so low, you would naturally assume that it would be cheaper than the produce sold in the suburban stores. Not so. Well, then you would assume that the rotten produce in the inner city stores would at least be the same price as the fine quality produce available to suburban residents. Not so. In fact, according to the Charleston Gazette on June 18, 2004, rotten, useless produce in the inner city stores averages 10% higher cost than the produce in the suburbs. Small stores in the inner city claim they charge more because they have some of the same problems with affordability as their customers. The Los Angeles Times September 9, 2004 explains, small grocery stores purport not to have the same purchase power that big chain stores do and, thus, they can't do things like eliminate the middle-man ... like Wal-Mart who buys mass quantities directly from the farmer and passes the lower prices on to their customers. Inner-city stores, simultaneously, work together to keep out chain stores and, then, pay more for their food than chain stores, and, then, raise the prices of their food in order to make a profit. Interestingly enough, these networks could work together to buy cheaper produce and pass along cheaper prices. In the mean time, their false market artificially raises the price of produce, and creates a cycle of poverty and bad diets that's hard to break.

Or is it? As equally valuable citizens, and equally hungry consumers, we have the ability to curb these injustices on governmental and local levels. First, it's been proven that the need for fresh groceries is apparent in the inner city, it's been proven that supermarkets can make more money with stores in the city, and it's obviously beneficial to all if the health of those in the inner-city is salvaged. Now, all we need is to convince people that change is a positive, relatively easy thing. And, local governments are already proving that this is possible. The US Newswire of July 28, 2004 outlines the story of inner city Baltimore, a city that proposed, in 2001, to bring at least six new supermarkets to the city ... and succeeded in getting 12 by offering tax subsidies. If your city doesn't provide these types of subsidies, talk

to your city council and encourage them to do so. Or, consider the stakeholder model.

When businesses do ban together to prevent chain stores from coming to their city, they end up NOT providing cheaper, better, food. In contrast however, The New York Times of September 12, 2004 documents the story of the Pathmark supermarket chain in New Jersey...who offered a community development corporation ownership stake in a new local Pathmark store ... then actively recruited and hired from the local community. The store has become a huge success since food prices have become affordable, and food quality has improved.

Finally if cities don't want to bring chain supermarkets to the city they should bring the city residents to the higher quality supermarkets. Newsday of March 27, 2004 explains that some public officials, like those in Hartford, CT have collaborated with supermarkets to provide free transportation from cities to suburban shops. In that city alone, citizens riding to shop for better food ... doubled their numbers the first year in operation. Clearly this is a program that could be beneficial in your city.

Having examined the problems of inner city food, the myths used to justify these practices, and some solutions, it's apparent that Lisa Ortega should have the same opportunities to eat produce that isn't rotten, to provide food to her children that won't make them obese, to taste a little bit of the golden opportunity that she hears driving by her apartment window each and every day. And with our help, she can.

Manuscript Delivery Copy:

Everyday trucks filled with delicious, fresh, produce pass by Lisa Ortega's home in the Bronx in New York City. **Too bad she'll never taste them *(emphasis)*.** Lisa, like millions of other low-income, inner-city, inhabitants, will only be able to buy half-rotten produce – tomatoes you can sink a finger into, carrots with mold growing on them, oranges shriveled and covered in bruises *(eye contact)*. Why can't Lisa get her

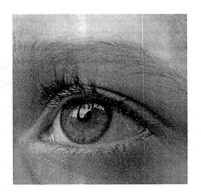

hands on decent food? *(pause)* Simply put she is too poor and she lives in the wrong part of town. If Lisa were to make triple her current salary **AND** live ten miles south, she would be able to get not only fresh produce, but organic as well. As it stands, Lisa is happy to get partially decayed food.

"You Put the Wrong Emphasis on the Wrong Syllable"

Inner city residents can't get access to quality groceries primarily because many supermarket chains believe they can turn a better profit in wealthier suburbs. According to the Business Wire of August 10, 2004 there are three times more supermarkets in wealthy neighborhoods and four times as many supermarkets in neighborhoods that are predominately white. Many inner city residents can't afford to own a car and taking a taxi to better suburban supermarkets isn't an affordable option either. So millions, like Lisa, settle for rotten groceries. To better understand how to stop this nutritional travesty, we must first examine why people are not given equal access to a basic necessity of life – quality food. Then we will reveal that the primary justifications of making more money are myths. And finally, we will examine some feasible solutions we can use to enact some change.

(physically move) So what do most inner city residents eat? Well, as we stated, supermarkets hardly exist in the inner city. But another food provider has filled the void left behind. Dr. Maya Rokeymoore, vice president of the Congressional Black Caucus Foundation, explained in her public address to the National Urban League on April 11, 2004 "It's easier to get a fatty piece of fried chicken that it is to get an apple," Junk food and fast food are often better economic options ... or the **ONLY** *(emphasis)* options for inner city residents. When it's easier to get to a fast food restaurant than it is a supermarket there can be disastrous effects on a population. The Daily News Tribune of August 22, 2004 emphasizes that 23% of lower-income Americans are obese, compared to 16% of the middle and upper class. This is something Lisa Ortega can attest to when she looks at her sixteen year old daughter who at barely five feet tall is 170 pounds. Lisa makes nearly twice the amount of money her neighbors make, yet she can only spend $110 a month on food. Hence, it makes greater economic sense for Lisa to buy off brand

frozen pizzas than high priced produce that will rot within a day of purchase.

And, according to Dr. James O. Hill, director of the Center for Human Nutrition at the University of Colorado in a PBS interview of April 8, 2004, obesity in lower-income communities is shown to cause diabetes, heart disease, stroke, and cancer. For a population that typically can't afford health care this is disastrous for them and for a 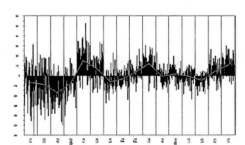 country who will ultimately pay for the health needs of the poor. All of these unnecessary health risks when research has shown that if given access to healthy produce the poor will buy it! *(voice intonation)* A 2002 University of Southhampton study showed that lower income neighborhood in Leeds ate 18% more fruits and vegetables once a supermarket opened in their area. Even those in Leeds with the worst diets, doubled their produce consumption after the supermarket opened.

(physically move) So now that we have realized the problem plaguing our poorer citizens, let's bust the 2 myths used to legitimate, thus facilitate, this caloric injustice: "demand for the supply," and "inability to lower cost." MYTH #1 **(eye contact — pause):** supermarkets claim that demand for produce has left the inner-cities … and they blame the white flight that started in the mid-sixties. The Los Angeles Daily News of March 18, 2004 explains that supermarkets in inner city Los Angeles, like most, large U.S. cities, experienced a 30% reduction between 1975 and 1991. Many supermarket owners claim they moved to suburbs for purely economic reasons. But, citizens of the inner-city do want good produce. And, if a supply is made available, demand has already

 indicated that it will rise. The Preventative Cardiology Conference of September 7 2004 reveals that the average inner-city family spends about $2,200 a year on groceries compared to $4,600 a year for the typical suburban family. But if suburban shoppers spend more on groceries, why is it that some of the most profitable supermarkets are located in inner cities? *(**Eye contact-pause**)* A 1998 report by non-profit Initiative for a Competitive Inner City, found that of all the Stop & Shop grocery stores in the country, the most profitable were located in inner-city Boston. A similar report in 1996 showed that a quarter of the overall profits of the Pathmark supermarket chain were brought in by the mere 22% of their stores located in inner-cities. Obviously, urban dwellers want good

produce, and when presented with the option to buy it, they will. It seems urban shoppers make up in population what they lack in income. And, apparently, more people spending less money individually still makes for a bigger profit in the inner cities than in the suburbs.

MYTH #2 (**Eye contact-pause**): It's impossible to lower prices on inner city food. Since the quality of the produce in the inner cities is so low, you would naturally assume that it would be cheaper than the produce sold in the suburban stores. Not so. Well, then you would assume that the rotten produce in the inner city stores would at least be the same price as the fine quality produce available to suburban residents. Not so. In fact, according to the Charleston Gazette on June 18, 2004, rotten, useless produce in the inner city stores averages 10% higher cost than the produce in the suburbs. Small stores in the inner city claim they charge more because they have some of the same problems with affordability as their customers. The Los Angeles Times September 9, 2004 explains, small grocery stores purport not to  have the same purchase power that big chain stores do and, thus, they can't do things like eliminate the middle-man ... like Wal-Mart who buys mass quantities directly from the farmer and passes the lower prices on to their customers. Inner-city stores, simultaneously, work together to keep out chain stores **AND** *(emphasize),* then, pay more for their food than chain stores, **AND** *(emphasize)*, then, raise the prices of their food in order to make a profit. Interestingly enough, these networks could work together to buy cheaper produce and pass along cheaper prices. In the mean time, their false market artificially raises the price of produce, and creates a cycle of poverty and bad diets that's hard to break. (**physically move**)

Or is it? As equally valuable citizens, and equally hungry consumers, we have the ability to curb these injustices on governmental and local levels. First, it's been proven that the need for fresh groceries is  apparent in the inner city, it's been proven that supermarkets can make more money with stores in the city, and it's obviously beneficial to all if the health of those in the inner-city is salvaged. Now, all we need is to convince people that change is a positive, relatively easy thing. And, local governments are already proving that this is possible. The US Newswire of July 28, 2004 outlines the story of inner city Baltimore, a city that proposed, in 2001, to bring at least six new supermarkets to the city…and succeeded in getting 12 by offering tax subsidies. If your city doesn't provide these types of subsidies, talk to your city council and encourage them to do so. Or, consider the stakeholder model.

When businesses do ban together to prevent chain stores from coming to their city, they end up **NOT** *(emphasize)* providing cheaper, better, food. In contrast however, The New York Times of September 12, 2004 documents the story of the Pathmark supermarket chain in New Jersey…who offered a community development corporation ownership stake in a new local Pathmark store ..then actively recruited and hired from the local community. The store has become a huge success since food prices have become affordable, and food quality has improved.

Finally if cities don't want to bring chain supermarkets to the city they should bring the city residents to the higher quality supermarkets. Newsday of March 27, 2004 explains, that some public officials, like those in Hartford, CT have collaborated with supermarkets to provide free transportation from cities to suburban shops. In that city alone, citizens riding to shop for better food … doubled their numbers the first year in operation. Clearly this is a program that could be beneficial in your city.

Having examined the problems of inner city food, the myths used to justify these practices, and some solutions, it's apparent that Lisa Ortega should have the same opportunities to eat produce that isn't rotten, to provide food to her children that won't make them obese, to taste a little bit of the golden opportunity that she hears driving by her apartment window each and every day. And with our help, she can *(eye contact)*.

Delivery Tips to Keep in Mind for Manuscript Speeches:

(1) Type the text out. Don't, we repeat, don't write out your speech in long-hand form because you risk not being able to read the text fluidly and there is nothing more damaging to your credibility than struggling to read your own hand writing for your own speech!

(2) Make the font readable. See the delivery copy above. Pay particular attention to letter size and spacing. Font size may appear to be a trivial detail, but when every word counts, making your text as easy to read as possible will allow you to fluidly read and powerfully delivery your speech.

(3) Arrange the text in such a way to maximize smooth delivery. This is your delivery copy – it should not look like an essay. For example, if an important line cuts off at the right margin, position it so that it only takes up one line to ensure the smoothest read possible.

(4) Provide delivery cues in the text. Make the manuscript delivery text your own. In addition to content, the text should provide delivery tips. Are there words or proper names you stumble over in practice? Spell them out phonetically. Do you find yourself speaking too fast in certain sections? Write *pause* in the margins or the subtext so you won't forget. Find yourself forgetting to look up from your text during practice? Remind yourself by putting *(eye contact)* before transitions. Bold important words or phrases that you want to emphasize. Develop your own system of delivery reminders. Remember, the delivery text is to help you perform the content in the most powerful and effective way possible, not just read the words.

fuh-net-ik

(5) Bold the source citations. Since this is a manuscript text, there are no excuses for inaccuracy. So make sure and bold the source citations in your text to ensure proper and complete citation.

(6) Don't staple your pages together. Unless you're the President of the United States or a Fortune 500 Executive (if so, congratulations), odds are you won't have a teleprompter at your disposal. Consequently, your text, with multiple pages, is your own teleprompter. However, if the pages are stapled together, you won't be able to effortlessly move from one page to the next. This will cause unnecessary glitches in the fluidity of your delivery. Not using staples will also allow you to place your pages in sheet holders.

(7) Number your pages. Once again, this sounds like a minor detail but it is essential if, for some reason, you inadvertently mix pages.

(8) Use your podium. Oftentimes the tops of podiums are at an angle. Given the temptation to read the manuscript text and forget about the audience, slide your text higher on the podium, so moving your eyes from your text to your audience is shorter, quicker, and easier.

Finally, while the manuscripted speech has its place, it should be limited in use. One of the cautionary elements to consider is that it is communicated and presented in a more 'stoic' manner. It is hard to infuse and weave emotion into a presentation when the speaker is continually focused upon reading the typed words to the tee. Many of my students, and I agree, have commented that manuscripted speeches indeed sound more robotic and unnatural in nature. It takes a well-practiced speaker, specific to a specific content, to pull off a well delivered manuscript presentation. Boyd (2007) confirms the previous cautionary statements by asserting the following, "…there is a misconception among some that since the speech is written, you don't have to spend much time in practicing – that because your speech is in front of you, all that you have to do is read it". Because you read it, your eye contact is limited and you will be tempted to read it in monotone". For more on the cautions of the manuscript presentation, please review Boyd's article here: http://www.speaking-tips.com/ARticles/Delivering-A-Manuscript-Speech.aspx.

Extemporaneous Speeches and Delivery

Most audiences expect extemporaneous speeches. Why? Extemporaneous speaking allows speakers to adjust, modify, and respond to audiences. In addition, audiences don't expect formalized and precise language as much as they expect speakers to use informal language and connect with them through a relaxed but prepared presentation. The speech sounds more natural and comfortable to the audience, as though you are 'getting to know' the speaker. Additionally, the number of speeches and speaking events expected in the business contexts, for example, make it difficult for contemporary speakers to deliver memorized speeches in the same manner as they did several decades ago. Finally, the ubiquity of media venues means that most speeches end up on *YouTube* or in print form. Hence, there are few reasons for speakers to deliver the exact same, memorized speech more than once since our hyper-mediated world emphasizes the introduction of new content rather than repetition of the same speech or speeches that can be easily saved and sent via a variety of means (email, pdf text, YouTube, et cetera). In other words, there is much to be said for variety.

Extemporaneous speeches, although not written out word for word, still require the speaker to prepare adequately. Informal delivery does not mean unprepared delivery. Remember, there is no substitute for preparation. However, audiences expect speakers to be well-versed on their speech topic or subject while not scripting out exactly what they will say, word for word, in advance. Consequently, an extemporaneous delivery seeks to combine advanced preparation with of-the-moment delivery spontaneity to account for the specific and real audience to which the speech is addressed.

If a speaker has practiced what points he/she want to get across, the examples to be used, and the order in which the points will occur, speakers are freed from the burden of having to get each word exactly right, thereby allowing for a speech presentation that demonstrates knowledge, sincerity, and audience-centeredness. This can be achieved in a well-organized, yet bulleted outline. Such an outline can encompass the knowledge aforementioned, yet also the delivery because each time you practice the presentation you have an organized, yet loosely structured direction. This allows for greater freedom to be 'yourself' in delivery, allowing the audience to connect to the person behind the words. For an example of a well-organized extemporaneous outline, please review: http://www.soapboxorations.com/educators/outlineguide.pdf.

"Public Speaking Video Tip – Extemporaneous Speech"

Impromptu

The third type of speaking style is referred to as impromptu. In impromptu speeches, there is little or no advanced preparation. Therefore, expectations from audiences are different than they are for manuscript and extemporaneous speaking. If you have little or no time to prepare and research, specific details cannot be expected. For example, when your teacher calls on you in class to answer a question about the reading for the day, this is an impromptu like scenario where you may have (hopefully) read the text for class, but did not know which, if any, questions the professor may ask. Without a script or even an outline to work with, eye contact is expected, but so too are basic organization structures and brief examples.

"How to Do an Impromptu Speech"

"Impromptu Speaking"

Impromptu speeches are one way to assess a speaker's ability to think on his/her feet – literally. A couple of suggestions to help you think and stand at the same time:

Delivery Expectations for Impromptu Speeches

(1) Keep it simple. Because you will have little or no advanced preparation time, simplicity is your ally. Don't make things more complicated than they need to be. A simple organizing structure can be applied to most impromptu settings.

(2) Organize your ideas. The basic organizing structure of an impromptu speech is similar to the organizing structures of other speeches. While the impromptu speech outline may resemble the extemporaneous outline in terms of the structural outline, the content in an impromptu speech will be less detailed. The only significant difference is that impromptu speakers are typically not expected to draw upon extensive, outside sources for evidence. However, evidence is still an expectation. The following two organizational formats provide basic templates.

I.   Preview (2 points)
II. Point #1
     A. Example
Transition
III. Point #2
     A. Example
IV. Conclusion

Introduction (Grab Attention/Preview)
I.   Point #1
     A. Example
     B. Example
     Transition
II. Point #2
     A. Example
     B. Example
Conclusion (Review/Closure)

(3) Start with specifics. One of the most challenging aspects of an impromptu speech is knowing where to start. If you try to cover everything, you'll end up covering nothing. Narrow your topic, think about two points you want to make, draw upon evidence from your own experiences to support your main points, and then remind the audience of what you told them. Yes, we know, easier said than done.

"Reagan's Impromptu Speech at 1976 GOP Convention"

Additionally, to view an impromptu student presentation, please review the following link: http://www.bing.com/videos/search?q=videl+example+of+impromptu+speech&view=detail&mid=92054F3A3D183732B1D792054F3A3D183732B1D7&FORM=VIRE.

Sample Impromptu Response:
(1) How do you think a friend or professor who knows you well would describe you?

Let's apply the principles above to this all-too common interview question (the ultimate impromptu context). This is a very broad question – most impromptu questions are. First, narrow it down. Think about two to three points you want to cover in your allotted time. Yes, there are probably a multitude of ways in which your friend or professor could describe you, but think about several specific ways. Be strategic given who you are talking to (i.e. an employer would not ask this question simply to know more about you – they're asking a roundabout question to find out how you see yourself and how these qualities might be a good fit with the organization). Let's say you come up with: (1) creative and (2) responsible. Okay, now fit these points into the impromptu organizing structure.

I.   Attention getter – What might artists and frugal spenders have in common?
II. Thesis: People who know me well, like my friends and professors, would definitely say that, among other things, I am not only creative, but also responsible.
III. Forecast / Preview – I'll be covering my artistic sides as demonstrated through my dancing, and my ability to shop for clothes on a budget.
IV. Relation – This relates to all of you because as college students, we all have to find an outlet to release our stressors, as well as being frugal without money to save for other expenses, like college.

Transition: Now that we know the major areas of focus, let's begin with my creative side.

V.   Point #1 – Creative
     A. Example from a class. Be specific. Tell them how the project demonstrated your creativity.

Signpost: Moving on to my responsible side

VI. Point #2--Responsible
     A. Draw upon an example from work experience that illustrates your responsibility. Be specific.

Transition: Let's wrap up the most important points that I covered with you today.

VII. Recap
     A. Reiterate your two points – others consider you creative and responsible. End on a strong note by saying why you believe these two character traits are important for the job you are applying for, etc.

End Attention-getter (e.g. joke or quote on responsibility.)

- **Note** – I am providing a 'written' out outline for the purposes of content understanding. However, an extemporaneous / impromptu outline is generally a bulleted list only.

Exercise: Respond to the following questions using the impromptu principles described above.

(1) In what ways have your college experiences prepared you for a career?

(2) How do you think a friend or professor who knows you well would describe you?

(3) Describe a situation in which you had to work with a difficult person (another student, co-worker, customer, supervisor, et cetera). How did you handle the situation? Is there anything you would have done differently in hindsight?

(4) In what ways do you think you can make a contribution to our organization?

(5) Describe a contribution you have made to a project on which you worked.

(6) What qualities should a successful manager possess?

(7) Was there an occasion when you disagreed with a supervisor's decision or company policy? Describe how you handled the situation.

(8) What two or three accomplishments have given you the most satisfaction? Why?

(9) Describe your most rewarding college experience.

Conclusion

This chapter examined the different ways to deliver a speech. Each delivery typology has its advantages and disadvantages for speakers. Typically, most speech assignments will be extemporaneous, thus placing the emphasis on your ability to examine your topic thoroughly and logically while also connecting and adapting to the immediate audience. Writing a manuscripted speech or completing an outline is an essential step in ensuring a quality speech, however, it is not the final step. As addressed in this chapter, the job of a speaker is to create a delivery note card set specifically designed to create the most compelling delivery for your speech content.

For more on the various speech styles, please review the following link: http://study.com/academy/lesson/types-of-speech-delivery-impromptu-extemporaneous-manuscript-and-memorized.html.

Suggested Websites

http://speaking-tips.com/Articles/Delivering-A-Manuscript-Speech.aspx (Boyd, 2007).

Chapter 9
The Informative Speech

"People demand freedom of speech as a compensation for the freedom of thought which they seldom use."

– Soren Kierkegaard

While you may or may not agree with the above quote, it is relevant in the sense that there is always hope to educate others – through speeches and communication of information. According to the writing center at Colorado State University, one of the main purposes of the informative speech is to allow you the opportunity to engage in and practice your extensive work in the area of research, your level of writing (which you always should want to improve, your use of the learned structure, and of course, your delivery skills (2016).

Revelatory and Explanatory Speeches

Let's begin with understanding a very important differentiation. It may be helpful to conceptualize informative speaking in terms of *revelatory* presentations and *explanatory* speeches. The informational speech, at its most basic level, is about conveying information to an audience in a way that can be easily ingested and digested by audiences. However, let us also not forget that the manner and mode through which information is conveyed usually depends, like any other speech, on the audience, context and speaker goal. For those who would like to split more hairs, Dr. Melanie Morgan (2007) builds on Kathy Rowan's earlier work that differentiates presentations focused on distributing information in terms of informative presentations and explanatory presentations. This typology outlines the two presentation forms accordingly:

A) Informative presentations are those speeches which provide structured news and/or basic instructions "to create awareness" for listeners regarding selected topics. To review a video example, please watch the video below.

"Good Example of an Informative Speech"

B) Explanatory presentations assume audiences already know something about certain concepts or issues and seek to expand the knowledge base of the audience regarding those concepts or issues. To review a video example, please view this link:

Describing and Translating Difficult Information: Transformative Presentations

Preparing and giving an informational speech is like working with a sharp object – you better know what you are doing or somebody, including you, is going to eventually get hurt. While I say this partly in jest, when you spend so much time researching, gathering and formulating evidence, what's often lost in the equation is how best to translate your information to audiences. Too often, we believe information speaks for itself. Or, we speak from our perspective. Information never speaks for itself. In fact, if you let facts speak for themselves and just "let the audience figure it out", all of your energy and hard work will be for nothing. You will only be creating confusion and mystery. The informative speech is intended to solve the mystery for the audience. Therefore, researching and gathering evidence from outside sources is the first essential step in creating an effective organizational speech. But, it is the first step. The translation process – gathering information from a variety of sources – needs to be put together in a way makes sense. After all, providing clarity is of the upmost importance for you to offer as the speaker. As such, consider the following:

Tips for Translating Information into a Speech:

(1) **Don't try to do too much in your speech:** If you try and inform your audience about a generic topic that is unfocused or too broad (i.e. health care, religion, global politics), you'll end up simply confusing the audience. Stay focused. Keep reminding yourself about your specific purpose. Remember to narrow your topic to 2-4 main points. You can't talk about everything. Your job is to highlight and communicate a specific part or portion of a topic as it would be impossible to inform an audience about everything there is to know about religion or health care. Ask yourself: What aspect of a topic do I most want to inform my audience about or what aspect of a topic does my audience most need to know about? In other words, put yourself into the audience's shoes – empathy will go a long way in terms of providing needed information.

(2) **Divide and speak:** Know which organizational structure (topological, chronological or spatial) makes the most sense in informing and explaining your speech to an audience? What point or points should come first? What point or points should come next? And last? Why? Be able to justify the logic of your arrangement. Clearly, the organizational structure you choose to organize your speech should guide you in this process. If you choose a chronological

organizing structure, chronology will guide your ordering. With spatial arrangement, you can decide which of the following makes more sense: beginning with left to right, or up to down, front to back, et cetera. Finally, topical structure, dividing the subject into thematic areas, requires you think long and hard about how best to divide your topic to address those elements of a topic that are most relevant to your audience. Know the differences!!! A little bit of research will go a long way in providing the audience the structure and the knowledge needed to create a common understanding.

3) ***Repeat. Repeat. Repeat.:*** By its very nature, information and explanation involve evidence such as examples and statistics and testimony, et cetera. The more information you provide the audience, the more you need to repeat. If each of your main points is connected to one another in a chronological format, for example, briefly retell the audience the essentials concerning step #1 and step #2 before you dive into step #3. Restate in different ways to keep the repetition fresh, but repeat to keep the audience's minds from going stale! Lastly, according to Wong (2014), "…memory is far more dependent upon technique and habit versus innate ability".

(4) ***No Evidence Left Behind:*** You've spent so much time researching and gathering evidence that you've even found a great statistic and riveting quote. And there they are, in your speech, perfectly quoted or paraphrased. Congratulations, you've just lost the audience and wasted effective forms of evidence! Don't ever let a piece of evidence stand alone because the audience

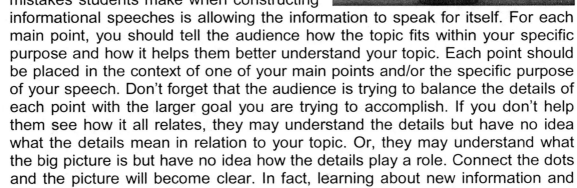

will leave it behind in their memories without your voice added to the mix. If you provide a quotation, then provide a lead in or follow up to explain what the quote means. If you provide what you believe to be a startling statistic, tell the audience why it is so startling. Leave them bread crumbs and they will follow!

(5) ***How Does it All Fit?*** One of the biggest mistakes students make when constructing informational speeches is allowing the information to speak for itself. For each main point, you should tell the audience how the topic fits within your specific purpose and how it helps them better understand your topic. Each point should be placed in the context of one of your main points and/or the specific purpose of your speech. Don't forget that the audience is trying to balance the details of each point with the larger goal you are trying to accomplish. If you don't help them see how it all relates, they may understand the details but have no idea what the details mean in relation to your topic. Or, they may understand what the big picture is but have no idea how the details play a role. Connect the dots and the picture will become clear. In fact, learning about new information and

details, according to the National Adult Learning Survey (1998), boosts ones' confidence.

Transitions are one specific strategy you should use to connect one main point to the next while reminding your audience how the points all fit together. Remember, transitions are linkages between points, a segway revealing the logic of your speech and helping the audience follow along with your thinking pattern. Don't underestimate the importance of these transitions. They are small, but mighty!

In this sample student speech, locate and evaluate the quality of transitions that both link one point to the next and help remind the audience how each point fits within the overall speech. For the purpose of example, this is exhibited in a manuscript format. Of course, the optimal format is outlined, in a bulleted format, but this allows for specificity.

The New York Times of February 2005 reported that math phenom Erik Demaine talked his way into *Dalhousie University* at the age of 12, despite having no grades to speak of. Then, as a math major he attended *Waterloo University*. Nine years, a PhD AND an MIT professorship later, Demaine is living it large in academe...due primarily to his math hobby – one of the world's most promising applications for everyday science: Computational Origami, the geometry of paper folding.

The January 2005 American Scientist reveals that this new math field holds infinite possibilities given that folding and unfolding is important to numerous material applications such as sheet metal fabrication, airbag storage, as well as scientific and mathematical theories for telescopic lens folding, robotic arm designs, and bioinformatics – the theory used to understand and predict how proteins fold.

"Sheet Metal Shearing & Bending"

Because this is one of our age's most innovative and revealing new math theories, we should have a look inside the complex world of computational origami by ... unfolding the convergence of origami and math, then examining the applications of the "math of folding," and, finally, assessing the pros and cons of this curious math application.

(1st) To better understand what Computational Origami is however, we must understand the origins of origami, and then the convergence of the art … with the science. The New York Times of June 22, 2004, explains that origami is "derived from the Japanese ori, to fold, and gami, paper, and [it's] come a long way from cute little birds and decorative boxes. Mathematicians … have begun mapping the laws that underlie folding, converting words and concepts into algebraic rules. Computational origami, also known as technical folding, or origami sekkei, draws on fields that include computational geometry, number theory, coding theory and linear algebra." The Hamilton Spectator last accessed February 10th, 2006, reveals that the origins of origami are controversial. Some believe it originated in China, other historians believe Japan. Paper was first invented in A.D. 105, and in the 6th Century Buddhist monks brought paper to Japan. Later, The Rock Hill South Carolina Herald online last accessed February 15th, 2006 explains, the Japanese samurai exchanged origami... and still later, Moors in the 8th century brought the art

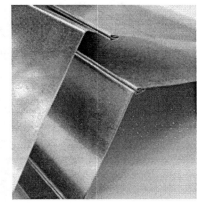

west. Today, as reported in an interview with Cabinet magazine in spring of 2005, a recently converted physicist-turned-computational origamist from CalTech, Dr. Robert Lang, explains that the traditional Japanese folk art is riding a wave of enthusiasm from scientists, mathematicians, and engineers around the world. Researchers have tapped into the rules of the craft, testing the angles and limits of paper to revolutionize the design and function of everyday things as varied as water bottles and cars.

According to the weekly updated encyclopedia site What is dot com, geometric and trigonometric principles were theorized and then applied to origami, when in the 1950's Japanese physicists created axioms, which are self-evident truths, that explain how folding creates three dimensional objects from a flat material. Humaiki Huzita, an Italian-Japanese mathematician, developed a sequence of six separate yet increasingly complex axioms which describe, at the most basic level, how any two points on a flat surface can be connected by a single line fold, and at the most complex level, the way in which four points on a flat surface can be interrelated. Extending those axioms, Erik Demaine stated in his meeting for the American Association for the Advancement in Science back in February of 2002 that being able to correctly align the outward and inward folds of the paper or other object is the key to making the theory work.

The previously cited New York Times of February 15, 2005 explains that Demaine has found that any shape can be made by simply folding

$$\varepsilon_0 \oint E \cdot dA = \sum q$$

$$\oint B \cdot ds = \mu_0 \int J \cdot dA + \mu_0 \varepsilon_0 \frac{d}{dt} \int E \cdot dA$$

$$\oint E \cdot ds = -\frac{d}{dt} \int B \cdot \cdot dA$$

$$\oint B \cdot dA = 0$$

it, snipping off a corner and then unfolding it. If the correct calculations have been made ... understanding the 'unfolded' flat shape is possible. The way in which Demaine has expanded on earlier axioms is by creating a mathematical system which explains the exact patterns and principles behind folding any shape, if the right numbers are factored in. These numbers are adjusted accordingly to factor in the shape size and hardness of different materials when folded. Hence, internal and external folds are made to match up correctly, and ostensibly flat surfaces of various sizes and hardnesses can be folded and unfolded efficiently.

(2nd) Well, efficiency is the theory's mantlepiece! Computational Origami has already predicted how many three dimensional objects can be unfolded into a sheet. Thus, the sheet metal industry's engineers and technicians practically apply these principles and theories to build cars or furniture often from a single sheet of metal, thereby saving costs on raw materials.

In an NPR interview on October 27, 2003 Demaine explains that one of the practical uses for computational origami is that it allows an airbag to collapse flatly into a steering wheel, pushing air into the compressed airbag, so that when it expands it will not be harmful to the driver.

And, the L.A. Weekly last accessed on February 11, 2006 explains that engineers and technicians can apply these principles any time in which a shape needs to change dramatically ... such as when a small shape needs to get very large. For instance, astronomers looking into deep space need very large telescopes to catch sufficient light. Scientists at the Lawrence Livermore National Laboratory are hoping to build space based telescopes with lenses up to 100 meters in diameter ... that can be folded and fit into the cargo bay of a space shuttle. Fortunately, flat film lenses like those in overhead projectors, are highly effective ... as long as the lens is folded without optics interference. Using computational origami, Robert Lang, a scientist who works with Erik Demaine, came up with a crease pattern resembling a spider's web...that will provide adequate alignment of interior and exterior folds for this particular material. What's more, such folding technology is already used in products such as tents, deployable shelters, telescopic lenses, and antennas.

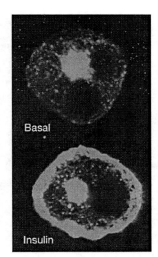

Basal

Insulin

(3rd) To assess the true potential of Computational Origami for the future however, we must look at the pros and cons of the theory. First, the cons...or should we cay Con? Outside of the difficulty in translating the theory to us non-math types, the challenge of Computational Origami is the newness of this theory. As shown on the daily updated Stanford University Official Website, technology has yet to catch up to the possibilities the theory has created. Thus, those mathematicians who are working with the theory are years ahead of the applications that can come from the math itself. Essentially, we have a bunch of math types sitting around waiting to fold the next thing that comes along! But considering that the theory holds a storehouse of future applications, however, the pros are quite encouraging! The Globe and Mail, updated daily reports that biologists are only starting to use computational origami to discover how proteins are folded...and it will one day help biologists create artificial proteins. This is important because scientists already know that a key element in the operation of natural proteins in the body is how they are folded, because proteins in the body generally only interact with the things around them through their unfolded surfaces. Learn how to unfold them, and voila! Increased protein interaction!

Today, we've explored Computational Origami by examining the convergence of origami and computation geometry, assessing its applications, and weighing its advantages and disadvantages. BBC News last accessed February 12, 2006 reminds us that the underlying principles behind folding a lens or a paper swan are the same. It's no wonder Computational Origami is revolutionizing the way we design, invent and experience our lives. And Erik Demaine? Well, his simple hobby of origami, has literally unfolded the way we think about the multidimensional world in which we live.

(6) ***Don't Forget the Set Up:*** Because all informational speeches require evidence, you will need to cite evidence in your speech. However, if not done right, citations can confuse and get in the way of audience comprehension. Ask any comedian and they will tell you that the set up is essential to the punch line. Likewise, the set up, or the citation, is essential to audience comprehension of the information you are providing. *Take a moment to locate and underline the citations in the sample speech. Note the clear and fluid use of evidence.*

At 14 years old, Blake Ross called himself the ultimate nerd. Having conquered several of the world's most complicated computer programming languages, Blake decided it was time to get a job. And according to Wired News of January 23, 2005, he didn't have to look far. Having spent most of his young life tinkering with programs and working on web pages, Blake was actually offered a job – not at the local grocery store, but as one of the chief programmers for America Online. Though he didn't know it then, Blake Ross would be at the forefront of the biggest news to hit the internet since Paris Hilton. It's called Firefox, a web browser with the potential to forever change the way that we surf the net.

To see why the *Chicago Tribune* of July 18, 2004 believes that Firefox is nothing short of a revolution in the making, we'll first hit the "back" button and take a look at the history of the web and web browsers we've come to know, love … and occasionally hate. We'll then explore the phenomenon known as Firefox and discover why it's been drawing some not-so-friendly-fire from Microsoft, before finally discussing – in some peer-to-peer fashion – the implications of this new world wide wonder. Even if you've already heard of Firefox or even downloaded it, stayed logged in – you might just learn something from this, a "People's history" of the web.

Now, back in days when spam really meant … uh … that gross meat-style stuff, a young British scientist named Tim Berners Lee, who was studying at the European Laboratory for Particle Physics or CERN as it's known in French, began working on an after school project to allow scientists from his organization to quickly post information in a

format that the rest of the faculty could see. According to *International Herald Tribune* of June 14, 2004, after several months of work, Berners-Lee completed what he called the World Wide Web, and with one stroke of the enter key, a new age in information sharing was born.

The web didn't gain real popularity until a few years later, when a couple of hobbyists created what was called Netscape, the world's first Web browser. As explained in the *New York Times* of January 27, 2005, a web browser is basically a program that allows all internet users to see the same information in the same way. It takes in coded data from a website, and according to previously set standards, reinterprets that data to show you a webpage. Now, Netscape became incredibly popular, and that drew the attention Bill Gates and his company Microsoft, who made the Windows operating system on which Netscape ran. They soon created a similar browser called Internet Explorer that would integrate into Windows, meaning that users were forced to use it. And … the browser wars had begun.

Since it didn't require a download and did everything that Netscape could, the growing internet public began to use Internet Explorer, which was already installed on their machine. PC World Magazine of January 23, 2004 explains that Netscape use plummeted, and by the late 1990's, Internet Explorer was being used by 95 percent of all internet users. As quickly as they had begun, the browser wars were over, and Internet Explorer was the clear victor.

It was about this time that 14 year old Blake Ross received a call from one of the nation's largest internet service providers – America Online – which had purchased Netscape a few years earlier. According to Agence France Presse of January 18, 2005, Blake was brought on board to head a spinoff of Netscape called the Mozilla project. Now, despite commonly being confused with one of those crazy monsters in the Godzilla movies, Mozilla was actually a revolutionary idea for the time. It was a part of a new movement of "open source" software which was free to anyone…as publicly available program code. After several popular test versions, Mozilla announced in November of last year the final iteration of the software. It's name is Firefox 1.0.

Well, several months and 23 million downloads later, Firefox has taken the computing world by storm. To understand why, we need to examine the 3 key components of its success – customizability, increased security, and ease of use.

First, Firefox is a lot like the ideal roommate – one who's reliable, who cleans up after themselves and only talks when you want them to. According to *USA Today* of February 4, 2005, the largest appeal of Firefox is the many ways to customize it. It can be as large or as small, as simple or as complex as the user would like. It's also cutting edge – by contrast, Internet Explorer hasn't had a major upgrade since 2001, so many of its features are slightly outdated. For example, it wasn't until late last year that Explorer added a pop-up blocker … to stop overly forceful advertising. Many other browsers, however, including the pre-release versions of Firefox, had supported this feature for years. By using what are known as "extensions," Firefox users can tailor their browser to do just about anything from the practical, such as playing music, to the bizarre – like one user-created extension that places a virtual marijuana joint on your desktop, just in case the stresses of the web really get to you.

Secondly, many individuals and businesses have chosen to make the switch from Internet Explorer due to security issues. Since Internet Explorer is by far the web's most popular browser, it's the one that most of the hackers try to attack. And attack they have. A CNet news report of November 17, 2004 notes that last year, security flaws in Internet

Explorer were found at the rate of about one every other day. Firefox overcomes these shortcomings in two ways. First, it's developed by enthusiasts and volunteers who enjoy programming and want to improve future versions of Firefox. Many of the hackers who would normally be attacking Internet Explorer are actually helping build Firefox, so there is very little motivation for anyone to attack the program they created. Secondly, according to InformationWeek of August 8, 2004, the Mozilla Foundation offers a 500 dollar reward to anyone who identifies a security flaw, giving extra incentive to hackers and the general public to put their efforts to good use. And according to a January 24, 2005 report from the excessively named US Computer Emergency Readiness Team, the Department of Homeland Security is even urging American citizens to consider switching away from Internet Explorer to browsers just like Firefox, simply because they aren't as susceptible to attacks.

Finally, the largest reason for Firefox's success is the price tag – it's free. This has enabled millions around the world to download and try it with no strings attached. And not only is it accessible, but it's easy to use. According to *The Washington Post* of November 14, 2004, IE users should be familiar with the program after just a few minutes of use. Once again, the internet is finally accessible to everyone.

But before rushing home and downloading your copy, we need to explore the implications of this technology – first, the challenges which Firefox faces to gain wider use, and secondly, the impacts that it will have on the larger open source movement.

According to Knight Ridder of December 29, 2004, the battle of Firefox versus Microsoft is nothing short of a David and Goliath contest. Since the introduction of the full version last November, Firefox has deeply cut into Internet Explorer's use, bringing it down from 95 percent of all web traffic to almost 87 percent – a substantial amount. And since Explorer is included with the Windows operating system, many users will continue to use it simply because they don't have to download anything extra.

The larger implications of Firefox, however, will be felt throughout the rest of the open source movement. As *Newsweek* of January 24, 2005 reveals, many have called the movement of free software which publishes its code for anyone to view the "democratization" of the internet, since it allows anyone from a college student living off week old pizza to a retired grandmother in Columbia Missouri to contribute. Firefox gained its initial popularity on Linux, another open source product, and as more individuals discover the uses and benefits of open source software, behemoths like Microsoft will be forced to begin paying attention to the little guy. And as *BusinessWeek* of January 21, 2005 explains, from Tim Berner Lee's original work from his dorm room to the millions of Red Bull addicted programmers across the globe, the greatest innovations in computing history have come from the minds of the next generation of tech savvy users. It may take more than a slingshot and five tiny stones, but open source software appears perched to revolutionize the way we think about and use computers.

And so ends the story of the "Little browser that could." In today's venture into geekdom, we discovered the history of the modern browser, the benefits that Firefox presents, and its implication on the internet and computing world as a whole. Remember Blake Ross, the 14 year old kid from the intro? Well, he's almost 20 now, and trying to balance the challenges of college, the world's fastest growing internet browser, and growing a goatee. But for Blake and the millions of other Firefox users, this revolution in computing isn't just a novelty anymore. It's about to change everything.

(7) ***Equality is Overrated:*** Tell the audience what's most important, crucial, for them to know. Not ALL evidence and information is created equal. Not ALL information is relevant. Yes, all of your evidence and information is important, but do your audience a favor and tell them what is most important. Or tell them what they should notice when you provide a graph of numbers. Point – literally and figuratively – at your evidence for your audience. Your audience wants this kind of help because processing and analyzing each piece of information is time consuming and difficult. By 'pointing' at evidence that is particularly important – "I'm going to repeat that statistic because It is so important" – you give the audience an opportunity to hang their hats on selected pieces of evidence that are crucial to comprehension.

(8) ***Keep it Interesting:*** Use metaphors, analogies and stories. Metaphors are an excellent source of evidence in informational speeches because they

help explain the unknown by using the language of the known. As the great movie philosopher Forrest Gump stated, "My momma always said, life was like a box of chocolates, you never know what you're gonna get." The wise Gump made sense of the sometimes intimidating, confusing, exciting, and frustrating experience called life by comparing it to something most of us know very well, chocolate.

"Those Must Be Chocolate"

Stories are also an essential way to impart information. Pieces of information tend to bounce off audiences – stories stick. Why? Audiences can relate to stories because stories humanize topics without explicitly having to state the message.

In the following student speech, note the story in the introduction. Does it help orient you to the goal and topic of the speech? Does it draw you in to the topic? If so, how? If not, explain. And, at the end of the speech, when the speaker returns to the story, does it help you put everything together?

In Shakespeare's much adored *Much Ado About Nothing*, prince Don Pedro pretends to be his friend Claudio to woo Claudio's lover because, it seems, Don Pedro is ... a heck of a lot sexier. Masked by this unusual story is a very unusual gardening technique that has recently become very important to the future of sustainable home building. Another character, Antonio, confesses his discovery of Don Pedro's disguise by recalling "walking in a thick pleached alley" in his orchard when he overheard the two discussing the plot. Who would've guessed that pleaching, the braiding of tree limbs, is making a comeback 450 years after it was used by our favorite literary son to describe a hedge in an absurd love story? To better understand why freedictionary.com updated daily refers to this arborscape act as an unusually important form of gardening, we'll unravel the mystery of how pleaching has made its way across centuries, then we'll examine how researchers are reinvigorating the art of tree weaving, so that we can finally posit the future implications of this forgotten, but important, sustainable method of gardening.

Well, to better understand how pleaching works, we need to explain it, then see how it's been used across the ages. According to *The GardenWeb Glossary of Botanical Terms last accessed October 26, 2004,* pleaching is a process whereby branches of woody plants are interwoven and plaited together to form an impassible hedge or very thick arbor. The process of pleaching involves three main steps. *The Rain Forest Centre Good Wood Guide of 2004* explains, "pleaching of inosculate trees (that is, trees that naturally grow together) [are] planted on a grid, like a small orchard. As they [grow], branches [are] pruned and trained along this grid, so that eventually the branch of one tree [meets] that of its neighbor. At that point, an incision [is] made in the bark of both branches and they [are] tied together, like blood brothers or sisters. The analogy is deserved in that not only [do] these branches grow together to form one member, but their support activities [such as water and minerals intake] merge, thereby joining the life processes of neighboring trees."

This rigorous artform has a long, celebrated history. T*he Daily News of October 8, 2004* explains that during Roman times pleaching was used to create living lattices, archways and screens. In mediaeval Europe, pleached trees were grown in fenlands and flood plains as living foundations for houses. The fused branches 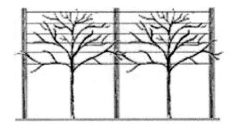 of a grid of planted trees provided support for floor bearers, several meters above ground and, theoretically, flood level. In the 16th and 17th centuries, the Dutch renewed an interest in the art form by pleaching hedges and arches around their cathedrals and government buildings. Pleached structures actually took on a survival quality as well. *Knight Ridder of December 28, 2003* explains, "In the medieval era, pleached orchards were supposedly planted in low-lying areas of Europe. When they flooded residents could put down wooden planks on top of the trees and built huts there to escape rising water." We should note, as well, that pleaching became an indicator of wealth since only those who could afford gardeners and plant weaving artists would employ it in their gardens and homes. And the strength of this art form can still be seen today as many of those living structures woven together centuries ago are still intact!

Considering the purposes and benefits of pleaching there has been a growing expansion of it in homes today. *Jerry Godspeed, a Utah State University Extension horticulturist explains (in a 2004 interview),* that pleaching can be an enjoyable activity that adds a little personality to the landscape. For instance, *Horticulture Magazine of May 1993* features craftsman Thomas Christopher discovering, for the first time, "a way to let nature be the builder." And Margaret Parker, an artist, gardener, and store owner recently contacted University of Michigan's Matthaei Botanical Gardens who helped Parker pull, push and tie young trees into aesthetic shapes to improve the look and environmental impact of her business.

But although pleaching has been deployed for decorative endeavors for several decades, its original purpose for living structures has been revived. *Mark Primack, writer for the Rainforest Information Centre of 2004* explains, the important structural focus of pleaching is being re-realized. Taking a cue from the gardeners of yesteryear, enter the Fab Tree Hab. *MIT professors of Human Ecology Design doctors Mitchell Joachim, Lara Greden, and Javier Arbona* have decided to start using an environmentally friendly housing idea they call Fab Tree Hab. Fab Tree Hab started about three years ago as a concept intended to replace the outdated design solutions of Habitat for Humanity International. The goal was to propose a method to grow homes from native seeds to enable local dwellings to be a part of an absolutely green community. During a personal phone interview of October 29th, 2004, Fab Tree Hab founder Mitchell Joachim explains, "Everyone uses the idea of green living but no one has any idea how it really ecologically fits into the environment itself. … Fab Tree Hab [has] decided to … essentially give back to the environment by using the idea of pleaching to form environmental housing."

"Fab Tree Hab by Terreform 1"

Stressing arborial farming in its process, the Fab Tree Hab embodies what it means to think and build ecologically. Tree trunks from the load-bearing structure are woven together with pleached, branch  'studs' to support a thermal clay and straw-based infill. The Fab Tree Hab plan accommodates three bedrooms, a bathroom, and an open living, dining and kitchen area placed on the southern façade in accordance with passive solar principles. The trunks of self-grafting trees, such as Elm, Live Oak, and Dogwood, are the load-bearing structure, and the branches form a continuous lattice frame for the walls and roof. Weaved along the exterior is a dense protective layer of vines, interspersed with soil pockets and growing plants. On the interior, a clay and straw composite insulates and blocks moisture, and a final layer of smooth clay is applied like a plaster to dually provide comfort and aesthetics.

Well, since the Fab Tree Hab process takes about 20 years of growing to complete ... we should examine the future implications of using pleaching in home structures. And while we should consider the disadvantages of time-to-move-in and increased insect control, it's clear that the positive potential of pleaching arrives in the form of environmental fitness, ecological discussion, and cost. First, in congruence with ecology as the guiding principal, pleached structures can be nearly entirely edible so as to provide food for organisms at each stage of their lives. While inhabited, pleached homes' gardens and exterior walls can produce food for people and animals. Secondly though, in departing from the modern sense of home construction, compilation of pleached homes opens the debate surrounding environmental cost decisions and green architecture. The New Ecological Home of 2004 explains that sustainable U.S. homes number in the tens of thousands due to more discussion of the importance of sustainability. And The Atlanta Journal and Constitution of February 20th 2004 acknowledges that energy efficiency makes us aware of compound savings over time, as well as both the future of national energy production and improved personal dwelling sustainability. The source goes on to explain that green homes like the Fab Tree Hab will be in increasing demand in the coming years as consumers seek more recycled materials and healthier, organic structures in which to live.

Mitchell Joachim explains that pleaching "is essentially chang[ing] our living culture and develop[ing] new living standards" as we employ it more and more as a construction method. Considering its history, current applications, and future implications, it's clear that unlike Shakespeare's passing references to folded limbs in the middle of a muddled romance, pleaching technology is truly finding its way into the way we will live our lives. Truly, it's growing on us!

* Note – So as we can see and to make it short and sweet, repeat and clarify the definition so it simplifies and elucidates to the audience what the foundation of the presentation is about.

(9) **Don't Intimidate:** Given the fact that the goal is to inform or explain an entity to the audience, the last thing you want is for the audience to get tripped up between one point and another. To help keep the audience clear on where you

are in the speech and properly distinguish between one point and another, use signposts such as *first, second, third,* and *finally* to help your audience see the paths amidst the forest of new information you are providing them.

Audience focus is partly a byproduct of making your speech logical and easy to follow. In many ways, signposts are like paragraphs. Have you ever looked at a document without paragraphs? How quickly did it take you to put it down and stop reading? Intimidating, isn't it? It reads and looks like one big blob! The same is true for speeches. That is, you want the audience focusing on your content, not getting lost. Audiences that get lost give up. They disconnect from the speaker and this affects your ethos. Also, when the audience gives up it means that all of your hard work is misused. Clarity is your best friend when trying to ask something of your audience: their attention, their understanding, and yes, even a change in the way they think or act. *In this sample student speech, locate the frequent use of signposts as a way of keeping the audience focused and preventing them from getting lost.*

What has no beginning, middle, or end, and touches every continent? Well the answer to the child's riddle is … The ocean! But, there's a new body of water that isn't touching anything but the curiosity of scientists and textbook writers across the world. The Hutchinson Encyclopedia stated on September 22, 2003 that there's a new region of water linking the Pacific, Atlantic, and Indian Oceans with the largest oceanic current. Wow! I had no idea that another ocean even existed! That's when I decided it was time I contact the International Hydrographic Organization and ask, "What's up with that?" Fortunately, Michel Huet, I.H.O. Representative, responded in an email on August 20, 2005. He told me that the Southern Ocean was unofficially declared in 1929, but they didn't think there was any political significance in sectioning off the region … until about the year 2000. Well … since our texts include, literally, no history for the sudden existence of a new ocean, we should first, explore the history of the Southern Ocean; next examine the relationship it has with the environment, and finally realize that naming the Southern Ocean significantly effects the rest of the world.

In order to understand the history of the Southern Ocean, we must first examine the importance of massive bodies of water, before next, analyzing why the specific region known as the Southern Ocean is

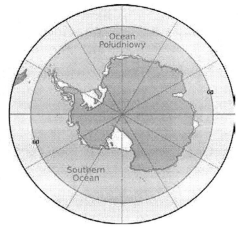

important, so we can finally understand why it was officially declared and is sometimes referred to as the world's 5th ocean.

But first, **the U.N. Atlas of the Ocean, accessed September 20th, 2005, clarifies** the significance of our oceans when they state that our future "and the future of the World Oceans are tightly connected. In fact, the oceans are the cradle of life on our planet." Aside from providing valuable resources for consumption, jobs to stimulate the economy, and awesome places to vacation and party it up, the most significant relationship the ocean has is with the atmosphere. The 6th Edition of the Columbia Encyclopedia, yes ... an encyclopedia, published June 7, 2005 explains that "The oceans act upon the atmosphere – in ways not clearly understood – to influence and modify the world's climate and weather system. The atmosphere receives nearly half of its energy supply for circulation from condensation of evaporated ocean water."

Oceans are important, but the Australian Academy of Science published an article in February of 1998 reporting that the Southern Ocean is the most important ocean for two reasons. It is home to the Antarctic Circumpolar Current, the most important ocean thermal current in the world, and it's the only ocean not blocked by land masses.

The Southern Ocean is quite distinct from the other oceans, thus it was no surprise when The CIA World Factbook Online, last updated July 28, 2005, reported that in the spring of 2000, the International Hydrographic Organization declared a 5th Ocean. Previously cited International Hydrographic Organization Representative, Michel Huet, would be helpful here to tell us why the Southern Ocean was declared, but he regretfully stated, "I have no definite source or background for the information you requested." Oh ... I get it ... I guess "Why do we have a fifth ocean?" really is a hard question to answer.

But now that we have established that the Southern Ocean is an official body of water, it's time to examine how it interacts with the environment. First, the temperature of the ocean is affecting the world's atmosphere. Second, animal life in the ocean is quickly diminishing. First, Ascribe Higher Education News reported on February 14, 2002 that the Southern Ocean is warming faster than the rest of the other oceans, and the temperature of the ocean significantly affects the carbon dioxide levels in the atmosphere. According to the Seattle Times on July 16, 2004 almost half of the carbon dioxide produced in the world ends up in the ocean. Dr. Taro Takahashi, Professor of Earth and Environmental Studies at Columbia University states in the previously cited article, that the bottom line is … warmer oceans won't absorb as much carbon dioxide.

Second, though, marine life there has become endangered due to the new interest in the Southern Ocean. The Kyodo World News Service on May 10, 2005 explains that commercial interest has peaked over stores of Patagonian Tooth Fish, a delicacy often sold as Chilean Sea Bass, causing the species to become scarce. Likewise, seagull populations in the Southern Ocean have also declined as they are often killed fishing for the Tooth Fish.

"Animals of the Southern Ocean – Wild South America"

Of course, there are dozens more issues concerning the Southern Ocean. However, the very existence of this body of water significantly impacts international policy, how we understand the environment, education, and even our symbolic life. First, the International Law Update reported on July 1, 2005 that the Japanese government has actively pursued permission to explore the Southern Ocean in order to obtain more whale meat, a cultural delicacy. As a result, the U.S. Department of State released a statement on June 24, 2005 reporting that the International Whaling Commission is now denying Japan's jaunts into the Southern Ocean to honor the 1986 ban on commercial whaling, in one of the prime whale environments in the world.

Second, the Southern Ocean is affected by serious environmental issues, Professor Sarah Gille of the Scripps Institute stated in a press release on February 12, 2002 that the Southern Ocean is currently acting as an image of what could happen to the other oceans around

the world. And given that the Southern Ocean is currently less able to act as a carbon sink, this trend extrapolated to other, untested oceans means that more carbon dioxide will remain in the atmosphere effecting the gas cycles of our world.

Third, educationally, the creation of the Southern Ocean will impact maps, textbooks, globes, and every other resource used in map studying classes everywhere! Even the Columbia Encyclopedias I cited earlier didn't get it right in its press release of June 7th of 2005. It states, "The Antarctic Ocean, also called the Southern Ocean, is sometimes considered a 5th separate ocean." Hello? Did they miss the memo from the official ocean declaring people? It exists. We have 5 now. Deal with it.

But joking aside, these publications AND the Daily Herald of September 29, 2004 shows us that there are significant rhetorical implications as a result of separating what scientists see as a singular body of water. The fact is all oceans are connected, technically making it one large body of water. The Daily Herald provides further explanation that the separation of this body of water is due to competing claims over fishing and resource rights, increasing ocean pollution, and international disputes over territory boundaries. As a symbolic construct, the Southern Ocean has become a territory for dispute, property to be fought over, and a bordered region with political interests. Hence, the implications of this simple act of naming will only be revealed incrementally and with much conversation, negotiation & litigation over the coming years.

Today, we've introduced ... the 5th Ocean, its significant relationship with the environment, and its policy & rhetorical implications. It may not have seemed like a big deal to explore a body of water that has always existed. But given that the National Science board reported in 2002 that only 15% of Americans know anything about scientific issues, it's pretty important we get this oceanic understanding right the first time. Especially since the 5th ocean was created out of thin air ... and already existing salt water.

Conclusion

In this chapter, we've discussed the different types of informative speeches and the special challenges speakers face when trying to impart information, outside sources, and evidence to audiences. Information and facts do not speak for themselves nor do they "naturally" fit within any speech topic. The job of a speech writer and/or presenter is to translate topic-related information and evidence so audiences can properly understand, comprehend, and follow your line of thinking throughout the totality of the informative speech. Enlightening and memorable informational speeches don't happen by accident. Rather, they are the byproduct of a speaker's careful forethought, effort, and diligence. For additional information on informative presentations, please review the following link: http://www.teachertube.com/video/informative-presentation-308773m.

References

Morgan, M. (2007). Presentational speaking: Theory and practice. New York: McGraw Hill.

Suggested Websites

http://www.princetontutoring.com/blog/2011/04/how-to-improve-your-long-term-memory/
   (Wong, 2014)
http://www.campaign-for-learning.org.uk/cfl/yourlearning/why_is_learning_important.asp
   (1998)

Chapter 10
The Persuasive Speech

"To be persuasive, we must be believable; to be believable we must be credible, to be credible we must be truthful".
— Edward R. Murrow

Persuasion. When we see or hear the word, it appears simple to define, right? We perceive it to be a 'thing' we do to others in order to get a need met. But, let's consider a more scholastic perception, as the communication field defines persuasion, from various perspectives.

Persuasion, according to communication scholars, is:

* a communication process in which the communicator seeks to elicit a desired response from his receiver:
* a conscious attempt by one individual to change the attitudes, beliefs, or behavior of another individual or group of individuals through transmission of some message:
* a symbolic activity whose purpose is to effect the internalization or voluntary acceptance of new cognitive states or patterns of overt behavior through the exchange of messages:
* a successful intentional effort at influencing another's mental state through communication in a circumstance in which the persuadee has some measure of freedom.

Combining these definitions, we have:

"Persuasion is a symbolic process in which communicators try to convince other people to change their attitudes or behavior regarding an issue through the transmission of la message, in an atmosphere of free choice" (Perloof, 20013).

Considering the above clarification, let's begin with a speech example below.

Two months before his death from bone cancer, college basketball coach and ESPN announcer Jim Valvano accepted the Arthur Ashe Courage and Humanitarian Award at the inaugural 1993 ESPY awards. During his acceptance speech, he introduced the "V" foundation, an organization he created to find a cure for cancer, and sought something else from the audience:

I just got one last thing, I urge all of you, all of you, to enjoy your life, the precious moments you have. To spend each day with some laughter and some thought, to get your emotions going. To be enthusiastic every day and [as] Ralph Waldo Emerson said, 'Nothing great could be accomplished without enthusiasm' – to keep your dreams alive in spite of problems whatever you have. The ability to be able to work hard for your dreams to come true, to become a reality.

Now, I look at where I am now and I know what I wanna to do. What I would like to be able to do is to spend whatever time I have left and to give, and maybe some hope to others. Alright, Arthur Ashe Foundation is a wonderful thing, and AIDS, the amount of money pouring in for AIDS is not enough, but it is significant. But if I told you it's ten times the amount that goes in for cancer research. I'll also tell you that five hundred thousand people will die this year of cancer. And I'll also tell you that one in every four will be afflicted with this disease, and yet, somehow, we seem to have put it in a little bit of the background. I want to bring it back on the front table. We need your help. I need your help. We need money for research. It may not save my life. It may save my children's lives. It may save someone you love. And it's very important.

"Jimmy's 1993 ESPY Speech"

Coach Valvano not only sought money for a worthy cause, but he also recognized the competition for scarce resources. Renowned social psychologist, Robert Cialdini, discusses as one of the six weapons of influence, that there is high persuasive value when one presents something as scarce. By human nature, the less available something is, the more we desire it (Kenrick, 2016). Understanding this influence, Valcano also sought to make his case that cancer research deserved more attention and more financial involvement. This is one of the defining characteristics of persuasion: persuaders help audiences attend to problems or harms associated with the way things currently exist.

"Robert Cialdini – The 6 Principles of Influence"

In the summer of 2009 at Cairo University, President Obama gave a speech regarding women's rights. In one section of his speech, he says:

The sixth issue – The sixth issue that I want to address is women's rights.

I know – I know – and you can tell from this audience, that there is a healthy debate about this issue. I reject the view of some in the West that a woman who chooses to cover her hair is somehow less equal, but I do believe that a woman who is denied an education is denied equality. And it is no coincidence that countries where women are well educated are far more likely to be prosperous. Now, let me be clear: Issues of women's equality are by no means simply an issue for Islam. In Turkey, Pakistan, Bangladesh, Indonesia, we've seen Muslim-majority countries elect a woman to lead. Meanwhile, the struggle for women's equality continues in many aspects of American life, and in countries around the world.

I am convinced that our daughters can contribute just as much to society as our sons. Our common prosperity will be advanced by allowing all humanity – men and women – to reach their full potential. I do not believe that women must make the same choices as men in order to be equal, and I respect those women who choose to live their lives in traditional roles. But it should be their choice. And that is why the United States will partner with any Muslim-majority country to support expanded literacy for girls, and to help young women pursue employment through micro-financing that helps people live their dreams.

"President Obama Speech in Cairo"

President Obama's speech also demonstrates another significant aspect of persuasion: strategic language choice and problem solving. In his speech, Obama characterizes women – often devalued as less than men – as sharing with men a common humanity deserving the rights of literacy and prosperity. Additionally, he offers American support to nations who choose to partnership in expanding educational and employment opportunities for women. Vella would assert that this form of persuasion arises from not only the strategic use of communication, but also the ability to present diplomatic persuasion. "…Diplomacy, being the art of communication, necessitates a thorough knowledge of human psychology, body language and a wide knowledge of the process of human thinking" (2013). Obama is identifying and connecting the need for human equality through persuasive modalities.

In 1950, at the height of the communist red scare that gripped our national politics, Senator Margaret Chase Smith urged the executive and legislative branches and both major political parties to come to terms for the sake of the American Character. Here is a section of her public statement:

> As a United States Senator, I am not proud of the way in which the Senate has been made a publicity platform for irresponsible sensationalism. I am not proud of the reckless abandon in which unproved charges have been hurled from the side of the aisle. I am not proud of the obviously staged, undignified countercharges that have been attempted in retaliation from the other side of the aisle.

> I don't like the way the Senate has been made a rendezvous for vilification, for selfish political gain at the sacrifice of individual reputations and national unity. I am not proud of the way we smear outsiders from the Floor of the Senate and hide behind the cloak of congressional immunity and still place ourselves beyond criticism on the Floor of the Senate.

> As an American, I am shocked at the way Republicans and Democrats alike are playing directly into the Communist design of "confuse, divide, and conquer." As an American, I don't want a Democratic Administration "whitewash" or "cover-up" any more than a want a Republican smear or witch hunt.

> As an American, I condemn a Republican "Fascist" just as much I condemn a Democratic "Communist." I condemn a Democrat "Fascist" just as much as I condemn a Republican "Communist." They are equally dangerous to you and me and to our country. As an American, I want to see our nation recapture the strength and unity it once had when we fought the enemy instead of ourselves.

Note Senator Smith's call to action to end the bickering, villain-making, and cowardice that consumed the political arena of her era. Clearly she indicated disappointment with behavior in the Senate and sought to reveal the problem of political division while calling for a solution of political unity.

Moreover, Senator Smith's speech highlights the third distinguishing characteristic of persuasion: a call to change behavior. Persuasion, and persuasive speaking in particular, is so difficult to accomplish because the speaker is not only asking for audiences to change their minds but also for a change in audience behavior. Impossible, you say? No doubt this task is difficult, but all the more reason for persuaders and persuasive speakers to be aware and take advantage of strategies of persuasion.

The remainder of this chapter explores the many tactical tools available to persuaders attempting to change audiences' beliefs and values and behavior, including strategic language use, attitude assessment, identification, and problem-solving.

Language Use and Framing

Nick Lund explains in his 2003 text, *Language and Thought*, that there are various ways to think about the relationship between language and the mind: Language constructs thought (commonly referred to as the Sapir Whorf Hypothesis), thought influences language (Piaget's research) and language and thought are somehow interdependent (according to Vygotsky). Though each of these theories has provoked some level of disputation, it is commonly held that language-use assessment is incredibly important in terms of conveying clear messages and attempting to persuade audiences. Translation: language – or the strategic use of language – is an essential tool for persuaders to master. Kurland states, "Just as authors must choose what to say, they must also choose how to say it" (2000). A more true statement could not be found in relation to presenters as well. You are tasked with this mastery for the most effective persuasion.

Language Use and Audience Appropriateness

Effective persuaders know that language use must be adjusted to account for who is in the audience. We have spoken to this earlier when we discussed audience analysis. More specifically, public speakers must stay attentive to what language is selected given the particular demographic and psychological makeup of the audience. Clearly, language found within the demographic social networks of your audience will make more sense to these particular groups than language that is specific to other social groups. This is to say that social groups tend to use their own vocabularies. From a communication perspective, we refer to this as convergent language – language that is specific within a group or context because the word/s emerge as a common understanding within that circle.

A rather radical example would be the use of the popular culture term "dude" in an Amish community. Given the surfing culture roots and the heavily mediated use of this term over the past thirty years, "dude" would find little traction if used in an Amish community because the Amish culture is insular, relies on little to no media technology, and is not often found adjacent to beaches.

George Lakoff and Mark Johnson explain in their well-known book, *Metaphors We Live By* (1980), that language and thought are wrought with metaphoric usage. Given that metaphors orient us to the world, shape our world and, perhaps, even compose our world, we must take particular care to use language wisely. Mary Midgley (2003) provides us a good example:

"...machine imagery, which began to pervade our thought in the seventeenth century, is still potent today. We still often tend to see ourselves, and the living things around us, as pieces of clockwork: items of a kind that we ourselves could make, and might decide to remake if it suits us better. Hence the confident language of 'genetic engineering' and 'the building-blocks of life'." (p. 1)

This particular imagery has provided both a general vocabulary for explaining systems (ex: assembly lines, workflows, internal structures) as well demonstrated cause and effect between interconnected activities in the world. In essence, language provides the conceptual framework for what we know and, likewise, how we know.

In the example provided above, machine metaphor usage guides description and prescribes our behavior in relation to other external factors (what is happening beyond my day-to-day life?) and internal factors (why am I so stressed and why does my anxiety affect my work?). We think in terms of cause and effect within a machine-like system precisely because we have been oriented to this framework for most of our lives. Hence, using machine language is very much speaking our language. In fact, think about the last time you referred the "the grind" of getting up and getting going to work every day. How about being "plugged into" a group? This very mundane language characterizes the act of doing what comes naturally in our everyday world to the friction between the gears in a machine.

In terms of specific language use, consider this excerpt from President Dwight D. Eisenhower's 1961 farewell speech where he used action language to evoke an emotional, patriotic response to get the U.S. audience involved in national affairs:

Throughout America's adventure in free government, our basic purposes have been to keep the peace, to foster progress in human achievement, and to enhance liberty, dignity, and integrity among peoples and among nations. To strive for less would be unworthy of a free and religious people. Any failure traceable to arrogance, or our lack of comprehension, or readiness to sacrifice would inflict upon us grievous hurt, both at home and abroad.

"Eisenhower – Farewell Speech 1961 Part 1"
"Eisenhower – Farewell Speech 1961 Part 2"

It is clear with the use of "keep" and "foster" in addition to "enhance" and "strive" that Ike was clarifying the active involvement of citizens in the processes of our national mission.

Now, consider the following poor word choice by Mitt Romney in 2012 when he was giving a speech: http://www.huffingtonpost.com/chris-weigant/romneys-very-poor-choice_b_1258556.html.

Knowing and understanding audience cultural reference points, dialect, language choice, and audience expectations is imperative when using language as a tool for persuasion. Although each speech is very different in content, what is variant between President Eisenhower's speech and Mitt Romney's speech is the careful consideration of language – given in the former speech and the apparent lack of consideration in the latter.

While President Eisenhower was speaking mostly to a middle-class demographic capable of owning a radio or television in the early 1960's, Mitt Romney was politicking for support in a live CNN interview. While the President needed to identify himself as a leader of a nation, Mitt Romney needed to present himself and the Democratic party as supporters of the American people, not excluding concerns for factions within the potential supporters.

An effective persuader understands his/her audience while an ineffective and unpersuasive speaker refuses to adjust his/her language to the specific speaking situation.

Traditional Persuasion Theory

Strategic language use, however, is not the only mode of influencing audiences. In fact, there is a lengthy history of studying the many ways through which human communication persuades individuals or audiences to change minds or behaviors.

Attitude Change

In their 1996 text *Attitudes and Persuasion*, Richard E. Petty and John T. Cacciopo provide guidance as to the manner through which attitudes are created and then changed via the process of influence. In terms of social influence, they explain that a person's attitudes can be changed when that person *centrally processes information*, arguments, or concepts that he or she happens to think about often. For instance, speaking on the need to increase parking spaces for students at the local university will be more persuasive in nature if presented to the students at that college versus the hopes of persuading those in your bible study class who have never attended the university. In short, we are more likely to be persuaded by information, and truly 'think' about it if it is relevant to who we are.

Peripheral cues, such as speaker attractiveness or fluid speaking ability, are also persuasive in the sense that we may be moved to action by elements which have little, if anything to do with the "content" of a speech or persuasive attempt. In the middle of a city council discussion of tax-raising, for instance, a smooth delivery may well be more influential than an angry tirade and a tall speaker may be more persuasive than his shorter counterpart. Personal cognitions that we may not fully be aware of oftentimes provide foundation for how we process information. In so doing, these information bundles help us organize and direct our thoughts about the world.

"Commercials with Peripheral Persuasion"

In sum, our frames of reality, or what I refer to as our frame of reference, is what counts as real, good, necessary, right and therefore guides our behavior. Recognize that our experiences and how we have interpreted those experiences creates such a frame. However, it is equally important to understand that your frame of reference is variant from the person sitting next to you. What each of you has experienced is unique not only to the context, but the individual responses to the event. As such, each person's frame of reality and/or reference is their 'truth'. This is important to grasp as audience members often seek some consonance or agreement between their own cognitions (i.e. attitudes) and the ideas or behaviors advocated by speakers.

In general, persuasive speakers should consider that traditional social scientifically researched persuasion theory has studied myriad modes of communicating change, and some important theories relevant to aspiring persuasive speakers include some of the following rules of thumb:

- Audience members will judge your messages (i.e. speeches) in relation to their previously held attitudes or what they already know or believe. The lesson: The closer your message is to the previously held attitudes, the more likely it will be received positively. No, we aren't advocating you cater to the beliefs and attitudes the audience already holds. However, we advocate that when you advocate for change in your speech you do so by building on or at least acknowledging what the audience already holds to be true. Want to persuade a class to wash their hands more often? Ask them to stop by the restrooms just down the hall only one additional time each day. Be realistic in what you can accomplish as a speaker in a matter of minutes. Think degrees of change rather than radical change. I often tell my students that even moving someone 1% can be considered persuasion. Ask yourself, "Can I plant a seed?" "Ask them to do a small action step towards the larger intent?" Such options are still forms of persuasion.

- People like the status quo. Who likes to change? Change means – well – change. Change is uncomfortable. Change is new. Change is unfamiliar. Change requires effort. To keep ourselves from having to change, we attempt to maintain some consistency between previously held attitudes and behaviors and currently held attitudes and behaviors. When a speaker advocates change to an audience, and that change doesn't match up with deeply held attitudes, the chance that the audience's attitude will be changed depends upon the reward received. If you don't clearly articulate the benefit of the change, that is, how the audience's lives will improve after they make the proposed change, then you have little to no chance of achieving a change in behavior. Consider the difference between saying, "Going to the gym benefits you" versus, "Going to the gym has shown to benefit your longevity of life and increase your overall self-esteem".

- Audiences will only experience shifts in personal attitudes when they try to make sense of the causes of certain actions taken both by themselves and others. "Well, I don't normally wash my hands after class. However, everyone else did it today…and H1N1 is running rampant. Well, I guess I should be doing that regularly." This triggered intrapersonal meaning-making influences how people respond to self and others.

According to Robert B. Cialdini (2008), communicators can follow six simple rules to gain compliance.

- *Reciprocation* – People tend to return favors – if you give someone a quarter to buy a Coke, eventually they will return the favor not simply with a quarter, but with a Coke itself. Speakers, think of your speech, or more specifically, helpful information and evidence the audience may not be familiar with, as a type of gift. Drawing attention to a danger or possible danger will be appreciated by audiences, and if you are adept at highlighting how your proposed change will make their lives better, the audience is more likely to return the favor with change – and then some.

- *Commitment and Consistency* – If people agree to make a commitment toward a goal or idea, they are more likely to honor that commitment. For example, in 1987, social scientist Anthony Greenwald approached potential voters on election-day eve to ask whether they would vote and to provide reasons why or why not. 100% said they would vote. On Election Day, 86.7% of those asked went to the polls compared to 61.5% of those who were not asked. Those who publicly committed to voting on the previous day proved more likely to actually vote (Polansky, 2016). Moreover, if you can highlight inconsistencies in the audience's current behavior, the audience will be more likely to change behavior to remain consistent. Effective persuasive speakers can provide a solution that will allow the audience to regain consistency.

- *Social Proof* – People will do things that they see other people are doing. Provide statistics and evidence that illustrates how popular or unpopular a trend is. Show examples of people the audience respects also adopting the solution you are proposing. We all look to others to see how we should act. Help your audience change their behavior by giving them evidence of others who have made the change or have adopted the solution you advocate.

- *Authority* – People will tend to obey authority figures. When articulating the problem or harms in your speech, providing statistics and evidence from established and well-respected authorities will go far in adding social proof to your claim that indeed there is a problem that necessitates a change in attitude and behavior.

- *Liking* – People are easily persuaded by other people they like. Cialdini (2008) discovered that we are more likely to purchase more Tupperware from the hostess if we like her, versus purchasing the same offered product from someone we don't have the same liking toward. Remember the concept of ethos? Ethos is the audience perception of your character, trustworthiness and goodwill. As a speaker, you have the opportunity to increase your likeability by demonstrating that you understand your audience and their

particular concerns and challenges. In fact, you need to demonstrate that you understand why they haven't changed their behavior or attitudes thus far, as this reinforces to the audience that their frame of reality is valuable. Audiences like speakers that seem to understand their particular situation and challenges.

- *Scarcity* – Perceived scarcity will generate demand. As a speaker, you must create urgency for your topic. When time isn't "running out," we delay and don't act because why should we when it can wait until tomorrow? The greatest threat to your proposed change is the audience belief that the solution can wait, until later.

Let's say a speaker would like to persuade a group to stop going to coffee house "A" and start using a different place of business, coffee house "B". Knowing that she only has one speech to give to try to change the audience's minds, she can still employ Cialdini's rules. She may hand out "free coffee" passes for coffee house "B" before or after the speech. She may tell the audience that she won't relinquish the podium until they agree to give coffee house "B" a try. She may show a picture of a very long line outside of coffee house "B". She may play an audio clip of a local, leading business person endorsing the second shop. She may talk about a special that coffee house "B" is offering for just 12 more hours after the speech. Finally, she may have spent all morning prior to the speech touching base with the audience to generate more positive affiliation. All of these persuasive tactic parallel Cialdini's rules. Free passes attempt to induce reciprocity. Gaining a promise of action may induce commitment. The picture demonstrates social proof. The audio clip introduces authority. The special offers something scarce and my work to make the audience like me fits the liking rule.

Of course, many of these activities are not simply part of the speech proper but go well beyond the speech delivering process itself. Audience persuasion cannot often be reduced to a particular strategy but a context of identification created and fostered by the speaker to enhance overall compliance.

Identification

Nowhere is the emphasis on social context more strongly examined than in the writings and work of famed twentieth century critic Kenneth Burke. In its simplistic form, identification is the manner by which we symbolically affiliate ourselves with others. Identification occurs because of our constant and overwhelming desire to become a part of a "we" that motivates us to speak, act, or imitate the behaviors of the individual or group we are seeking to become incorporated into.

Identification is similar to persuasion in that the end result is conversion. However, persuasion involves explicit strategies speakers use upon audiences whereas identification induces self-persuasion so the audience wants to be a part of something the speaker is advocating and thus persuades him/herself internally. In his 2002 State of the Union Address, George W. Bush utilizes a clear example of identification:

> The Iraqi regime has plotted to develop anthrax, and nerve gas, and nuclear weapons for over a decade. This is a regime that has already used poison gas to murder thousands of its own citizens – leaving the bodies of mothers huddled over their dead children. This is a regime that agreed to international inspections – then kicked out the inspectors. This is a regime that has something to hide from the civilized world.

> States like these, and their terrorist allies, constitute an axis of evil, arming to threaten the peace of the world. By seeking weapons of mass destruction, these regimes pose a grave and growing danger. They could provide these arms to terrorists, giving them the means to match their hatred. They could attack our allies or attempt to blackmail the United States. In any of these cases, the price of indifference would be catastrophic.

> We will work closely with our coalition to deny terrorists and their state sponsors the materials, technology, and expertise to make and deliver weapons of mass destruction. We will develop and deploy effective missile defenses to protect America and our allies from sudden attack. And all nations should know: America will do what is necessary to ensure our nation's security.

It is evident within this section of Bush's speech that the axis is neither allied to the U.S. nor militarily impotent. In fact, the language the President used to frame this group – as evil – clearly casts a negative evaluation upon them. Of course, the 9/11 commission later found fault with some of the claims against Iraq, but the we/they characterization coupled with the characterization of evil made the president and the state department's case to go to war much easier in terms of public support.

"2002 State of the Union – President George W. Bush"

In addition, consider this celebration speech provided by Larry Rayfield Wright from August of 2006 upon being enshrined in the National Football League's Hall of Fame:

> Now, offensive linemen are taught to protect the quarterback the same way that the secret service protects our nation [sic] President. In this case, Roger Staubach was our president. And the Director of the Secret Service was our offensive line Coach Jim Myers. He built an offensive line that was unmatched. And today I cannot accept this honor without bringing Coach Myers and his offensive line into the Hall with me. That line consists of John Fitzgerald, and Tony Liscio, and Dave Manders, and Ralph Neely, John Niland and Blaine Nye.
>
> Gentlemen, I'm proud to call myself your teammates, and I share this enshrinement with you.
>
> And to our defense, you were the "Doomsday." And I'm thankful that I only had to face you guys in practice. I remember Coach Landry once telling me that, Rayfield, no matter how many awards or accolades you receive, that you will be never greater than the team. The Dallas Cowboys was a team, and what a team the Cowboys had during the dynamic decade of the '70s ... But we played together as a team in 12 playoff games and five Super Bowls. Guys, you know who you are. I know who you are. The Cowboy fans around the country know who you are. I always remember that we were winners, and I treasure those moments and memories.

(Audio of Rayfield Wright's Speech)

While Mr. Wright is speaking historically about the great Dallas football team of the 1970's, he uses the language of team both to clarify the fact that his Hall of Fame enshrinement is a product of the whole Cowboys team, as well as the fact that he was part of the an offense set over against a great defense with great coaching at the helm. Thus, Mr. Wright is still being a good member of the Cowboys team as he recognizes that, despite his individual award, his accomplishments are byproducts of a "we" greater than himself.

Finally, let's examine a student persuasive speech text where language is used as a way to induce self-persuasion in the audience.

According to the July 24, 2006 edition of the Ottawa Citizen, computers nowadays generally go obsolete after only two years of use. Every year more and more tonnage of obsolete technology gets sent to less developed nations like India, China, and Africa. And why not? For US retailers and manufacturers it is justified by the powerful trinity; cheap, easy and effective. Yet, much like sweeping dust under the rug, exporting electronic waste, or e-waste, to other countries is solving one problem, at the cost of creating many more. When e-waste is shipped to these countries monumental health and environmental problems abound. The February 10, 2006 edition of the University Wire reports that the central nervous system is what's at risk the most since extreme exposure to e-waste toxins like lead, mercury, and cadmium cause intestinal cramps, birth defects, and irreversible brain damage. Given the impact to millions of poor who live in or close to the dumps where e-waste is reposited and/or reprocessed AND given that children are the most effected physically, mentally and emotionally, we must put an end to e-waste abuse. To do so, we will surf the world wide web overseas and see how horrible e-waste is. Then we'll upgrade our intel to find out how this problem was created, before we crash the system with solutions to help us stem the e-waste problem.

When we hear the term e-waste is probably sounds like something out of a Star Trek episode, but in fact it is very real. Every time a piece of technology is thrown out it has to go somewhere. For most of the world's technology, that place is Guiyu, China. According to the April 9, 2006 Seattle Times, there are 21 villages with 5,500 family workshops handling e-waste in Guiyu. All in all the city's businesses use over 60,000 workers to process 1.5 million tons of e-waste a year, pulling in $75 million dollars in revenue. Obviously massive amounts of money are made from this, but how? The May 17, 2006 edition of the New York Times tells the story of a woman named Renee St. Denis, a worker for Hewlett-Packard, who revealed that there are several precious minerals which are combined into ores that are used for computers. Per ton of ore, there are more minerals to be extracted than there are in most industrial mines. There are about 8 to 10 ounces of Gold, Silver, and Palladium in every ton of ore, compared to the 6 ounces that are collected in most mines.

This almost seems too good to be true for most companies. Not only do they not have to spend money on recycling their product, but they are allowing people to have a job, which will keep them paid, happy, and quiet. Unfortunately for these manufacturers, there is a catch. The same jobs that create so much revenue for Guiyu and the recycling importers, also decimate the entire area. The previously cited New York Times article tells us that TV's and computers are dangerous when burned or dumped. The toxins in the products – like lead, mercury and cadmium – endanger health as well as air and water quality. On April 17, 2006 the Boston Globe reported that once these items are melted down, or bathed in lead, they release a stew of cancerous toxic waste. This toxic waste is then dumped into the local water supply where it harms the environment and creates massive health problems for the people living in Guiyu.

The previously cited Ottawa Citizen article revealed that the water in Guiyu is so contaminated that it is undrinkable for any animal. Is it any wonder, with all the lead baths and powdered computer parts being dumped into that water? Even without drinking the water, there are still

health issues that accrue. The Philadelphia Inquirer reported on April 8, 2006 that last year a study, performed by a Professor Huo Xia of the Medical Sciences College of Shantou University, discovered that out of 165 children from the Guiyu area, 136 or 82% of them had excessive levels of lead in their systems, a condition inhibiting neurological development.

With these working conditions and subsequent physical atrocities one can only wonder how and why we haven't already ended this nightmare? Well, the reasons are twofold: Legal ambiguity and ignorance. First … while the aforementioned profiteering is an incredible motivator, a legislative problem prohibits the U.S. from doing its part to end the e-waste abuse. The previously cited Boston Globe reports that on the international level confusing laws, corruption, and mismanagement allows the majority of e-waste to slip through customs. Meanwhile on the national level there is no legislative action being taken at all. This means that over a million tons of e-waste is shipped out of the U.S. annually and the federal government isn't doing anything helpful. Even when the government tries to take action they are unable to. The June 4, 2006 edition of the St. Louis Post-Dispatch reported that the E.P.A. couldn't draft a proposal on the issue, because the manufacturers and retailers couldn't agree on a proposal. Allow me to repeat that. The E.P.A., a *federal* agency, couldn't pass legislation, because *private* retailers and manufacturers couldn't agree on one. I pose a question to you: Aren't we a government for and by the people??

But governments and companies aren't the only reason that this problem is what it is today. The biggest reason for e-waste abuse is … U.S. public's ignorance of the issue. Everyone in the U.S.A. is partially responsible for this problem whenever they throw out an old computer instead of recycling it. Jim Puckett, the coordinator of the Basel Action Network, a Seattle-based group that advises consumers about sustainable methods to dispose of e-waste stated in an interview in April of 2006 that most people just don't know what to do with their old technology. They just throw it out since they don't know how bad things are and they don't know of any other way to dispose of their technology.

Fortunately, there is still hope. It is not too late to help stem the ever growing tide of e-waste on both a Federal level as well as a personal one. On an institutional level there is action occurring right now, which could help decrease the amount of e-waste being exported from the U.S. Currently the United States has entered into an international treaty called the Basel Treaty, which was created by the United Nations in 1992. The Basel Convention is designed to limit the amount of hazardous materials that are shipped between countries, and prevent the shipping of hazardous materials to less-developed countries. Unfortunately, the United States is one of the countries that has signed the Basel Convention, but not ratified it into law. Hence, we can take action. Write a letter to your congressperson to inform them that you support the Basel Convention and wish for it to be signed into law. For more information you can direct your browser to the Basel Convention's main website at www.basel.int. Ask our government to back up words with deeds.

Another way to help on a federal level is to show support for policies that senators are trying to pass in Congress. In the June 11, 2006 edition of the St. Louis Post-Dispatch is was reported that U.S. Senator Jim Talent supports the idea of using tax breaks for an incentive to recycle your old computer properly. Unfortunately Talent has had little support in Congress, but still wishes to add it to legislation later this year. Write a letter to your congressperson to show support for Senator Talent's idea or write a letter directly to Senator Talent himself, and show your support for an initiative like this.

Finally, on a personal level, all it takes is a little time and initiative to put an end to e-waste abuse. Simply get in touch with the manufacturer who made your old technology and ask about their recycling policy. Dell, for example, has made the biggest move yet by announcing in June of 2006 that it would start a new recycling policy to take back any of its products for recycling, even if you are buying a new computer from a different company. Apple and Hewlett-Packard also have recycling programs available and all three companies have made pledges only to disassemble their products here in the U.S. instead of shipping them overseas. These facilities are able to handle the materials since they have safer and better disassembly methods. Instead of ripping computers apart with children's' bare hands and contaminating local reservoirs, U.S. companies are able to spend their money and use modern tools and dispose of the materials with minimal risks.

Technology is the fastest growing industry today. Unfortunately technological waste is the fastest growing product in its arena as well. This neglect has created the huge e-waste problem that we have seen today. Thousands of people in a single city are slowly killing themselves and their environment. Not only does the U.S. make up a majority of the e-waste contribution, but it doesn't show any signs of slowing down in the near future. But, by following these easy steps we can all feel a little bit better knowing that we have done our part in helping the e-waste problem, become outdated.

This sample speech reveals three specific strategies of identification. First, consider carefully the language used in the speech preview: "…we will **surf** the world wide web overseas and see how horrible e-waste is. Then we'll **upgrade our intel** to find out how this problem was created, before we **crash the system** with solutions to help us stem the e-waste problem." This language also draws closely from the vocabulary of computer and net users as a kind of gimmick to help audience members remember the main points of the body. Surfing, upgrading and crashing are all conceptual and

technical terms familiar to contemporary technology users. Similarity of the terminology creates connection and potential liking.

Second, this particular speech tended to use affective language in the sense that e-waste is a "tide," "abusive," and a "problem." In fact the very name for electronic waste is shortened to "e-waste" in a way that makes the term more accessible, easier to remember, and more like the vocabulary of technology – "e-mail" or "e-commerce" anyone?

Finally, did you notice the "we" language at the end? "But, by following these easy steps we can all feel a little bit better knowing that we have done our part in helping the e-waste problem, become outdated." The call to action after solutions and moving into the conclusion clearly works to include audience members with the language of "our" and "we." Hence, this student clearly selected language to induce identification.

At minimum, then, the speaker manifests "we" language to affiliate both speaker and audience members into a membership in need of action, relies on affective language to draw attention to this important issue, amends language so that the named problem sounds as if it part of the technological culture, and then extracts a few pieces of jargon from the playbooks of technology speakers to punctuate the body of the speech. And given that the speaker indicates how ubiquitous technology use is for us here in the U.S., the speech indicts us all.

While identification doesn't guarantee persuasion, it does provide the right context and incentives for persuasion to occur. Thus, all speakers benefit from creating opportunities for audience identification.

Strategies of Creating Identification

(1) **Establish rapport with the audience**. When advocating change of any kind, drawing upon personal experience is an important step toward creating identification with the audience. For example, if you are asking the audience to join a local gym, the first question an audience will ask (or think) is whether you, the speaker, have joined a gym. If you haven't, why should the audience? And if you haven't, there goes your credibility! But, if you haven't but you acknowledge that, given the research you have gathered in the process of creating your speech, you recognize both the need to work out more and have  found the perfect gym in town for students to join, your credibility will soar as will the identification or bond you created with your audience. Acknowledge your own limitations, your own temptations, your own struggles, as it pertains to the subject matter at hand, as a way of acknowledging possible audience objections, but then clearly demonstrate how and why you were convinced to change.

(2) **Use language, references, dialect, and dress similar to that of your audience will elicit sympathy.** However, sympathy derived from delivery or physical appearance is short-lived. Additionally, it doesn't bode well for your credibility if you're seeking connection based upon this factor. What is just as important, however, is the identification you can create through the types of evidence you choose to use in your speech. Will your audience be most sympathetic to examples? To quotes from experts? Statistics? Stories? Lastly here, consider UCCS (2016) states about attire for a presentation. "Your message is always the

most important part of a public speech; however, everything else about your speech will affect how your audience perceives you & your message. Your voice, your gestures, your grammar, your movements, your mannerisms, your clothes, and your style all create the impression you leave on the audience & how much of your message they hear and subsequently, remember".

(3) **Use inclusive language rather than exclusive language.** Sounds simple enough and it is but too many speakers speak *at* their audiences rather than *with* audiences. Small language choices, such as "we" rather than "you" can go a long way to remind your audience that you are like them, but for the fact you have taken the time to research and construct a speech that will make their lives better. Also,  don't exclude members of your audience with slang such as "you guys" or "you girls" (these are considered ad hominems: a Latin word that asserts one is attacking a character rather than an argument). These slang distinctions may seem harmless but they create needless divisions within your audience. Finally, the second person "you" rhetorically implies a distinction between speaker and audience like that between a teacher (i.e. "you have to do this…", "if you want a good grade, avoid this…" and student. In our experience, speakers who have all the answers and only use the second person "you" when talking to audiences are less likely to achieve identification with audiences. However, speakers who are strategically different while acknowledging they are similar to the audience in many ways (i.e. "we"), are more likely to achieve identification with their audience.

(4) **Creating identification by antithesis, or creating similarity by rallying together against a common "enemy" serves to deflect attention from the differences between you and your audience and highlights the similarities you share.** Use with caution. We are not, repeat, we are not advocating speakers create enemies for the purpose of creating identification with your audience. However, a speaker can take advantage of identification by antithesis when talking about the problem that requires change. If done right, the problem can be constructed as a type of enemy, such as a physical or psychological enemy, that is felt by both audience and speaker alike. For example, students and speaker alike can rally against the all-too common student affliction called procrastination or the seemingly universal problem of finding a good job after graduation.

"Public Speaking Tip – Identifying Your Audience"

Structuring the Persuasive Speech

Traditionally, the persuasive speech has been structured so that the main points are much like a problem and solution structure where the problems you articulate naturally (or logically) lead to your solution. *Read the following two persuasive speech introductions and see if you note the problem-solution structure.*

"Persuasive Speaking Tips: Problem & Solution Persuasive Speech Styles"

Speech #1

In the fall of 1993, 18-year-old Jennifer Koon was carjacked in suburban Rochester, New York. She somehow managed to dial 911 from her cell phone, but the operator at the other end of the line couldn't hear anything but muffled voices. She kept the phone line open in hopes that Jennifer would answer, but no answer came. The car was found 2 hours later with Jennifer's body inside.

The FCC reported on September 22, 2005 that 30% of 911 calls, about 50 million calls annually, are placed by people using wireless phones, and that percentage is increasing every year. At the time of Jennifer's abduction, the technology to trace cell phone calls did not exist, and since she was unable to give any location, the electronic enhanced (or E911) operator couldn't have sent help. Sadly, the technology to trace cell phone calls does exist today. However, even though all of us cell phone users pay a monthly surcharge for E911 services, many local counties don't have the equipment necessary to locate callers. A good example of this is Greene County, where all of us are currently sitting! Because it is imperative that we all receive the emergency services we're paying for ... and the safety we deserve, we must first understand the consequences of missing e911 services, then we will examine the causes, so that we can finally enact some solutions to increase public and personal safety.

You can tell from simply reading the introduction that the main points of the body of the speech will articulate e911 problems, uncover causes, and, of course, provide solutions for the specific problems outlined in the speech. One more speech introduction example is provided to help demonstrate the structure.

Speech #2

85-year-old retired refinery worker, Lester Tomlinson, was dying of mesothelioma – an especially painful form of lung cancer. After making known his wish to receive all pain medications, Tomlinson entered a hospital with shortness of breath and intense chest pains … and never received consistent around-the-clock pain control. His family advocated his medication, but his physician and nurse practitioner continually ignored their calls despite chart notes that Tomlinson was "screaming in

pain" and "yelling at night". Two weeks later, the doctor made his first and only visit to Lester Tomlinson, noted that "the patient seems to be in pain," and ordered medication for "breakthrough" pain. Four excruciating days later, Lester Tomlinson died. While few of us will ever experience pain as extreme as Lester's most of us believe that when pain is unmanageable we can go to the doctor for help, right? According to an article in Nursing Magazine from August 2005, "Pain is the most common reason people seek medical care." But, it's one of the most under treated health care issues. And given that the August 2005 *New Yorker* explains that Americans spend … "almost two and half times the industrialized world's median expenditures on health" yet almost none of it for pain treatment that a majority of patients need, we must remedy this situation. To do so, we will first explore the problem of under treated pain, then we will diagnose this … misdiagnosis, before we, finally, prescribe a few steps to make the pain go away.

Once again, based only on a reading of the introduction, you can probably discern that the main points in the body of the speech will articulate problems regarding the treatment of pain, uncover causes, and, of course, provide solutions for the specific problems outlined in the speech.

The traditional structure of the problem/solution model makes sense for persuasion speeches because strategic speakers want to help audiences solve a problem by "nipping it in the bud" so to speak. The success of this model depends, in large part, on the ability of the speaker to convince audience members that a) there is a problem b) the problem is a relevant problem and c) it is a problem that warrants a solution that can actually reduce the problem.

Here is a complete example of a persuasive speech using the problem/cause/solution structure to induce action in the audience.

"When [Sister Barbara Pfarr of the National Interfaith Committee for Worker Justice] walked two flights of rickety steps and stepped onto the cramped, dimly lit sewing factory floor, the Latino women didn't pause or ask questions. Their eyes and hands stayed focused on their machines – nothing else. Their pay was less than state-mandated minimum wages. [a violation of the 1938 Fair Labor Standards Act] Their stifling [northside Chicago] workplace had no amenities – no drinking water, no toilet tissue or soap in the rest room." In the June 21st, 2004 *US Newswire*, Sister Pfarr reports that this Cintas workspace models the sweatshop conditions of 3rd world countries. This raises the question, how can a laundry company with "more than 500,000 clients and more than 5 million people who wear their uniforms" still engage in these types of practices? With "365 facilities in the U.S. and Canada, employing more than 27,000 people" Cintas is a VERY large company … with the power to help thousands of people live happy and successful lives. YET, it doesn't. In fact, according to www.uniformjustice.org last updated October 27th, Cintas has been "cited over 100 times by OSHA for violation federal health and safety laws and workers have filed 42 discrimination lawsuits in 16 states." To address the wrongs that this company has committed against its 27,000 employees we will first air this cleaning company's dirty laundry, then we will examine the underlying causes, so that we can, finally take action to 'redress' this issue.

The primary problem with Cintas is its lack of respect for its workers … via compensation, prejudice, and poor work environment. Marta Cuervo, an employee of Cintas, expresses in online interview in the summer of 2004, that "It's with our labor that their millions grow." And she's right, but for most Cintas workers it is almost impossible to get a wage they can use to support themselves and their families. According to the City News Service of February 17, 2004, Gloria Servin has worked for Cintas for 27 years and is still only making $8.25 an hour, a wage on which it is almost impossible to support a family in her native Southern California. Low wages are not they only problem for the average Cintas worker though. Many deal daily with discrimination, unsafe work environment, and long hours … with very few breaks. Coretta Silvers has worked in the accounts receivable department of Cintas' Raleigh North Carolina facility for years. But according to a 2004 report by UNITE HERE she earns 50 cents to one dollar less per hour than her white coworkers for performing the exact same job. Many people assume that such injustice is a thing of the past; however, (source here) substantiates that Cintas continues to operate as if it's above those laws which mandate a workplace free from discrimination.

Uniformjustice.com of October 2004 explains … that Cintas workers in San Leandro, CA experience injuries at a rate of 8 times higher than the rest of the laundry industry." The increased injury rate may be due, at least in part, to profit engineering. According to Maria Colon, a Cintas worker in Branford, Connecticut, "The company says we need to make up every minute of lost time, no matter what the reason – even if it means working through lunches and breaks." By now the problem seems obvious employees are forced to work in an unfit environment for very little pay, while constantly being exposed to discrimination and long hours.

But what causes this problem and how has it been overlooked for so long? Well, let's imagine that we are Cintas workers and we wish to solve a problem with low pay due to discrimination. The first step to solving such a problem typically is to go within the ranks of the company – tell a supervisor or appeal to a committee – however, at Cintas this just isn't feasible. It is difficult for a minority employee to explain discrimination when, as reported by a 2004 UNITE HERE, "eight of nine members of Cintas' Board of Directors are white men and 30 of Cintas' 31 corporate officers are men." There seems to be very little hope within the company, but even if a worker could correspond with company officials it doesn't seem that we would have much sway. According to the Forbes 400 list accessed online from September 23, 2004, Richard T. Farmer, owner of Cintas Corp. is the 203rd richest American with a net worth of 1.4 billion dollars. Not only is he very wealthy but according to the Washington Post as of May 17, 2004 "he and his wife had donated 3.1 million dollars to the Bush campaign over the past 15 years." You might say … Mr. Farmer is incredibly wealthy and enjoys donating money to President Bush, there's nothing wrong with that. But you might wonder about a *Washington Post* article of November 2003 which points up an EPA decision to allow woven shop towels to be treated as regular laundry instead of toxic waste … the latter being the designation they've held for years. Advance notice to the industrial-laundry lobbyists aided them in supporting the change. Meanwhile, the bill's opponents received no such opportunity. This decision gave Cintas, who provides these shop towels to companies, an advantage over the competition.

So what when this company harms the environment with toxic pollution, AND continues to rack up OSHA violations? Well they get fined. But, how do you give a substantial fine to a company that according to the Sept. 24th, 2004 Cincinnati Post expects full-year revenues for 2004 to be within 3 and 3.2 billion dollars? With that amount of revenue they can build the fines into their budget … as overhead costs.

We now know that the problem at Cintas is a lack of respect for employees and we have seen that the causes of these problem stem from a company whose upper ranks is permeated with white apathy, anti-environmental proponents, and political and financial insulation. The question then becomes: what can we do to stop these violators in their tracks … and how soon can we do it? Quite simply the answer is … stop supporting Cintas right now. If the company you work for uses Cintas as their uniform provider ask your management not to renew the contract. Spread the word to fellow employees and encourage them to make the same request. Do not support companies that use Cintas, ask companies that you have done business with for a long time if they use Cintas; if they do, explain the horrible worker conditions and ask them not to renew their contract with Cintas. Tell family members and friends: the only way we stop this corporation is if we all work to do so. You can also contact your representatives, tell them that fines are not enough for this company. Further action must be taken. Listen to the plea sent up by www.zmag.org "If we let Cintas win, it will send a message to all employers – if you want to beat me bad enough, you can, if you have enough money." I'll make available after my speech contact cards with Cintas violations. Feel free to take them, hand them out, and stop this injustice.

Sister Barbara Pfarr has decided she will do everything in her power to bring an end to injustice by bringing an end to Cintas. She and the National Interfaith Committee for Worker Justice have registered complaints with the federal government, and they are spreading the word through organizational documents

and press releases to the public. Understanding Cintas' dirty laundry and the dire organizational circumstances that propagate them, we too can redress such grievances. Say no to Cintas.

In full outline format, the Cintas speech would look something like this:

Speech Title

General Purpose: To Persuade
Specific Purpose: To Persuade the Audience to Redress Cintas
Thesis Statement: We should seek to diminish Cintas' grip on service laundry by considering the wide-ranging problems, assessing causes, and suggesting very focused solutions.
Organizational Pattern: Problem, Cause, Solution

Introduction

I. **Attention Getter:** "When [Sister Barbara Pfarr of the National Interfaith Committee for Worker Justice] walked two flights of rickety steps and stepped onto the cramped, dimly lit sewing factory floor, the Latino women didn't pause or ask questions. Their eyes and hands stayed focused on their machines – nothing else Their pay was less than state-mandated minimum wages. [a violation of the 1938 Fair Labor Standards Act] Their stifling [northside Chicago] workplace had no amenities – no drinking water, no toilet tissue or soap in the rest room." In the June 21st, 2004 US Newswire, Sister Pfarr reports that this Cintas workspace models the sweatshop conditions of 3rd world countries.

II. **State topic:** Because Cintas does not help its workers or community the way it claims, we should reveal and reject this company.

III. **Audience Relevance:** In the June 21st, 2004 *US Newswire*, Sister Pfarr reports that this Cintas workspace models the sweatshop conditions of 3rd world countries. This raises the question, how can a laundry company with "more than 500,000 clients and more than 5 million people who wear their uniforms" still engage in these types of practices? With "365 facilities in the U.S. and Canada, employing more than 27,000 people" Cintas is a VERY large company … with the power to help thousands of people live happy and successful lives. YET, it doesn't. In fact, according to www.uniformjustice.org last updated October 27th, Cintas has been "cited over 100 times by OSHA for violation federal health and safety laws and workers have filed 42 discrimination lawsuits in 16 states."

IV. **Preview Statement:** We will first air this cleaning company's dirty laundry, then we will examine the underlying causes, so that we can, finally take action to 'redress' this issue.

Transition: *To begin…*

Body

I. The problem with Cintas revolves around its lack of respect for its workers.
    A. Cintas' compensation is substandard.
        1. Gloria Servin makes $8.25 after 27 years. (City News)
        2. Coretta Silvers makes $1 less than white counterparts. (Unite Here)

    B. Cintas' management and organization demonstrate prejudice.
    C. Cintas provides a poor work environment.
        1. Workers experience 8 times more injuries. (Uniformjustice.com)
        2. Maria Colon confirms that tight time management increases localized injury and accident.

Transition: But what causes this problem and how has it been overlooked for so long?

II. The causes of the Cintas problem lie in no managerial recourse and little in the way of political or financial punishment.
    A. Managerial recourse is non-existent at Cintas, minority workers have little say. (Unite Here)
    B. Political recourse is slim given the company's executive branch connections. (Washington Post x 2)
    C. Company profit is so large that OSHA violations can be written into overhead costs. (Cincinnati Post)

Transition: We now know that the problem at Cintas is a lack of respect for employees and we have seen that the causes of these problem stem from a company whose upper ranks is permeated with white apathy, anti-environmental proponents, and political and financial insulation. The question then becomes: what can we do to stop these violators in their tracks...and how soon can we do it?

III. The solution to Cintas' continuing injustice? Stop supporting them!
    A. Organizationally, ask your manager to support them no more.
    B. Do not support other companies who support Cintas.
    C. Tell your family and friends to stop based on principle.
    D. Contact Lawmakers and get them involved.

Conclusion

I. ***Closure:*** Sister Barbara Pfarr has decided she will do everything in her power to bring an end to injustice by bringing an end to Cintas. She and the National Interfaith Committee for Worker Justice have registered complaints with the federal government, and they are spreading the word through organizational documents and press releases to the public.

II. ***Summary Statement:*** Understanding Cintas' dirty laundry and the dire organizational circumstances that propagate them, we too can redress such grievances. Say no to Cintas.

(Note that this conclusion structure if flipped in comparison to some of the other speeches we have examined!)

This more traditional problem-cause-solution structure follows the basic pattern of exposing a problem, uncovering the driving causes behind the problem, and encouraging solution steps to reduce the problem by curing the causes. *This time, outline the following speech, using the problem/cause/solution structure.*

> In the fall of 1993, 18-year-old Jennifer Koon was carjacked in suburban Rochester, New York. She somehow managed to dial 911 from her cell phone, but the operator at the other end of the line couldn't hear anything but muffled voices. She kept the phone line open in hopes that Jennifer would answer, but no answer came. The car was found 2 hours later with Jennifer's body inside.

>  The FCC reported on September 22, 2005 that 30% of 911 calls, about 50 million calls annually, are placed by people using wireless phones, and that percentage is increasing every year. At the time of Jennifer's abduction, the technology to trace cell phone calls did not exist, and since she was unable to give any location, the electronic enhanced (or E911) operator couldn't have sent help. Sadly, the technology to trace cell phone calls does exist today. However, even though all of us cell phone users pay a monthly surcharge for E911 services, many local counties don't have the equipment necessary to locate callers. A good example of this is Greene County, where all of us are currently sitting! Because it is imperative that we all receive the emergency services we're paying for ... and the safety we deserve, we must first understand the consequences of missing e911 services, then we will examine the

causes, so that we can finally enact some solutions to increase public and personal safety.

One of the most common reasons why people carry cell phones is in case of an emergency, but if you are unable to verbally give your location to the person on the other end of the line, help may not arrive in time. Why? Well, according to ABC's Primetime Live of August 25, 2005, only two thirds of the nation's 25 largest cities have upgraded their equipment to be able to trace calls from cell phones. And, the state of non-metropolitan e911 is much worse. But it's not due to a lack of payment. Mobile Radio Technology reported on April 1, 2005 that all but 3 states – Hawaii, Missouri, and Wyoming – collect wireless 911 surcharges ranging from 50 cents to 2 dollars per phone each month.  This adds up to hundreds of millions of dollars annually. But the 911 surcharge we 190 million U.S. cell users pay monthly isn't being used for 911 services. Instead, in most states, the money you pay to your service provider for the surcharge is sent to the state, who in most cases, sends the money to a general fund for public safety. And, this fund covers fire, police, and other safety-related programs in addition to 911 services. The consequences are clear: people pay and think they are safely, effectively protected only to find out, under the most dire circumstances, that they are not.

But if the technology and funding is available, why are we not receiving the emergency services we pay for? Well, there are three main causes to this problem: lack of government regulation, inconsistency between wireless carriers, and ignorance on our part. First, the FCC has put into place a plan to make wireless 911 services available everywhere in the U.S., but they have failed to enforce their plan. Wireless News reported on December 12, 2005 that despite the FCC's mandate that 95 percent of wireless customers have location-capable handsets by December 31, 2005, many wireless companies, including Verizon, Alltel, and Sprint Nextel have been granted waivers pushing the deadline back one year to December 6, 2006. And all indications point to the fact that these waivers could happen again for future years. So even if your area has the equipment to trace your cell phone's location, your phone may not have the technology to give them the information they need, even if it does have a camera and mp3 player.

Secondly, the technology to trace cell phone callers is much more complicated than tracing a call from a landline phone. According to the Federal Communications Law Journal of May 1, 2005, basic 911

service identifies a caller's phone number through Automatic Number Identification, matches it to a physical address, then sends it to the nearest Public Safety Answering Point. With wireless 911 services, the Automatic Number Identification requires the wireless carrier to provide both the number of the wireless user and the location of the caller by longitude and latitude before the call can be routed to the nearest Public Safety Answering Point. This can be done via two methods: GPS and triangulation. According to the FCC's Consumer Advisory's September 26, 2005 publication, Verizon, Sprint-Nextel, and Alltel use enhanced GPS capability within the phone itself to pinpoint callers within 50 to 150 meters 67% to 95% of the time respectively, whereas Cingular, T-Mobile and AT&T use towers and antennae to triangulate the location of a caller within 100 to 300 meters 67% to 95% of the time respectively. GPS location is more accurate in rural areas where towers are further apart, whereas triangulation is more accurate in urban areas where the towers are closer together. And, most wireless companies operate in both rural and urban areas – so no matter which method of location they use, their accuracy is compromised in at least part of their coverage area.

Finally, we are ignorant cell phone consumers. Most us look at our cell phone bills and see we pay a surcharge for wireless emergency services, and we assume we're getting what we pay for. But that assumption could turn out to be a deadly mistake. In Philadelphia in 2003, resident Reinaldo Zayas dialed 911 from his cell phone after being kidnapped. In the ensuing minutes, dispatchers listened helplessly as he was tortured and stabbed to death. His body was found a day later, due in no part to his e911 service. But if he had had the E911 services he paid for, emergency services would've found him.

Even though it's too late for Jennifer Koon and Reinaldo Zayas there is hope for the rest of us. The E911 vacuum can be solved at the national, local, and personal levels. First at the national level, the FCC needs to buckle down and force wireless companies to meet the deadlines that were initially set and standardize the location identification systems used. According to the Federal Communications Law Journal of May 1st, 2005, the FCC's constant revision of the rules has created uncertainty for the industry, hampering deployment of the e911 program. Pushing back implementation deadlines may be beneficial to wireless companies, but it's devastating consumers who trust that those same companies who are acting selfishly are providing the services intended to increase personal safety. Additionally, the FCC should mandate that all cell phones be equipped with GPS technology so that wireless companies can use either GPS or triangulation to locate wireless 911 callers whether they're in the middle of nowhere or at the bottom of an urban canyon.

Secondly at the local level, you should check to make sure your community is covered. You pay the fees, make sure you get the coverage. According Mobile Radio Technology of April 1st, 2005, the FCC has no authority over call centers. The responsibility to get the money to its intended destination is in the hands of local officials and state boards. The cities of Chicago and San Diego are excellent examples of how local, enhanced 911 services should work. The Chicago Tribune reported on February 11, 2005 that Chicago will have thousands of video cameras on its streets by mid-2006, making it the most high-tech 911 call center in the world. When you dial 911 from a cell phone in the windy city, not only will the dispatcher know where you are, he or she will also be able to see you, thus increasing the ability to aid responding officers and get help to you faster. And in San Diego, recent triangulation upgrades in various parts of the county have already helped California Highway Patrol find incapacitated drivers to help them to safety.

Finally on a personal level, there are many ways to help ensure that you get help as soon as possible during an emergency. Check with your wireless phone service to see what steps they've taken to make you, the consumer, safer. Ask if your phone has a GPS system on it, and if not, consider purchasing one that does. Make sure you always find out if your destination has e911 that works. Finally, if you are in an emergency and you call 911 from your cell phone, an FCC Consumer Fact Sheet of September 22, 2005 encourages you to give your location and cell number to the operator immediately in case the call gets disconnected. That way the dispatcher will be able to call you back.

We can't go back and save Jennifer Koon or Reynaldo Zayas, but now that we've recognized the problems associated with our current 911 system, discovered the causes, and explored some solutions, we can make sure that the E911 services we pay for have all the information required to send help … and save us when we most need it!

Of course, this is not the only way to structure a persuasive speech. A tried and true method of structuring a presentation to induce immediate action in an audience was developed by Alan Monroe of Purdue University in the 1930s and can still be useful for speakers today. Again, consider that this structure calls attention to the problem that needs to be addressed, shows the audiences that solutions can assist in solving the issue, provides a visual for the solution and then calls the audience into action (within a realm of their ability). See below for an extended explanation.

Monroe's Motivated Sequence (MMS)

Monroe's Motivated Sequence (MMS) speech structure organizes the entire persuasive speech, not just the body of the speech, around a sequence of steps for the speaker:

1. **Attention:** An effective speaker will use various methods such as emotions and narratives to pull an audience into a presentation. This step also provides an understanding of the issue (history, definitions for clarity, past laws or statistics…).

2. **Need:** An effective speaker will generate a clearly indicated need for action that highlights the harms of the status quo. If done effectively, after hearing of the harms associated with the problem, the audience will feel motivated to want to satisfy the need.

3. **Satisfaction:** An effective speaker will provide a clear roadmap for meeting the need such than an audience knows exactly how to satisfy the need (i.e. harm(s) or solve the problem. Present at least two viable options; your own or researches, or a culmination of them both!

4. **Visualization:** An effective speaker will help the audience "see" what benefits will result when the need is satisfied through the satisfaction steps. This section is like a test drive when contemplating buying a new car. Specifically, when the dealer encourages you to "drive the car for yourself," you are able to feel the comfortable seats and push the pedal to see how quick and agile the car is. Visualization is an important step in helping an audience mentally "try on" the solution.

5. **Action:** An effective speaker will provide a specific and detailed call to action so that the audience will understand, through the additional motivation of the visualization step, the importance of acting ... and then act.

Some speakers prefer this particular structure both because the call to action demonstrates immediate results of the persuasive strategy as well as the fact that this structure closely aligns with the ways through which people reason to take action. Additionally, the visualization step provides a persuasive boost to the somewhat "flat" solution step of the problem/cause/solution structure given that a picture is painted for an audience to "see" what good/positive/appropriate/beneficial things will accrue with the acceptance of the action challenge.

"Monroe's Motivated Sequence Group"

Imagine if the Cintas speech above followed Monroe's Motivated Sequence. What changes would the speaker make to the original speech? It is clear that the need and satisfaction are clarified, as is the call to action. Even the offering of the information card encourages solution activity on the part of the audience. However, an effective speaker delivering this speech may choose MMS and expand the speech to include the visualization of enacting the steps. Applying MMS in this way would allow the speaker to "paint a picture" regarding a world post-Cintas, a world where less injustice, prejudice and worker injury occurred.

Exercise: Please outline the following speech using MMS.
Sample speech:

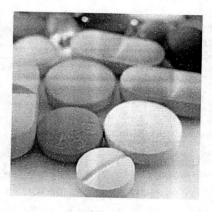

85-year-old retired refinery worker, Lester Tomlinson, was dying of mesothelioma – an especially painful form of lung cancer. After making known his wish to receive all pain medications, Tomlinson entered a hospital with shortness of breath and intense chest pains ... and never received consistent around-the-clock pain control. His family advocated his medication, but his physician and nurse practitioner continually ignored their calls despite chart notes that Tomlinson was "screaming in pain" and "yelling at night". Two weeks later, the doctor made his first and only visit to Lester Tomlinson, noted that "the patient seems to be in pain," and ordered medication for "breakthrough" pain. Four excruciating days later, Lester Tomlinson died. While few of us will ever experience pain as extreme as Lester's, most of us believe that when pain is unmanageable we can go to the doctor for help, right? According to an article in *Nursing Magazine* from August 2005, "Pain is the most common reason people seek medical care." But, it's one of the most under treated health care issues. And given that the August 2005 *New Yorker* explains that Americans spend "… almost two and half times the industrialized world's median expenditures on health" yet almost none of it for pain treatment that a majority of patients need, we must remedy this situation. To do so, we will first explore the problem of under treated pain, then we will diagnose this … misdiagnosis, before we, finally, prescribe a few steps to make the pain go away.

First let us examine how widespread and harmful under treated pain is. According to the August 2004 *Associated Press*, "painkillers known as opioids are considered standard care for serious pain from cancer, AIDS, and among the terminally ill … yet about 40% of … patients are under treated." 40% of Americans who are already dealing with the psychological pain of having a serious disease are being failed by our medical system … and even more of us deal with under treated pain every day … leading to extra stress in our everyday lives. According to *Hospitals and Health* from April 2005, "Chronic pain affects 50 million 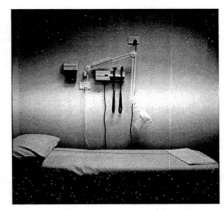 Americans and costs the country $125 billion or more each year in treatment, disability compensation and lost productivity." Apparently, we can increase our recognition of treatment for people with chronic pain … and this can increase productivity and allow individuals to go back to work. We've also seen that in the case of Lester Tomlinson not only were his last days spent in agonizing pain and the pleadings of his

family members ignored, but his suffering cost the hospital a tremendous amount of money. And consider the case of Californian William Bergman, an under treated pain sufferer whose family received $1.5 million for his suffering. This is money that could have been put to better use if the hospital had just treated its patient appropriately … for a life deserving of such treatment!

So, what causes under treatment? For each individual, exact causes are sometimes hard to recognize. However, there generally are two main causes: first … a lack of understanding between patient and physician ... and second ... the fear of liability if a patient becomes addicted to pain medicine. In order to better understand why communication is so important in the treatment of pain we must first understand what pain is. A 2004 article from the *Journal of Palliative Medicine* states, "Pain is not just the physiological response to tissue damage, but also includes emotional and behavioral responses based on individuals' past experiences and perceptions of pain." Part of what creates pain is the patient's life and how their pain has been treated in the past. The only way to discover these things is through communication. Hence, we must recognize that pain is different for everyone. We often forget this, especially when asked to empathize with someone who experiences pain differently. Physicians must be able to recognize and empathize by openly communicating with the patient and putting aside their own biases. This is not happening; doctors and nurses are often unaware of their misperceptions of the patients' pain so they feel the pain is being adequately treated. Many doctors have read the article in the 2004 issue of *International Council of Nurses* which states that "pain is whatever the experiencing person says it is, existing whenever the experiencing person says it does." While this is absolutely true it leaves physicians vulnerable to the ploys of drug-addicted patients with little protection. Hence secondly, doctors fear liability. You see, by understanding the subjective nature of pain tests, we learn that there is little room for objectivity in doctors' examinations. Especially since most of what makes up the pain response is subjective. In a study done by the Southern Medical Journal published on October fourth 2005, more than half of the seniors graduating from medical school believed addiction risks are substantial and one third feared malpractice investigations." If students just graduating from medical school enter the medical profession with such fears it is unlikely they will be able to adequately treat pain because of that fear.

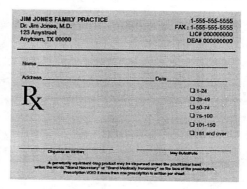

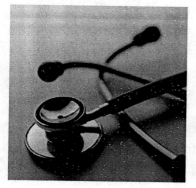

Because pain mistreatment is wrong, we must take steps to solve for this painful problem at the federal level, educational level and finally at the personal level. Doctors may hesitate to prescribe strong medication for fear of being held liable for an addiction. In February of 2005, *The Reason Foundation* explained that in August of 2004 the DEA released a pamphlet laying out some guidelines for doctors so they could adequately treat their patients without fear of a lawsuit. This was removed two months later, though, claiming that it had been misused. The DEA must resubmit this pamphlet or one very similar to it so that doctors can feel safe in treating their patients. But doctors must also take responsibility for their actions; it is their job to treat the patients. That is why we need to take educational steps as well. Pain must become what JCAHO describes as the fifth vital sign, being monitored and charted accurately.

According to the aforementioned study by the *Southern Medical Journal* by integrating pain management into classroom curriculum and clinical experience misperceptions about pain management can be improved allowing physicians to address these problems in medical school before they become a danger to their patients. We must teach our future doctors that pain is subjective and as such they must listen to the patient in order to assess it properly AND they must listen with unbiased ears. This lack of understanding between patient and physician must  also be addressed. The best way to accomplish a better understanding of pain under treatment is to create an environment of open communication. This would include standardized pain evaluations and specific treatments once pain has been assessed, including consultation if pain is considered extreme. Patients should not remain "patient!" Instead, we should continue to call and visit doctors until they listen, or deal with the problem. It is also important that you take an active role in your treatment. Doctors are not mind readers and if we don't tell them we are in pain we offer them no chance to treat it.

Whether it's a minor scrape or a chronic disease, pain affects our lives We have seen that pain isn't being appropriately treated, seen why it's misdiagnosed, and we've envisioned the steps we can take to remedy this ill. After Lester Tomlinson's doctor cut off communication with his family and Lester passed away, the Tomlinson family won a legal suit against the hospital. But no amount of money can ever make up for the death of a loved one, nor the excruciating pain … no one should suffer.

The Transformative Capacity of Invitational Communication

As we have stated previously, it is helpful for effective speakers to think in terms of all the persuasive tools available to them in their tool box. When Aristotle wrote *On Rhetoric*, he was quite pleased to inform students of the necessity of studying ethos, pathos and logos: ethics and credibility, emotive usage, and language matched with reasoning. Persuasion research and thinking for most of the past century has included very technical, rigidly structured recipes for communicators to conceptualize the process of delivering a speech and having an audience consume it with some positive outcome. Whether in terms of attitude adjustment, emotional impact, or sophisticated self-other identification, persuasion has tended to be taught and practiced in terms of trigger mechanisms to influence others.

It would only seem appropriate at this late point in the chapter to mention some important work accomplished more recently in the communication field by Sonja Foss and Cindy Griffin. In their article, *Beyond Persuasion: A Proposal for an Invitational Rhetoric*, Foss and Griffin provide us an introduction to a mode of communication they believe is effective even though the goal is not to mandate changes of attitude or behavior in other individuals. Rather, they argue that invitational communication is of a type that encourages greater participation while providing opportunities for group learning and problem solving. In essence, an invitational communicator is not a speaker who seeks to control and dominate through words and evidence as much as someone who seeks to provide opportunities for audiences to co-participate problem-solving and working around issues that may harm everyone in a given speech situation.

Of course at this point, it is hard to imagine what an invitational speech might look like given the time constraints of our speaking laboratory/classrooms as well as the structures we have used up to this point to help students grasp speech construction. However, we offer this notion of invitational communication as a kind of reflection on the "what" that we as strategic speakers would like to get out of the speaking process. What do we want to accomplish? Are our goals ethically sound? Do we have the audience in mind, in addition to their interests? For a specific example of invitational speeches, please review the following: http://www.bing.com/videos/search?q=video+examples+of+invitational+speeches&view=detail&mid=C9BA42EA7A6C9A34C7F9C9BA42EA7A6C9A34C7F9&FORM=VIRE.

References

Aristotle. (1991). *On rhetoric: A theory of civic discourse*. George Kennedy (trans.). New York: Oxford University Press.

Cialdini, R. B. (2008) *Influence: Science and practice* (5th ed.). Boston: Allyn & Bacon.

Foss, S. K., & Griffin, C. (1995) *Beyond persuasion: A proposal for an invitational rhetoric*. Communication Monographs 62, 2-18.

Lakoff, G. & Johnson, M. (1980) *Metaphors we live by* Chicago: University of Chicago Press.

Lund, N. (2003) *Language and thought* New York: Routledge.

Midgly, M. (2003) *The myths we live by* New York: Routledge.

Petty, R. E., & Cacioppo, P.T. (1996) *Attitudes and persuasion: Classic and contemporary approaches* Boulder, CO: Westview Press.

Suggested Websites

http://journalism.uoregon.edu/~tbivins/stratcomweb/readings/persuasion_def.pdf (Perloff, 2003).

https://www.psychologytoday.com/blog/sex-murder-and-the-meaning-life/201212/the-6-principles-persuasion (Kenrick, 2016)

http://www.diplomacy.edu/resources/general/persuasion-importance-trust-relevance-small-states-and-limitations-computers (Vella, 2013)

http://www.criticalreading.com/choice_of_language.htm (Kurland, 2000).

http://www.influenceatwork.com/wp-content/uploads/2012/02/E_Brand_principles.pdf (Polansky, 2016)

http://www.uccs.edu/Documents/commcenter/Dress.pdf

Chapter 11
The Art of Effective Speaking and Effective Arguments

Penguin motivational speakers.

While penguins are not aliens, in the summer of 2009, aliens invaded, just like they did in the summer of 2007. Thankfully, this invasion was a cinematic invasion; the kind of invasion to be enjoyed with a soft drink in one hand and popcorn in the other. Originally introduced in 1984 by the Hasbro toy company, these highly popular mechanical aliens called Transformers were recently rebooted in the form of a sequel called *Transformers: Revenge of the Fallen*.

"Transformers 2: Revenge of the Fallen"

Prior to the latest 2009 summer release of *Transformers: Revenge of the Fallen*, there were many predictions and opinions about future of the lucrative franchise. In particular, Tan Hee Teck CEO of Resorts World in Singapore, said:

> It is great that Asia will be the launch pad for the first Transformers attraction. Transformers was introduced in the United States in 1983, but traces its roots to Asia. Optimus

Prime, Bumblebee and Megatron are familiar names to Asian audiences, who grew up with the robot toys and love the movie. When Transformers opens in Universal Studios Singapore in 2010, it will be the first of its kind in the world. We may see a surge of Transformers mania. http://www.mania.com/dreamworks-uni-team-for-transformers-ride_article_110642.html

A world-wide "surge of Transformers mania"? Really? Upon what is his prediction based? How does Tan Hee Teck arrive at this conclusion? Tan Hee Teck wasn't the only one making bold statements.

In the 2007 movie, *The Transformers*, Optimus Prime explains why the good alien robots must protect humans from the bad alien robots. He tells his fellow transformers, "They're a young species. They have much to learn. But I've seen goodness in them. Freedom is the right of all sentient beings." Not to pick on a Transformer, but what is the logic behind Optimus Prime's bold assertion? And how does he know humans have "goodness in them"?

In an academic text entitled *Transformers and Philosophy* (yes, academics can write about Transformers!), John Shook (2009) states that if we were to come into first contact with an alien species we should neither assume that they would be concerned with our human appreciation of life, nor should we assume they would automatically arrive peacefully or militaristically. Basing his analysis on a long history of human cultural evolution in which humans have foraged for food for survival, endured cycles of war and peace, and embraced contact and competition, Shook argues that we have to assume extraterrestrials will be as surprised as we are about first contact and their reaction to us would likely fall anywhere along a spectrum between being absolutely warlike or absolutely peaceful. After reading Shook's analysis, do you agree with his conclusion? Or do you question the grounds or evidence he uses to make such an assertion that aliens would mirror human evolution? Considering the questions and the above statements you may even change your view on the existence of aliens in general.

Who knew that a movie could inspire so many arguments? So far, the following claims have been made:

- Tan Hee Teck, CEO of Resorts World in Singapore, predicted that a history of product and media connection provides enough evidence to conclude that local audiences will want to support a Transformer theme park.

- The Transformer, *Optimus Prime*, believes humans are worthy of protection because freedom is a right of all beings.

- Academic John Shook contends that the natural state of alien culture mirrors human culture.

Each and every one of these public comments is a type of *argument,* or a *basic claim supported by some form of evidence*. Which claim do you believe? Are they all right? Are they all wrong? How do we determine whom to believe? And on what basis is one prediction or assertion more believable than the others?

While arguments are made all the time, we don't always critically analyze the quality, accuracy, or logical reasoning of arguments because, more often than not, illogical arguments, inaccurate opinions, and unfounded claims become confused with truth simply by default. We often don't 'break down' the argument in the moment either.

In the comically portrayed "Monty Python Flying Circus" short, *Argument Clinic*, a man goes to a professional office to pay for an argument. The scene turns humorous when the professional simply disagrees with everything the customer says with "yes it is" or "no it's not." In fact, it is the customer that has it right when he points out that the professional arguer is not constructing a full argument, he's just being contrary. In all aspects of life, most disagreements end up looking and sounding like the "Yes it is" or "No it's not" illustrated in *Argument Clinic*. Watch the hilarious clip for yourself below:

"Monty Python – Argument Clinic"

Before we address how to construct arguments and support your own ideas, it is important to take a look at how and why, as audience members and consumers of other people's arguments, we make judgments that determine the difference between agreement/disagreement, buying/selling, and believing/disbelieving.

More Than Meets the Model: Stephen Toulmin's Model of Argumentation

A formal logician, British intellectual Stephen Toulmin (1958) realized early in his career the need for a way to construct, assess and understand everyday arguments. After assessing fields of study such as legal thought and scientific research, Toulmin came to the conclusion that not every persuasive argument follows the exact rules of formal logic. Rather, he believed that there was a general form for competently constructing and assessing arguments that transcended differences in content, background, and expertise. Namely, a layperson, according to Toulmin, should be able to assess the quality of a medical doctor's arguments about whether or not to have surgery even though he/she does not have expertise in medicine. Consider the importance and need for this based upon a 2015 government census bureau report. Roughly 88% of our nation has a high school diploma or the equivalent, but only 32% have a Bachelor's Degree. The statistics drop exponentially for a more advanced degree to only 12 percent!

Toulmin articulated his now widely studied argument model by using the following terms for argument features: claim, grounds, warrant, backing, qualifier and rebuttal. Just like when learning a new language, understanding each component is essential before trying to create and assess these terms in more complex forms.

"The Toulmin Model of Argumentation"

A Model of Argumentation

Claim

A *claim* is an assertion about how the world works or should work. We make claims, or assertions, all the time.

Examples:
   Transformers is the best movie of the year.

   Transformers is the worst movie of the year.

   George W. Bush was a successful president.

   George W. Bush was an unsuccessful president.

The above statements are claims, or simple opinions or assertions. Claims are important because they are declarative statements about what we think or believe, and it is based on our claims that others know where we stand, what we believe, and what we think about a person, idea, movie, and so forth.

However, if you haven't already noticed, take caution here because assertions are mere opinions if they are not substantiated with anything more than opinion. It is impossible to argue with someone or change someone's mind when all they provide are claims or assertions. For example, if you are a fan of the movie *Transformers,* it is impossible to convince your friend with only a claim. Your claim – "*Transformers* rocks!" – tells your friend how you feel or think about the movie, but it does not provide any evidence or reasons to support your assertion. The claim simply reflects your tastes, nothing more, thus telling your friend more about you than the movie itself.

Claims alone do not suffice for argumentation. They are an important ingredient in argumentation, but without evidence, or grounds, they imply more about your tastes than they do about the subject matter of the claim.

Grounds

Grounds is the portion of the Toulmin model on which claims are founded. The metaphor of 'ground' in Toulmin's model is apt because a claim needs to "stand on" something. The ground, oftentimes referred to as evidence, includes anything that supports or substantiates a claim.

Examples:

> *Transformers* is the best movie of the year *because it earned more in box office receipts than any other movie.*
>
> *Transformers* is the worst movie of the year *because there was no substantial dialogue and character development in the movie, just one action scene after another.*
>
> George W. Bush was a successful president *because, after September 11, 2001, there was not another terrorist attack on U.S. soil.*
>
> George W. Bush was an unsuccessful president *because, after September 11, 2001, he wasted much-needed U.S. resources and money to attack Saddam Hussein in Iraq.*

As you can see from the examples, a claim becomes an argument when evidence, or grounding, is provided to support the claim. Each of the statements above is an argument because there is evidence to support the claim or point of view. Consequently, if you disagree with any or all of the above statements, you can point to the evidence provided when disputing or rebutting the claim. Thus, unlike a mere assertion – a claim without grounds – a claim with grounds gives audiences the opportunity to critique, rebut, or contest another's claim by pointing to their evidence, not their tastes! Giving those mere, yet crucial evidentiary examples fertilizes the ground on which the claim can grow.

As a caution and for greater success, make certain to pay attention to what the ground of a claim is

> The "rules" of academic argument exclude the following as support: – Because it is my personal opinion – Because my friends or relatives think so or most people think so – Because it's always been, it's

tradition – Because it's obvious – Because it's morally right (Odegaard Writing and Research Center, 2016).

According to the above, your ground needs to have evidence that can be verified and authenticated as imminent evidence to be credible.

Warrant

Warranting is the reasoning or inferencing process that connects grounds to a claim. Typically, warrants are rules or principles that connect the claim to evidence. The warrant is often unstated, but is assumed to be true by the arguer because if the unstated principle or rule is accepted, then logically, so too is the claim.

Examples:

Transformers is the best movie of the year *because* it earned more money in box office receipts than any other movie.
Unstated Warrant: Movies that have higher box office returns are good movies.

Transformers is the worst movie of the year *because* there is no real character dialogue and development in the movie, just one action scene after another.
Unstated Warrant: Movies that have dialogue and character development are better than movies that don't.

George W. Bush was a successful president because, after 9/11, there was not another terrorist attack on U.S. soil.
Unstated Warrant: Presidents should be judged on whether or not they provide for the safety and security of the American people.

George W. Bush was an unsuccessful president because, after 9/11, he wasted much-needed U.S. resources and money to attack Saddam Hussein in Iraq.
Unstated Warrant: Presidents should be judged on the quality of their decision-making.

To conclude, warrants are the essential link between evidence and claim. Warrants provide the unstated principle or pattern of reasoning that allows for the logic of the particular claim-evidence relationship.

Backing

If a warrant is questioned or disputed, backing provides support of the warrant. Consider these two warrants from the examples above:

Transformers is the worst movie of the year *because* there is no real character dialogue and development in the movie, just one action scene after another.

Unstated Warrant: Movies that have dialogue and character development are better than movies that don't.

Backing: Consider, for example, *Pulp Fiction*'s extensive dialogue and multiple character episodes versus the much maligned and choppy *Waterworld*.

George W. Bush was a successful president because, after 9/11, there was not another terrorist attack on U.S. soil.

Unstated Warrant: Presidents should be judged on whether or not they provide for the safety and security of the American people.

Backing: As Benjamin Franklin once said, "They that are on their guard and appear ready to receive their adversaries, are in much less danger of being attacked than the supine, secure and negligent."

In both instances additional information may be used to bolster the reasoning process used to make the original claim based on the original evidence. Thus, providing evidence for the warrant in the form of backing provides a stronger case for the claim. In the backing for each of the examples above, neither is incredibly strong because both appear anecdotal at best. Stronger evidence and/or backing relies on the quality and quantity of supporting material. Most likely, a random quotation from a man who was never president (Benjamin Franklin) isn't as powerful as would be backing from a modern president who was of a different party than George W. Bush.

Qualifier

A Qualifier is a term used to characterize the strength of the claim-ground relationship. Qualifiers are usually expressed in words such as, "probably", "ostensibly", "necessarily", "sometimes", and the like.

Examples:

Transformers is the best movie of the year probably *because* of the incredible special effects, especially the last fight scene.
Qualifier: 'Probably'

Transformers is the worst movie of the year necessarily *because* there is no real character dialogue in the movie, just one action scene after another.
Qualifier: 'Necessarily'

George W. Bush was a successful president probably because, after 9/11, there was not another terrorist attack on U.S. soil.
Qualifier: 'Probably'

Ostensibly, George W. Bush was an unsuccessful president because, after 9/11, he wasted much-needed U.S. resources and money to attack Saddam Hussein in Iraq.
Qualifier: 'Ostensibly'

Qualifiers help audiences determine how confident the arguer is concerning his/her claim, while also alerting them to any extenuating circumstances that may modify or contradict the claim.

Rebuttals

Rebuttals are those questions about the claim that deal with counter claims or opposing examples that may call a claim into doubt.

Examples:

Transformers is the worst movie of the year *because* there was no real character dialogue and development in the movie, just one action scene after another.
Rebuttal: Unless you count the increasingly tense dyadic relationship between Megatron and Starscream used to demonstrate the problem of tyrannical leadership.

George W. Bush was a successful president because, after September 11, 2001, there was not another terrorist attack on U.S. soil.
Rebuttal: Unless you consider the increased likelihood that new, U.S.-led conflicts abroad may provoke foreign fighters onto our soil.

Now that you've been introduced each of the ingredients of the Toulmin model, let's revisit one of the arguments regarding *Transfomers* provided at the beginning of this chapter and apply Toulmin's argumentation model.

Example: Tan Hee Teck, CEO of Resorts World in Singapore, said:

It is great that Asia will be the launch pad for the first Transformers attraction. Transformers was introduced in the United States in 1983 but traces its roots to Asia. Optimus Prime, Bumblebee and Megatron are familiar names to Asian audiences, who grew up with the robot toys and love the movie. When Transformers opens in Universal Studios Singapore in 2010, it will be the first of its kind in the world. We may see a surge of Transformers mania.

Claim: Singapore may see a surge of Transformers mania.
(Hint: One way to discern the claim is to look for the thesis or point of the argument.)

Qualifier: 'May'
(Hint: Remember that the qualifier characterizes the strength of the claim-grounds relationship.)

Grounds: Singapore will be the location of the new Universal Theme park addition.
(Hint: Remember that the grounds include the data and facts, otherwise known as evidence.)

Warrant: When Transformer entertainment is present, mania ensues.
(Hint: Remember that warrants are rarely explicitly stated. So, to come up with the warrant, ask yourself: what principle must be true for the claim to connect to the evidence?)

Backing: Local toys with familiar sounding names, like the Hello Kitty line of products and merchandise, have traditionally induced loyal patronage
(Hint: Remember that the backing is a type of evidence for the warrant.)

Rebuttal: Unless robot or toy sentiment has changed.
(Hint: Remember that the thinking process is involved.)

Now let's examine another example, this time, from a public speaking student's persuasive speech. In her speech, this student claimed that consumers must take the steps necessary to conserve energy with appliances, given the lack of manufacturers activating the energy-saving measures within the machines:

The *Newsday* of February 17, 2005 states that a downside to our national energy conservation program – the EPA's Energy Star – is that after buying products with the Energy Star logo, consumers feel they have done their part. But as it turns out, product manufacturers don't take all the steps necessary to make the energy saving options understood, or easy to use.
According to the Energy Star website updated monthly, Energy Star standards only require that appliances have an energy saving function. Yet, for many appliances and domestic tools, such as TVs and laptop computers, Energy Star features are not even turned on before

shipping! All too often, it's up to the consumer to find the Energy Star function, figure it out, and enable it.

Claim: It is up to the consumer to turn on the Energy Star function.
Qualifier: 'Most of the time'
Grounds: Manufacturers do not turn on the Energy Star function.
Warrant: If it is probably not turned on, there is a good chance it is not functioning.
Backing: Manufacturers are only required to supply the energy saving function, not turn it on.
Rebuttal: Unless some manufacturers do turn on the energy saving function.

Finally, one more example is provided to make sure you can locate the parts of Toulmin's model. This example is from another sample student speech from a few years ago discussing home theft. This student relies on a case study as evidence that local policy actions do have efficacy:

According to the previously cited National Notary Association report, although home theft is an issue that affects the entire nation, it is best dealt with at the state or local levels where regulations are implemented and enforced. The first thing communities must do to protect themselves is to implement a system of secure notarization, which requires notaries to collect and preserve the fingerprints of anyone who signs a deed in a journal that most states already require notaries to carry. After such a system was implemented in Los Angeles County, it proved so effective that the cases of real estate fraud dropped dramatically, and in some instances, ceased all together. Its efficacy motivated the California state legislature to implement the system statewide. Criminals – many of whom already have established police records – are forced to think twice before providing incriminating evidence.

"Tips to Protect Your Home from Burglars"

Claim: Secure Notarization forces criminals to think twice before engaging in home theft.
Qualifier: 'Probably'
Grounds: Secure Notarization maintains a fingerprint record.
Warrant: Fingerprint records ward off criminals.

Backing: Los Angeles County used this system and it worked.
Rebuttal: Unless criminals find a way around fingerprint record keeping.

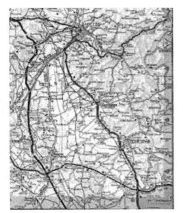

Toulimin's model provides a language for assessing other's arguments. As speakers and creators of arguments, this model provides a road map to ensure the proper ingredients in the construction of effective arguments. And, from the audience's perspective, this model provides the necessary tools to evaluate the quality of evidence and reasoning. However, locating parts of arguments for evaluation is only part of the story. Thus far, we have spent much of this chapter addressing only one form of proof. Aristotle (384 BC-322 BC), in his famed book, *On Rhetoric* (1991), referred to this form of proof as *logos*, or the form of proof having to do with reasoning and evidence. This means of persuasion is demonstrated through logical means of reasoning – from evidence to claim – and by the effective and appropriate use of evidence.

Some of you may object; however, and claim that there is more than reasoning involved when you evaluate other people's arguments, persuasive attempts, messages, infomercials and music. In fact, many of you might argue that you aren't just listening for their ground-claim relationship, let alone considering their use of warrants or backing. You're not alone.

Toulmin was not the first theorist to provide a road map for audiences when creating and analyzing other's texts. Long before Toulmin, Aristotle explained that public communicators would be most effective and persuasive when appropriately deploying appeals to analytic and quantitative reason (logos), *and* emotion (pathos), *and* edifying character (ethos). In fact, Aristotle defined rhetoric, or public persuasion, as "the faculty of observing in any given case the available means of persuasion" (1991, ln. 14555b26). To better understand *all* the available means of persuasion – not just the argumentation model – the following section explores all forms of proofs speakers use to influence and affect audiences.

Types of Proof

The first type of proof articulated by Aristotle, logos, is closest to the argumentation model. In fact, Aristotle highlights logos because it is through a speaker's arguments and reasoning that audiences make judgments. Consider the following student speech sample taken from an introductory speaking course. The student makes the argument that immediate action must be taken to deal with the growing problem of elderly suicide. His grounds (or evidence) are the comparative, escalated rate of elderly suicide.

When most of us think of suicide, we usually think of a troubled teen or a distressed college student – the ones we most often hear mentioned in the media. However, according to the August 2003 edition of the Internet Journal of Mental Health, the suicide rate for elderly men is 50% higher than that of youths. In 2001, close to 6,000 elderly Americans committed suicide – a number expected to rise rapidly as our society continues getting older. By the time this speech is over, another older American – possibly your grandparent or the grandparent of someone you know – will have taken their life. The clock is ticking – something must be done.

"Signs and Symptoms of Suicide"

As demonstrated in the use of quantitative assessment and comparison, this speaker attempts to persuade his audience by using logos as a mode of contrasting the higher rate of elderly male behavior against the behavior of younger people. Although reasoning and arguments are essential to making public and persuasive arguments, other forms of 'evidence' must complement this form of proof. Audiences are not moved by reasoning and evidence alone. As audience members, we also need to feel connected to the topic at hand.

Pathos, another form of proof articulated by Aristotle, refers to the creation of an emotion in the minds and hearts of audiences. As audience members, we pay attention to, and make decisions differently, based on emotional connection. Emotions change our judgments and thus, can't help but affect, influence, modify, and color our judgments. In the student speech above, the speaker specifically references 'your grandparent or the grandparent of someone you know' in hopes of connecting the audience to the demographic most at risk: older Americans. Arguments an audience cannot identify with or empathize with might be logical, but also unpersuasive. Thus, pathos is important because, when used appropriately, it can predispose audiences to interpreting a speaker or writer's arguments in a manner most beneficial to the arguer.

For example, a prosecutor attempting to argue for a death penalty verdict in a drunk driving case will employ pathos in closing statements to elicit the emotion of anger in the minds and hearts of the jury. Anger, in this case at the drunk driver, is an appropriate emotion to manifest because it is more likely to necessitate a judgment of death more than other types of emotions such as love or empathy will. On the other hand, the defense, in attempting to argue for a punishment of a life sentence in jail instead of the death penalty, will seek to use pathos to elicit pity and sympathy in the minds and hearts of the jury by focusing on the fact that the defendant was a good person, like you and me, who simply made one mistake.

Arguments and reasoning matter, but so too does our emotional connection to the reasoning and evidence provided by the speaker. It's no surprise that during the trial of Timothy McVeigh, the perpetrator of the worst act of domestic terrorism before the September 11 attacks, prosecutors solicited testimony from victims in what is called the victim-impact phase of the trial. In this stage of the trial, jurors listened to witness after witness discuss the pain, loss, nightmares, fears, and grief experienced at the hands of Timothy McVeigh. After he was found guilty of killing 168 people at the Murrah Federal Building in Oklahoma City, emergency medical personnel talked about what it was like minutes after the explosion at the Murrah Federal Building. They talked of hearing screams, not being able to get to victims, and in one case, having to saw off a victim's limb with a pocketknife to free them from the rubble.

Jurors also heard testimony from families who lost spouses, friends, co-workers, and, in the most emotionally difficult testimony, parents talked of losing their children who were killed while at the pre-school in the building. Parents showed pictures of their children, talked about the lives their children were going to lead, and tried to give the jury an idea of what it was like to have to endure holidays and birthdays without them.

After hearing such testimony, what frame of mind would you be in? If you were the defense and were attempting to argue for a life sentence rather than the death penalty for McVeigh, what emotional state of mind would you try to elicit in the jury? And, how would you go about doing so?

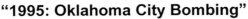

"1995: Oklahoma City Bombing"

Ethos, the final proof of persuasion articulated by Aristotle, is oftentimes the most difficult to pinpoint because it defies quantification. According to Aristotle, we are more likely to be believe "good men [and women] more readily than others" (1991, ln. 1356a10). Character, or credibility, is a result of three interrelated factors: expertise in a subject matter, goodwill, and good moral character.

Expertise in a subject matter can be demonstrated by the knowledge expressed in the speech, the types of arguments and evidence used to make a point (see the connection to logos), and by an overall perception that the speaker understands his/her topic. In other words, are the arguments logical? Is there a clear beginning and ending to a person's speech or presentation? And, does the persuader appear to know what he/she is talking about?

Goodwill, the second aspect of ethos, is the disposition of the speaker toward the audience. As an audience member, have you ever felt like the speaker did not have your best interest in mind? That the speaker was out to make a buck or profit at your expense? Or have you felt that the speaker truly cared about your well being and wanted you to understand what he/she was discussing? Did how you feel about the speaker affect how much you believed what they said (or didn't say)? According to Aristotle, your perceptions of a speaker's intentions are essentially important.

An excellent example of ethos in action occurred in 1962 when General Douglas MacArthur, addressed West Point students as he stepped down as a military commander after fifty plus years of service. In that speech he eulogized reverence for U.S. soldiers:

> I regarded him then as I regard him now – as one of the world's noblest figures, not only as one of the finest military characters, but also as one of the most stainless. His name and fame are the birthright of every American citizen. In his youth and strength, his love and loyalty, he gave all that mortality can give. He needs no eulogy from me or from any other man. He has written his own history and written it in red on his enemy's breast. But when I think of his patience under adversity, of his courage under fire, and of his modesty in victory, I am filled with an emotion of admiration I cannot put into words. He belongs to history as furnishing one of the greatest examples of successful patriotism. He belongs to posterity as the instructor of future generations in the principles of liberty and freedom. He belongs to the present, to us, by his virtues and by his achievements. In 20 campaigns, on a hundred battlefields, around a thousand campfires, I have witnessed that enduring fortitude, that patriotic self-abnegation, and that invincible determination which have carved his statue in the hearts of his people. From one end of the world to the other he has drained deep the chalice of courage.

Clearly, General MacArthur's arguments cannot be separated from his reputation and his previous accomplishments. As such, it is not surprising that *who* utters an argument is an extremely important factor in *how* we interpret the argument.

Ethos is so important to the reception of messages that organizations such as MADD, Mothers Against Drunk Driving, are very careful in who they solicit to speak to high school students. You be the judge. Imagine two speakers, each of which are asked to speak to an audience of high school students (ranging from ages 14-19) about the dangers of drinking and driving. The first speaker is an eighty-year old man who talks of the dangers of drinking and driving, but acknowledges that he hasn't driven in twenty plus years, and even more, he hasn't ever had an alcoholic drink. He provides startling statistics on the dangers of drinking and driving, reviews the laws against such activities, and warns the audience of how drinking and driving can affect people's lives.

Contrast the eighty-year old man's speech with that of a nineteen-year old speaker. She, like the eighty-year old speaker, provides startling statistics, reviews the current laws concerning drinking and driving, and warns the audience of the long-lasting consequences of drinking and driving. However, there is one significant difference between the speakers, and it has everything to do with ethos.

Unlike the first speaker, the nineteen-year old speaker speaks from experience. She discloses to the audience of high school students that she knows from first-hand experience what it's like to drink and drive because she has. She claims she drove drunk, just one time – after a high school senior graduation party at one of her friend's houses. It was on her drive home, which was only five miles away from the party, that her car crossed over the yellow line and hit a car head on. Or at least that's what the police told her, as she had no recollection of the accident. While she spoke to the students she began to cry as the pictures of the victims, the passengers in the other car, a 4-year old, a mother, and a father, were displayed for the audience to see. Then, she revealed that all of them had died because of the one and only time she had gotten behind the wheel of a car intoxicated. She had become a murderer.

Both speakers made similar arguments. Both speakers tried to elicit the emotion of fear. However, who would you more likely believe? Why? How does your judgment about speaker believability relate to Aristotle's conception of ethos?

Conclusion

Too often we are told to be better listeners. Unfortunately, few tell us how to listen or, more specifically, what to listen for even though our public life is wrought with arguments, some very clear, others not so much. In this chapter, we have discussed the important elements of Toulmin's model of argumentation. While this model can be used to improve create logical arguments, it can also be used to help you better evaluate the quality, logic, reasoning, and effectiveness of other's arguments. In addition, the three modes of proof postulated by Aristotle also provide a means of evaluating speakers, and what they say, by adding the components of emotion and character to the important assessments of logic.

References

Aristotle. (1991). *On rhetoric.* Aristotle: A theory of civic discourse. (Trans.) Kennedy, G..

Shook, J. R. (2009) First contact In J.R. Shook & S. Stillwagon (Eds.), *Transformers and philosophy* (13-27). Chicago: Open Court.

Toulmin, S. (1958). *The uses of argument,* Cambridge, England: Cambridge University Press

Suggested Websites

http://depts.washington.edu/owrc/Handouts/Claims%20Claims%20Claims.pdf

Chapter 12
Public Speaking and Beyond

© 2000 Randy Glasbergen. www.glasbergen.com

"WHEN YOU WANT TO GET SOMEBODY'S ATTENTION, THROW A ROCK AT HIS HEAD. IT'S THE LATEST THING IN WIRELESS COMMUNICATION!"

Modem. Fax machines and payphones. Black and white transmitted television shows. While most students reading this chapter haven't experienced the last 50 years of mass communication introductions into our society, you have experienced the speed at which technology and therefore, communication, has changed within the past decade or so. Computers, cell phones and data quickly expire. MySpace is now a dead source, while Instagram and SnapChat are the current trending social media forms for communication. Phones and computers with touch screens and streaming via the web for meetings, seminars and even classes is becoming more prevalent. Sterkenburg asserts, "What sets us apart as humans is the speed at which our communication develops and innovates" (2013). Yet, let us never forget the importance and impact that public speaking has as a means of communication. Throughout this book, we've talked about public speaking as a means of connecting with audiences by communicating yourself and your ideas, your passions, knowledge, and insight to audiences beyond yourself. And, we hope we've given you the knowledge to effectively communicate your ideas in the forum of public speaking.

Sometimes, however, when you spend so much time talking about the details of *how to do something*, it's easy to forget the big picture. Imagine staring into a microscope every day, eight hours a day, examining microscopic bacteria. If you continue to stare at that magnified slide of microscopic bacteria too long, you might forget that your slide is only a small representation of the world, not a complete world unto itself. In other words, it is a sum of the parts, not the whole.

In spending so much attention on the details of *how* to conceive of a rhetorical situation, *how* to gather and situate compelling evidence and arguments, *how* to construct a speech, and *how* to deliver a memorable speech, we don't want to give you the impression that public speaking is somehow distinct from the art of communication. While public speaking is a distinct area of communication with its own rules and ways of acting, public speaking is inexorably linked to human communication because none of us can escape the fact that we are simultaneously speakers and audiences.

Public Speaking and Communication

All of the above mentioned modes of communication were and are 'leaders' in the current trends of modes of communication. In our experiences, students who are the most effective public speakers understand that public speaking can't be reduced to speaking alone or even stand alone. In other words, whatever the specific reason or reasons that public speaking compels us to share – to celebrate our commonalities, to

highlight our differences, to change others' minds, to change our own minds – public speaking shouldn't be separated from what happens when you acknowledge others in the communication process: you become more connected with some people (audiences) and disconnected from others.

Close your eyes for a moment and think of an important leader in your life. A pastor? An instructor? Coach or politician? Okay, you can open your eyes now. Wasn't the leader you conjured in your mind a memorable public speaker? Even in our technology-laden culture, leadership can't be separated from public speaking. In order to be able to lead people to change, the speaker must encapsulate the ability to speak 'to' them. So, in learning about how to communicate publicly with audiences, we've also been talking about one of the essential ingredients of leadership: creating and maintaining a public persona with an audience. Let's be honest: What is a leader without his/her ability to address audiences, to inspire people, to organize ideas for people to rally around and against, and, of course, to persuade others? You may be thinking, "Public speaking is important for leaders of social movements like Martin Luther King, Jr. and Cesar Chavez, but not someone like me!"

Leadership occurs in your everyday life even though you may not call it leadership. In small group communication, for example, leaders emerge from groups of at least three to twenty people (Tubbs, 2008), largely determined by how well they present themselves to their peers. Once again, it's hard

to imagine removing public speaking from the small group communication experience. Think of one of your class projects where your teacher required you to work with fellow students. Without a leader, how would your group accomplish its tasks, maintain effective harmony within the group, and create a vision for the entire group that was consistent with the individuals within the group and the goals of the assignment?

Similarly, the relationship a speaker develops with his/her audience is analogous to the types of interpersonal relationships you develop in less formal everyday interactions. In many ways, public speaking draws upon essential principles and practices of interpersonal communication – communication with another person – and applies them to the formal public speaking situation. Of course, when you are giving a public speech, you aren't just speaking to one individual and perhaps there isn't the expected reciprocity of spontaneous communication from the listener.. As we've discussed throughout this book, the idea of speaking to one individual probably wouldn't make you very nervous or apprehensive, especially if you knew the person intimately. However, when speaking to a class of individuals, or even hundreds and perhaps thousands of people, the interpersonal elements of trust and goodwill that are present in any healthy interpersonal relationship, are also essential in the public speaking environment. Yes, you may never meet Conan O'Brien or Ellen DeGeneres personally, but your perception of how trustworthy they are, how similar or dissimilar you believe they are to you and your values, and their overall goodwill – do they have a particular political predisposition, or are they equally "rough" on all the political candidates – plays a vital role in how you perceive them from afar.

Publicly Presenting – Yourself

Almost every time you apply for a job you are engaging in some form of public speaking. The only element a prospective employer or organization knows of you prior to an interview is your resume – bullet pointed action verbs that are designed to seemingly represent essential parts of yourself and your skills. However, how is it that employers attempt to distinguish you from others in making the final hiring decision? Interviews! Correct, the dreaded interview. Employers want your narrative, in your own words. They want to know if you can put a sentence together, let alone if you can organize your thoughts about your previous experience. Can you articulate why you want to work at this particular organization? And most importantly, they want to know if you can convincingly persuade them that you would be a valuable asset to their organization.

"Any other people skills, besides 400 Facebook friends?"

"Silly Job Interview – Monty Python"

We hope you noticed that the skills we've talked about thus far are similar to those of public speaking that we have addressed throughout this book. So, maybe you didn't notice it up to this point, but presenting yourself and your ideas to an audience, like that in a formal interview process, is organizational communication's equivalent of the 'big speech" – the only difference being that instead of applause, you're hoping for a job! Did you know according to AARP – Workplace Information Center (2016), communication is a primary reason you are hired, as well as what is 'reviewed' during your interview process. "Employers look for people who **communicate well both orally and in writing**. You need communication skills to sell yourself during the interview. Being able to convey your thoughts both verbally and in writing helps you to be understood by your coworkers. Good communication means better relationships in the work environment. **Listening** skills involve not only hearing but understanding. The sign that you were listening is that you can act on the information that you heard. Listening means gaining information and understanding information."

By your very willingness to speak with others in public, you are also inviting others to participate – setting off a chain reaction that allows you to join a public conversation that began before you walked up to the podium, and will inevitably continue long after your speech is over. That's the point. While we've spent much of this book discussing what happens inside the speech, we can't forget that that so much exists before your speech, and after your speech, that determines not only how receptive audiences are to your words, but also how they experience your words after the applause ends. After all, as we have discussed, perception matters! In fact, according to Goman (2011), it takes a mere 7 seconds to make a first impression of someone! As well, consider what her research finds. "First impressions are more heavily influenced by nonverbal cues than verbal cues. In fact, studies have found that nonverbal cues have over four times the impact on the impression you make than anything you say". This means that as a public speaker, we have a very limited time to create a positive impression upon the audience. No pressure, right?!

The Changing Public Speaking Landscape

Times and trends are always changing. What once wasn't cool becomes cool once again (think neon color and balloon pants from the 80's. Grunge is out, and glamour bands will soon be back in style. So it should be no surprise that public speaking, and what counts as public speaking, also changes. Nothing does and should stay the same. After all, human beings are designed from birth, to evolve. The days of a lone individual standing behind a podium, speaking to an audience of people physically present for hours on end still occurs, but this traditionally defined context of public speaking is becoming more and more rare. In the hopes of connecting the history and tradition of public speaking to the 21st century, let's briefly examine

four important developments that are changing what's expected of speakers and audiences in the public speaking situations of the 21st century.

The 21st Century Dilemma?

Discussion Exercise: Is presenting yourself and your ideas on social networking sites like Facebook, Instagram and SnapChat, an example of public speaking? You are creating images and words with friends and possible employers in mind. Check off the public speaking box that requires you to consider an audience. You are contemplating how best to organize your home page – do you want to show pictures of your latest vacation, and if so, which pictures are most appropriate, and how best should you share

your thoughts about Proposition 13 in California on your Facebook wall given that the subject is so controversial? Check off the public speaking box that requires you to organize your thoughts and ideas in a coherent manner. Is an audience capable of judging what you are saying/creating? Your friends won't judge what you are saying/creating with rounds of applause and a possible change in public policy, but couldn't it be argued that signing up to be a friend on someone's Facebook page or consistently visiting a blog on your friend's homepage is the equivalent of audience applause and the beginning of a grassroots movement for social change? Check off the public speaking box that requires that audiences be able to respond. But what about the nervousness? What about walking up to the podium? What about the audience hearing your voice? What about your face turning red when you're looking out into your audience's eyes? And what about the evidence and arguments that seem to distinguish public speaking from other types of communication that require little, if no, preparation?

Before we can fully answer the above exercise, let's talk about what used to count as public speaking, and consider how some of those definitions have already changed, or should change, to meet the new demands of the 21st century – like the Facebook question we posed above.

Ancient Definitions of Public Speaking

According to Barry Brummett (2006), public speeches in Ancient Greece were composed of four specific ingredients. First, public speeches had to be verbal. That is, the ears of the audience were essentially important for a speaker because it was through the ears – not only the eyes – that a speaker connected with audience members. A speaker's voice was perhaps the most important communication channel, by which a speaker could communicate his ideas to a physically present audience. The tenor,

projection, rate, intonation and quality of a speaker's voice all mattered because the voice was the only way in which audiences could hear, interpret, and make judgments about what was being said. The voice of the speakers was the sole mode of transferring the message.

Second, for the Ancient Greeks, all public speeches were expected to include claims, evidence and examples, and have a semblance of organization – a beginning, middle, and end – so audiences could follow the speaker's arguments and ideas. Makes sense, doesn't it? After all, since we were young we were taught that the proper structure of an English paper was to have the same format. So it would be assumed that a speech

would follow the same structure. Imagine yourself trekking through the heat of an Athenian summer to hear Socrates speak about the importance of the city-state. Like we said, imagine is the key word here. But here's the important part – you're only going to hear this speech once, and you're far away from the speaker because there is a large crowd. The wind is blowing, and it's hot outside, and you're thirsty and hungry because you've walked so far in the midday sun to hear this speech. That's a lot of distractions to put up with even before the speaker begins speaking. As this example illustrates, in Ancient Greece, the burden was on the speaker to make the speech as compelling and clear as possible so audiences could follow along, relate to the examples presented, and walk away from the speech remembering the main points without any way of writing down, or recording, what was said. If the speech was disorganized, poorly planned, jumbled, and seemingly irrelevant to the cares or concerns of the audience, what would have been the point, and would you have cared to remember what was said?

Third, public speeches in Ancient Greece all occurred in a clear time and space context. Simply put, the speeches occurred at a specific time, for a specific audience, and it was a one-shot deal. A particular speech with a particular speaker only occurred once. Yes, a sophist travelling from city to city may have given the same exact speech, using the same exact words, memorized of course, countless other times to countless other audiences in different city-states. But, no matter how many times that speaker delivered that speech to audiences, it was never the same. It may have been similar to previous speeches, but it could never be the exact replica. The mood of the speaker could never be replicated, the weather changed, the composition of the audience was different – maybe there was a heckler at one of the speeches and an audience of his students on another occasion – and alas, the speech was different.

In Ancient Greece, you didn't have the luxury of waiting for a speech to come out on YouTube to watch it. You were either at the specific speech location, or you weren't. There were no other options other than being informed or caught up to speed on the content from someone who actually attended the speech. Other people could describe or attempt to summarize what they heard, and what their impressions were, for those who were not physically present at the speech, but that would mean that it was a second hand interpretation – not an authentic public speech where a speaker was speaking directly to you, at a specific location and time, for a specific purpose. And as discussed numerous times, your perception is your truth, thus creating your reality.

Finally, the last characteristic of public speeches in Ancient Greece was the fact they were hierarchical. One person, the speaker, was always considered "in charge." This specific ingredient helped distinguish public speaking from other communication experiences – like talking to your partner, talking to yourself, or talking to a friend where the communication exchange is informal and relatively unregulated. In Ancient Greece, when you gave a speech to an audience, you were expected to be "in charge" because others attended for the sole purpose of listening to your thoughts, your ideas, and your words. That's right – this is the very reason we get so nervous when we speak. It's hard to imagine that a group of people, let alone complete strangers, would ever want to listen to what we have to say on a topic, uninterrupted for minutes, or even hours, on end.

Audiences in Ancient Greece didn't expect a give and take, back and forth exchange, like you indulge in when talking over dinner with friends. There was no simultaneous reciprocation. Speeches were explicitly designed to be uninterrupted because the speaker knew the audience's job was to listen, and the audience expected the speaker to speak on a topic or an important issue – uninterrupted. The job of the speaker was to inform, persuade, or enlighten, and the role of the audience was limited to response – either in the form of applause, questions after the speech, falling asleep, jumping up on their feet in approval, walking away, or of course, the always popular throwing rocks at the speaker. Whatever the specific audience response was, however, one thing was always clear: the speaker was speaking because he (we're talking Ancient Greece here that's why we are using the 'he') was expected to lead the audience, know what he was saying, be accurate in what he was saying, be compelling in his use of examples and illustrations, and, of course, be relevant (Brummett, 2006).

But times, they are a changing, aren't they? So why wouldn't public speaking? Can you remember the last time you heard a speaker speak without a visual – either a flag waving in the background or a news script running underneath highlighting the most-up-to-the minute breaking news? "Words. Just words?" to quote President Obama. I'm sure you can remember a time when a speaker told a story – no arguments where there is a clearly discernible claim with evidence that can be verified. Perhaps comedians like Kevin Hart or Chris Rock fit in this category? Would one of Chris Rock's classic comedy sketches be considered a speech with expositional argument by the Ancient Greeks?

Hart and Rock's stories have a point – oftentimes weaving critical social commentary and societal trends in and around the laughter – and in so doing, weren't their humorous stories both humorous and persuasive? Most likely you answer 'yes'. You find yourself laughing at the content because you can connect, as well as see, the humor in the content. So, did you believe you were going to a traditional public speech the last time you saw them in concert or watched one of their performances on satellite?

"Obama in Washington: Words Matter"
"Chris Rock – Doctors & Drugs – GRAPHIC, VIEWER DISCRETION IS ADVISED"

Think about not being able to see, or hear, or read the latest presidential debates between Donald Trump and Hilary Clinton. Or a press conference from your favorite band, unless you were physically there, actually at the Presidential Inaugural, or at the band's latest gig in Boulder, Colorado. Think about how often you experience speeches without being present when the speaker, or the singer, or the politician, or the comedian actually spoke those words or sung that song? Your physical absence is not that relevant anymore because you can download, or even unload the presentation via a search engine on our laptop or even phone. Yet, according to the Ancient Greek definition, you had to be there, physically, for it to be a public speaking event. But what about now? Does your physical presence matter? What, if anything, is lost or gained in translation when you experience a speech via another medium that allows you not to have been physically present when it was actually given? In fact, in recent times, a term coined "separation of content from presentation" is used to denote a differentiation of meaning versus how it should be presented to the listeners (e.g. a common example is <em> to denote a phrase element in HTML which refers to emphasis) (Choen, 2004).

What's Different Now?

We don't even have to travel all the way back to Ancient Greece to realize that our conceptions and expectations of public speaking have always evolved to meet new demands and changing audience expectations. Throughout history, two major elements in particular are responsible for changing what audiences expect from public speakers and speeches, and what speakers and speeches can do to audiences.

First, technology has changed, and will continue to change, how speeches (and speakers) reach audiences. As was mentioned before, Abraham Lincoln's voice was the only means available for him to reach audiences clamoring to see him at his First and Second Inaugurals. Of course, his tall and slender frame helped him reach more members of his audience, but he could only be heard and understood as far as his human voice would take him. Additionally, he had what was considered a low, baritone voice, making it perhaps harder for the listener to understand at a distance. Obviously, we've come a long way since then.

Not only did the invention of microphones and other voice-amplifying devices empower speakers who might have been previously excluded from the public speaking experience, these technological inventions also changed how speakers interacted with audiences. While Warren G. Harding became the first president heard on radio, and President Coolidge became the first president to deliver a radio broadcast from the White House, it was President Franklin Roosevelt's "Fireside Chats" that radically changed how audiences experienced public speaking. Between 1933 and 1945, Roosevelt delivered over thirty radio speeches directly to the American people, across different time zones, and across social class barriers.

"Fireside Chat 1"

Moreover, the technology of radio allowed a speaker to speak to audiences not physically present. Allowing speakers to speak or broadcast their voices to "mass" audiences is the first obvious change. However, while providing more access, technological inventions such as the radio also allowed for a more intimate connection – or at least a changed connection – between speaker and audience. The medium of the radio, and later the television, allowed for a speaker's words (and face) to be seen and heard in a context other than the formal occasion of the speaker. In addition, in the 1950's, politicians such as Dwight Eisenhower were no longer restricted to specific audiences in specific locations. Rather, they spoke to you in your living room, as an individual, where the now familiar voice and image of the speaker's face was transmitted to you in the midst of your daily activities. As an audience member, you could guarantee complete fidelity to the message. You could tune others out (including the weather and the immediate situation) simply by turning up the volume of the radio or television. The microphone or the camera had already served to edit out the very situation in which the speaker spoke.

"Eisenhower Reacts to Integration"
"Political Ad"

Now, in the 21st century, with the internet, Skype and smart phones, as well as all other attenuating technologies, physically attending a speech in which the speaker is speaking to us is the oddity. The norm is to watch a presidential address or watch a coach's press conference from the private confines of your own living room or your cell phone. You can access speakers when you choose to – not at the specified time and location chosen by the speaker. And when you do access them, your attention is expected to be divided – while you're watching and listening to their speech on YouTube, you can also easily check your email with the television on in the background, and friends in the room with you. Speakers know that. Just as our definition of what counts as a public speech changes, so does the composition of the speech, and the speakers themselves. It is much like the evolution of the 'split screen' of today's televisions. Many viewers can attend to multiple shows and content at one time.

Unlike the Ancient Greek public speaking situations, the possibility of the repeat and the replay is not only possible, but expected in your mediated environment. When you want to see a commencement speech that Steve Jobs, President of Apple Computers, gave to the graduating class of 2005 at Stanford University – the one your friend told you that you should watch because it was so inspiring – all you have to do is access YouTube and the speech can begin and end when you want it to. You can begin it, pause it two minutes into his address to take a call from a friend, continue, and then stop the speech again when you feel you have watched enough of it. Once again, advances in technology have shifted the locus of control away from the speaker, and have placed it in the hands, literally, of audiences who can interrupt, and thereby edit, speeches that are rarely experienced in their entirety from beginning to end (Gitlin, 2007).

What does this mean for prospective speakers? You don't have to be a Stanford graduate to hear and watch Steve Jobs' speech, let alone be anywhere in particular to be an audience member. However, there is a price to pay for not being anywhere in particular because it places the speaker in a challenging, and relatively new predicament that was not faced by the Ancient Greeks who devised the traditional public speaking situation model. Specifically, who does Steve Jobs write his speech for? For the Stanford graduates  and family members who were present on that sunny day in beautiful California on June 12, 2005? Or for other commencement speakers who will follow him in upcoming years, who will want to know what previous speakers said, how long they spoke, and what they focused on? Or is he writing his speech to a high school student who is contemplating even attending college?

"Steve Jobs' 2005 Stanford Commencement Address"

In addition, how should you, as an audience member, interpret Jobs' speech? You weren't there, so you couldn't have been inspired by the applause and laughter of others. You are alone when you watch and listen to his speech, and you're not a 2005 Stanford graduate, you're simply looking at a speech stripped of its original location and purpose. Is that fair to you as an audience member?

Thus, the technologies that have made possible the democratization of access to public speeches, also makes it more challenging for the speaker who must write for a more universal audience – an audience that won't be present, an audience that will watch and listen to the speech years or decades in the future, an audience that may not understand the particular references that may make his or her speech popular with the live, physical audience, but unfamiliar and outdated to the audience connecting from afar and watching via YouTube or other streaming media (Gitlin, 2007).

Consider what Blair and Miller (2014) allude to. Because the gadgets of communication have so rapidly advanced, the role of the speaker has changed in that the audience demands les time. The lag time, and patience of that lag time, has become less and less as technology increases. Blair and Miller assert that our role as speakers is different now. We must be more concise, present and connected to the material and our audience. They describe this as being authentic to your audience. Why does this matter so much, you ask? Consider this – if not you, then someone else. With so many options, ideas and modes of going about acquiring information in today's times, the more authentic (which creates connection) you are to your audience, the more they will trust and follow you.

Blair and Miller delve further and also assert that today's public speeches the presenter must present agility in their delivery. Because so much can be contextual 'off site' of the presenter, tone, intonations, and your overall emotional connection to the topic must come through.

Lastly, these authors assert that a presenter must be nimble, or flexible. If your technology fails you in a presentation, adapt and implement a level of improvisational speaking in your presentation. Because we can't predict how fast things will continue to change, today's presents must be open to possibilities.

Given what we have talked about in regards to the changing landscape of public speaking, let's return to the question that we began this discussion with – is your

Facebook page an example of public speaking? Given that our conceptions of public speaking have definitely changed, what do you think? What do your peers think? What should and should not count as a public speech these days? What are the implications of our evolving conceptions of public discourse?

To conclude, public speaking, and all of its technologically-driven derivatives, is still an essential cornerstone of democracy. At its very core, public speaking is an essential component of community building and of individuals connecting. While this is not often advertised in public speaking classes – be proud to take public speaking and learn how to build and sustain a community and impact relationships – it is the side effect that is as important as learning the craft of publicly thinking and speaking. Caring to speak by connecting to your internal sense of pathos, anticipating how audiences might react and respond to your ideas, translating your pure ideas into a compromise that accounts for the differences of backgrounds and experiences of your audiences, and standing up in front of others to present your ideas, highlights what the Greeks would call the dialectic – the unending dialogue that must take place by each of us, and between us, to allow for the introduction and evolution of ideas, thought, change, and of course, the sharing of substance we call community. A community which you can help grow, change and alter for the betterment of yours and others' future. For more on changes in the roles of the public speaker, please review the following website: https://medium.com/@life_binge/future-of-public-speaking-bcdf080fc77e#.fs3epclyf.

References

Brummett, B. (2006). *Rhetoric in popular culture 2nd edition*. Thousand Oaks, CA: Sage Publications, Inc.

Gitlin, T. (2007). *Media unlimited: How the torrent of images and sounds overwhelms our lives*. New York: Hold.

Tubbs, S. (2008). *A systems approach to small group interaction*. New York: McGraw-Hill.

Suggested Websites

http://thenextweb.com/media/2012/07/15/whats-the-future-of-communication-lets-ask-the-experts/ (Sterkenburg, 2016)

http://www.aarpworksearch.org/Inside/Pages/HowEmployableAmI.aspx (2016)

http://www.forbes.com/sites/carolkinseygoman/2011/02/13/seven-seconds-to-make-a-first-impression/#5b476ca8645a (Goman, 2011)

http://alistapart.com/article/separationdilemma (Cohen, 2004)

http://www.beinkandescent.com/articles/2136/Future+of+Public+Speaking (Blair and Miller 2014)